Kauai

A Paradise Guide

By Don and Bea
Donohugh

Cover design by Sharon Carter
Illustrations by Janora Bayot

Published by
Paradise Publications
Portland, Oregon

In affiliation with
Prima Publishing and Communications

Distributed by
St. Martin's Press

S0-BUF-485

"KAUAI KILOHANA"
(Superb Kauai)

This book is dedicated to the memory of Mary Kawena Pukui.

Paradise Publications
8110 S.W. Wareham
Portland, OR   97223   U.S.A.

Copyright © 1987 Donald L. & Beatrice I. Donohugh

First Printing: May 1988

ISSN # 0895-9382
Printed in the U.S.A.

COVER DESIGN: Sharon Carter
Sharon Carter received her BA in fine arts in 1972 from the University of Texas. Currently a resident on the Big Island of Hawaii, she is involved in a variety of freelance multi-media activities including cartooning and weaving and has been featured in a number of exhibitions.

PEN & INK SKETCHES: Janora Bayot
Janora Bayot is a freelance artist who especially enjoys cartooning. In addition to having her work appear in numerous publications, she spent six years with the Columbian newspaper in Vancouver, Washington. In her spare time she volunteers on behalf of animal agencies. Janora's keen sense of humor and vivacity is personified in all her artwork.

MAIKA'I KAUA'I

Maika'i Kaua'i hemolele i ka malie.
Kupu kelakela ke po'o o Wai'ale'ale,
Kela i ka lani kilakila Kawaikini,
Ka no ka helekua linohau Alaka'i,
Malo'elo'e ka la'au huli 'e mai ka pua,
Ke 'ike iho ia Maunahina.

–Mele Kuo

INCOMPARABLE KAUA'I

Beautiful is Kaua'i beyond compare.
She sends forth a bud in the summit of
Wai'ale'ale,
She flowers in the heights of Kawaikini,
Her strength radiates in awful splendor
from Alaka'i;
Though I weary, though I faint, she renews
my strength in her soft petals;
I have myself beheld Maunahina!

–Ancient Chant

ALOHA NUI NO

Bunt Baldwin

John Clark

John Dillon

Hobie and Nancy Goodale

Henry Gomez

Lucille Kawaihalou

Bill Kikuchi

Valdemar Knudsen

Bobbie Waterhouse McCord

Clare Miller

Eric and Beryl Moir

Jim and Nancy Morgan

Bruce Morehead

John Plews

Carmen "Boots" Panui

Debbie Wilcox Pratt

Warren & Arlene Robinson

Barnes & Ba Riznick

Adele & David Silver

Frederick B. Wichman

Maili and Paul Yardley

And to Kathy Gotzenberg, who has the unique ability to type and think at the same time.

We would like to express special appreciation to Director Kenneth Kapp of the Kauai Museum, and to our fellow Directors of the Kauai Historical Society.

TABLE OF CONTENTS

V. WHAT TO SEE

VI. WHAT TO DO

VII. RECOMMENDED READING

VIII. INDEX

X. READER RESPONSE – ORDERING INFORMATION

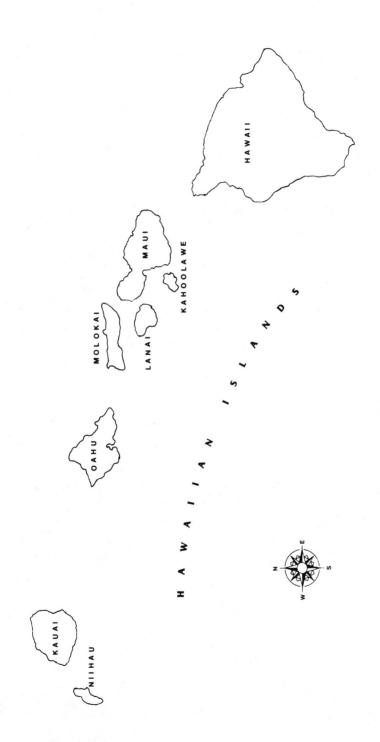

KAUAI

8

INTRODUCTION

You chose well when you selected Kauai for your vacation. The ancient Hawaiians referred to this island as "Kauai Kilohana" - superb Kauai. And today, while vacationers come from everywhere to Hawaii seeking paradise, Kauai is where Hawaiians come to find theirs.

Hollywood has also found Kauai. "South Pacific" was filmed at Haena, Hanalei and Kahalahala Beaches. At least forty other films and television shows have been made here. You have seen them, or heard of them. A few are: "Fantasy Island,", "10", "Pagan Love Song", "Blue Hawaii", "Islands in the Stream", "Donovan's Reef", "The Old Man and the Sea", "Miss Sadie Thompson", "The Thorn Birds", "Raiders of the Lost Ark", and the new "King Kong."

Kauai is the oldest of the major Hawaiian islands, so there has been time to etch its mountains, shape and color its canyons, deepen its hanging valleys, and to spread a lush green over all. It has more rivers and waterfalls than any of the other islands, and truly deserves its sobriquet "The Garden Island."

When you step off the airplane from busy Honolulu, you step back half a century in time to the truest Hawaii that is still to be found on a major Hawaiian island. Life is simpler here and the pace is slower. Our first traffic light didn't appear until 1973! But it would seem that Kauai wasn't made for the automobile. Even our "belt road" doesn't go all the way around, and during commuting hours, the two-lane roads in and out of Lihue choke up with the traffic. It seems we already have hardening of our major arteries!

Kauai must have been made instead for those who climb its peaks, feel its mists in the mountains, inhale the fragrance of its flowers, walk the remote beaches where there are no other footprints, and dive into the clear waters to see the coral formations and exotic marine life.

We have been coming here as tourists for over twenty years. The last twelve were to our own condominium, and two years ago we built our permanent home here. This background gives us the advantage of having the visitor's point of view as well as an intimate knowledge of the island. As you read our guide, you will see that the opinions we express are our own - we have not received a single cent or favor from any commercial interest.

This guide book is as complete and accurate as we could make it at the time of publication. We have tried to tread the fine line between exhaustive and exhausting. But things are constantly changing. We welcome your suggestions and comments to make the next edition even better. A quarterly newsletter, *THE KAUAI UPDATE*, from Paradise Publications, is available to bring you the most recent changes. (See READER RESPONSE for details).

The Hawaiians have always felt that there are three Kauais - the wet and windy north and east shores, the sunny south and west shores, and the chilly but awesome Kokee area in the mountains. However, the coming of civilization has created four. The places to stay, restaurants, and stores are clustered in the north (Princeville/Hanalei), the east (Kapaa/Waipouli/Wailua), the central area (Hanamaulu/Lihue/Nawilwili/Puhi), and the south and west (Koloa/Poipu/Hanapepe/Waimea/Kokee). So we have grouped and discussed them this way. Each of these areas is little more than an hour by car from any other, so you can easily enjoy all of them while you are here.

As our guide features pen-and-ink sketches, we thought we would list four books featuring color photographs of this incredible island: *Hawaii's Garden Island: Kauai.* Fabulous photographs, but an excessively exhortative text by Robert Wenkam. This is a large coffee-table book which can be purchased at many bookstores for about $25. *Kauai, A Many-Splendored Island,* by Douglas Peebles and Ronn Ronck. This is a bit smaller, but almost as beautiful and with an excellent text for about $20. *Kauai, The Garden Isle,* by Allan Seiden. A trade paperback with gorgeous photographs for $6. *Kauai,* by Bob Krauss and Bill Gleasnor. Also a beautiful trade paperback for about $6.

One other, *The Kauai Album,* by Carol Wilcox, has only black-and-white photographs and concentrates on the historical buildings of Kauai, but the photographs are well-done. Several other books with incidental illustrations are listed at the end of this guide. And, of course, you will have your own photos and some of the free or inexpensive brochures available everywhere to help you remember the beauty of Kauai.

Most visitors who come here also stop off on one or more of the other islands. For those who are Maui bound, we recommend the companion Paradise Guide, *Maui, A Paradise Guide,* by Greg and Christie Stilson. The best guide to all of Hawaii is *The Maverick Guide to Hawaii,* by Robert Bone. The *Insight Guide to Hawaii,* by Hans Hoffer, is the most artistic with photographs and essays on various aspects of Hawaii, but contains surprisingly scant travel information. *Hidden Hawaii* and *Hawaii on $45 a Day* are good for the backpack set. We can't recommend any others. There is no other guide to Kauai that makes an effort to be comprehensive and accurate. Other books about Hawaii and Kauai are recommended throughout this guide and in the bibliography.

Four free publications available once you arrive are *Spotlight Kauai, Kauai Drive Guide, This Week Kauai,* and *Kauai Beach Press.* Look these over - you may find some good tips. But remember that they are advertising publications and most of their content is made up of ads. A secret beach or secluded waterfall is not advertised, so most of the best things about Kauai will not be listed there. The coupons are good for discounts, however, and the maps serve well enough for main-road tours.

You will need a better map of Kauai. The best is published by University of Hawaii Press, 2840 Kolowalu Street, Honolulu, HI 96822. It costs about $2.50 and can be purchased at several places on Kauai.

GENERAL INFORMATION

OUR PERSONAL BESTS

GOLF: Kukuiolono Golf Course, Kalaheo

EXCURSION: Pacific Tropical Botanical Garden, Lawai

BODY BOARDING: Brennecke's Beach, Poipu

ANNUAL EVENT: The Hanapepe River Raft Race, Hanapepe

BOARD SAILING: Anini Beach Park, Kalihikai

BEAUTIFUL BEACH: Kalihiwai Bay

HAMBURGER: Duane's Ono-Char Burger, Anahola

SAIMIN: Hamura Saimin Stand, Lihue

SUNSET: From a spot about a mile up the road out of Waimea to Kokee, with Niihau and Lehua in the distance

HISTORICAL TOUR: Grove Farm Homestead Museum, Lihue

SHAVE ICE: Halo Halo, Lihue

LUAU: Tahiti Nui, Hanalei

SCUBA DIVING: Sheraton Caves, Poipu

SNORKELING: Outside the reef at Waioli Beach, Hanalei   *133*

SAIL: To Kipu Kai from anywhere

NUDE SWIM: The pool at Hanakapiai Falls

KAYAK TRIP: Huleia River, Nawiliwili

HIKE: Na Pali Coast

VIEW: Kalalau Valley from Puu O Kila

SUNDAY BRUNCH: The Waiohai Resort, Poipu

SHOPPING: The Kong Lung Store, Kilauea

RESTAURANT ATMOSPHERE: Plantation Gardens, Poipu

OUTRAGEOUS DESSERT: Hula Pie

BOAT RIDE: Na Pali Coast with Clancy Greff, "Captain Zodiac"

ICE CREAM: Lappert's Aloha – made on Kauai

THRILL: Helicopter ride over Waimea Canyon and into the remnants of Waialeale Crater

MOST MOVING EXPERIENCE: Hearing The Lord's Prayer – Ka Pule A Ka Haku – sung in Hawaiian by the choir of the Waioli Huiia Church, Hanalei

HISTORY OF KAUAI

No one knows when it started – not even within a million years. Nor exactly how. But eons ago, a defect near the middle of the huge Pacific tectonic plate – the outer crust of the earth sixty miles thick – allowed molten lava to escape and emerge hissing and boiling onto the ocean floor seven miles down. The seamount thus formed rose slowly until, thirty million years ago (we *do* know that date), the volcano that was to form Kure atoll rose from the dark sea into the bright sun.

Kure atoll is now the northernmost island of an archipelago that stretches 1,800 miles from the northwest to the southeast. During the millions of years after Kure was formed, the Pacific tectonic plate moved to the northwest over this defect at a little less than four inches per year. As magma flowed forth intermittently, the individual islands of the archipelago were formed to the southeast. The process is still continuing. At this moment, seventeen miles southeast of the Island of Hawaii, the defect is erupting and has formed Loihi, a seamount already 8,000 feet above the floor of the ocean.

The eight major Hawaiian Islands comprise the last 400 miles of this archipelago. Of these, Kauai and Niihau are the oldest, and Kauai itself is the fourth largest. Surface samples tested by the potassium-argon method range in age from 3.8 to 5.6 million years. By the time Kauai rose from the sea, most of the islands to the northwest had already sunk or become eroded to become little more than rocks. On some, coral formed atolls. Others were only sand shoals beneath the surface.

Kauai, and its small satellite island Niihau, emerged from the surface of the sea together. They are actually compound domes separated by a shallow channel 17.2 miles wide. Kaula, a small tuff cone nineteen miles southwest of Niihau, and Lehua, a small island a half mile north, were also part of this great upthrusting.

When first formed, Kauai was much larger than it is today, with a north-south diameter of over thirty miles. Crashing waves from the trade winds and northern storms have eroded the north shore to form the dramatic Na Pali Coast – cliffs that plunge 2,000 to 3,000 feet to the sea. The diameter in the north-south direction is now twenty-five miles, and with an east-west diameter of thirty-three miles, Kauai still has a nearly circular shape 553.3 square miles in area and a coastline of 137 miles.

Many major events occurred on Kauai in the millions of years after its birth. A huge fault broke open, forming the Waimea Canyon, which was then eroded further by the Waimea River. Deep valleys formed along the canyon's eastern slope from the action of rivers flowing from the summit plateau of Alawai. The great Olokele shield volcano itself, which once soared over 10,000 feet into the sky, sunk and formed a crater, or caldera, nearly thirteen miles across. Then most of the rim collapsed, leaving the eastern ridge with the two peaks of Waialeale and Kawaikini. The entire Makaweli area sunk, forming a huge graben, or depression. Erosion of all the high mountain ridges continued from rainfall and rivers. Coral grew along the southwest coast, then with a great tilt, that area rose to form the dry plains of Mana backed by the ancient sea cliffs. Alluvial flows flattened the floors of Hanalei and other valleys. Subsequent eruptions formed Kilohana and the cinder cones in the Koloa area. Then the island grew quiet after the last eruption 1.5 million years ago at Kaluahonu Crater on the flank of the Haupu Range near Koloa.

Life came slowly to the island. The first must have been in the form of tiny spores of ferns, mosses and lichens borne by the jet stream that sweeps out of Southeast Asia. The small seeds of orchids and other plants probably arrived that way too. Insects tossed about by storms may have come next. Sea birds and then migratory land birds blown off their course by severe storms then arrived. Some bore larger seeds of plants, grasses and sedges embedded in the mud on their feet, and sticky seeds of various plants and trees caught in their feathers. From time to time, floating seeds arrived. Some were in rafts of plant material, some in driftwood, and larger ones floated long distances by themselves.

This coming of life to Kauai – and the other Hawaiian Islands – did not happen as rapidly as the above may suggest. If one divides the number of known indigenous species into the time involved, one species became successfully established on an average of every 30,000 years. Yet here they flourished, turning the island green, while around the island coral quietly grew.

How the first Polynesians came to Hawaii has always been something of a mystery. The first attempts to solve it, late in the nineteenth century, were from the oral traditions and genealogies of the Hawaiians themselves. Then early in this century, the science of comparative linguistics was brought to bear. This was followed by physical anthropology and ethnobotany, which added much to what we knew. Still, much of the mystery remained. Sometime in the future, DNA analysis (genetic fingerprinting) will probably resolve this fascinating mystery. But for now we have to be content with what is presently the most reliable source of information – archeology – and combine this as best we can with all that we learned before.

Archeology did not become a systematic study in Polynesia until about 1950. The classic methodology used elsewhere relied upon seriation studies of pottery. Here there was very little pottery, so seriation techniques were attempted on fishhooks and other material. But this was fraught with difficulties. In the 1950's, radio carbon dating of artifacts shed much light, but this provided only ranges of time, and not precise dates. During the 1980's, the new technique of hydration-rind dating of volcanic glass chips (produced when tools were made) has added the accuracy we needed.

The outline of the story, at least, is now apparent. It started during the ice ages about 50,000 years ago when Negroid hunter-gatherers from Africa and Madagascar crossed the land mass that was then solid (because the ocean level was some 300 feet lower) into Australia and New Guinea. Subsequent short sea journeys carried them only as far as New Britain. These people were warriors, not seafarers.

Some 30,000 to 40,000 years ago, Mongoloids moved south into Southeast Asia and the Malay Peninsula. Then Caucasian groups began migrating east from India, passing south of the Himalayas, to arrive on the Malay Peninsula. Once there, they mixed with the Mongoloids to become the Proto-Polynesians. It was in the islands of Indonesia that the Proto-Polynesians developed their skills at seafaring, horticulture and fishing. They also developed a unique pattern of pottery known as Lapita that has helped us learn this story. As their seafaring skills developed further, they built outrigger canoes with sails shaped like crab claws capable of going before the wind, but not against it.

The prevailing winds in Indonesia are from the southeast, but now and then westerly winds lasting ten to twenty days occur. Small exploration groups chose these times to sail east, and when the wind once again came out of the southeast, they were able to return to their home islands by simple dead reckoning. If they found suitable islands to the east, they returned to settle.

In New Guinea, New Britain, and by then the Solomons, the Proto-Polynesians encountered the Negroid race already established there. Undoubtedly, a degree of mingling occurred with some interchange of seafaring skills, because this race we now refer to as Melanesians then settled islands to the east as far as Fiji. However, the Proto-Polynesians moved on. This was probably because of conflict with the Melanesians and perhaps also because of their greater susceptibility to malaria, to which the Negroid peoples were more resistant.

The Proto-Polynesians arrived in the Tongan Islands about 1500 B.C. and in Samoa about 1000 B.C. These islands were free of malaria and beyond the reach of the Melanesians.

It was here during the next thousand years that this race truly became Polynesian. Their seafaring skills were further developed in journeying from island to island, and there is clear evidence that they acquired the skills necessary for long voyages during that time. To sail between Tonga and Samoa, they built large twin-hulled canoes and altered their sails so they could sail them with the wind on the beam. They also studied the stars and, by the end of the thousand years, knew the names of some 150 and could use them for navigation.

As their skills improved, the pattern of easterly exploration and return was apparently repeated over longer and longer distances. Coconuts served the voyagers for both food and water. They preserved other food by drying and fermentation so it could last twenty to thirty days, and became skilled at fishing at sea using trolling lures. They carried water in gourds and bamboo joints and caught rainwater in their finely-woven pandanus mats to supplement this. As population pressure pushed them on, they settled the islands they found to the east and evidence indicates that they arrived in the Marquesas northeast of the Societies about 200 B.C.

But life was hard in the Marquesas. There were no coral reefs for them to fish and little level land to cultivate. The deep valleys allowed scant sunlight to reach their crops. It is probable that this combination of factors, along with overpopulation, is the reason that the Marquesas became the major dispersal point in the Pacific at that time. This dispersion continued until major improvements were made in their farming and fishing skills.

What we now call the Society Islands, including Tahiti, were settled shortly after the Marquesas. Easter Island presents a perplexity – it lies almost alone to the east of the Marquesas in the vast reaches of the Pacific. The finding of Easter Island was probably fortuitous.

It is possible that some canoes reached Central and South America. One bit of evidence supports this: the sweet potato, known botanically as *Ipomoea batatas*, that some botanists believe had its origin in what we now call Peru. Other botanists believe as strongly that it may have come originally from Eastern Polynesia. All that we are certain of is that it was found by the earliest European explorers in eastern, but not western, Polynesia. It is possible that some adventurers stranded on the western shores of South America attempted to return to their home islands, and a few reached eastern Polynesia bearing the sweet potato with them.

By about 400 A.D., the Marquesans probably became convinced that there were no more islands to the east of what we now call the Tuamotos because the canoes that had gone beyond either never returned or reported that they had found no new islands. They did know, however, of the annual northward migration of the small land bird, the golden plover, as the sun moved north, and its return to the Marquesas when the sun moved south. This meant land lay somewhere to the north. The golden plovers still migrate every year from the Marquesas and other islands south of them, straight to Hawaii and then beyond to the arctic. Pushed by population pressures and perhaps by societal conflicts, it is certain that one or more Marquesan canoes set out from there heading north about 400 to 450 A.D., on the path of the plover, prepared to settle whatever lands they encountered. This date is from recent archeological finds. During the month or so it took to make the trip to Hawaii, they undoubtedly encountered storms which would have dispersed the canoes.

At first they sailed before the prevailing winds which set them to the west, and near the equator they were set farther to the west by the equatorial current. If the doldrums were wide, they would have had to paddle. At least one canoe continued to follow the path of the plover, guided at night by what their legends called the two "pointer stars" of the seven, the Pleiades, and by the sun during the day. When the skies were overcast, a northerly course could be maintained by observing the constant "long swells" formed by the trade winds sweeping over a thousand or more miles of fetch. The northeast trades pushed the canoes still farther to the west, lining them up on a direct course to Hawaii.

During the latter part of their voyage, there must have been one night when they first saw a star that was fixed in the heavens. This the Hawaiians call Hoku Paa – the "steadfast star" – our North Star. By then their food must have been nearly gone, their water low, and undoubtedly they were in desperate straits. Perhaps they regarded this star as an omen and it gave them courage to carry on.

The tall peaks of Mauna Loa and Mauna Kea can be seen at least thirty to forty miles at sea on a clear day. Clouds gathering over them could extend this range to more than sixty miles. If a volcanic eruption were taking place, the loom at night could be seen from at least a hundred miles. One way or another, they sighted the Island of Hawaii, made their way toward it, and landed there.

With the recent resurgence of interest in Hawaiian culture and history, we hear more of the Hawaiian legends that tell of several back-and-forth voyages, especially at later dates of 1200 A.D. - 1400 A.D. Unfortunately, there is no objective evidence to support this.

About 1000 A.D., Raiatea, known then as Hawaiki, became a second center for dispersal. The natives of this island, by now fearsome warriors, conquered many of the nearby islands. Tahiti was one of them, where the natives referred to themselves in their own language as "Manahunes." The Raiataians adopted this term to refer to them, which became one of derision. The Marquesans, including those who had gone to Hawaii, had no such word in their language.

For reasons that are not known but were probably similar to those of the Marquesans, a second group of canoes sailed north from Raiatea about 1000 A.D. also prepared to settle the islands they found. When they arrived in the Hawaiian Islands, they set about subduing the Marquesans who had settled there. Some fled, as evidenced by archeological finds on Necker and Nihoa, others were exterminated, and the rest became the working class under the new alii.

Although mingling undoubtedly occurred, it is interesting that at the time of the first census on Kauai in the 1820's, there was still one group of sixty-five natives living in the upper Wainiha Valley that referred to themselves as Menehunes. The earliest Hawaiian legends about menehunes refer to them as lower in status, not stature, and as having prodigious strength. Only post-contact legends describe them as small in stature and possessing supernatural powers. When the early westerners came and asked who had built certain heiaus, fish ponds, and irrigation ditches, all of which were hundreds of years old at the time and whose origins were lost to the Hawaiians by then, it was natural to reply that the workers or menehunes, did. We westerners are responsible for the myth of tiny men who labored through the night producing stupendous feats. Our own mythology is replete with small people doing such things, and there is nothing comparable in any Hawaiian myths before western man arrived. No skeletal remains have ever been found of small humans, or any other objective evidence for that matter. So the myth of the menehunes is just that – a myth – but a delightful one.

The new arrivals were to have nearly 800 years to settle the other Hawaiian Islands, develop their agriculture, social organization, customs and legends before the coming of western man was to change their way of life forever.

The period from this point to the present is the one that most history books cover well while slighting the foregoing. So let us refer you to some good references to shorten our story here. The best history of Kauai is, *Kauai, the Separate Kingdom*, by Edward Joesting. For all of Hawaii there is no better reference than the classic, *Hawaii, A History*, by Ralph Kuykendall and A. Grove Day. *Shoal of Time*, by Gavan Daws, is also authoritative and well-written.

This brief history will only include two or three observations on the landing of Captain Cook at Waimea, Kauai on January 20, 1778 and a few subsequent events.

Let's hear about the coming of Cook from the other side for a change. Kamuela Kamakau tells us that the Hawaiians at Waimea awoke, saw the ships at anchor, and:

> "All were astonished...trees moved on the sea...a floating forest..."

> "The men have white wrinkled faces and three-cornered heads...speak in a confused tongue...fire comes from their mouths...they have doors in their bodies into which they thrust their hands and draw out knives, bells, and pieces of iron..."

Indeed, the Hawaiians already knew of iron. Driftwood containing nails and bolts had come to Kauai from Spanish galleons broken up by storms at sea, and it was highly valued.

It was entirely fortuitous that Cook discovered Hawaii. Spanish galleons had plied the Pacific from Panama to the Philippines and had passed both north and south with the trade winds for nearly two centuries without suspecting the Hawaiian Islands were there. Cook had been instructed to search for a northwest passage from the Pacific side, and sailed first to Tahiti to gather stores and prepare for the long, grim trip north. He finished his preparations early so leisurely sailed through the Society Islands and then the Tongas, where he happened to be when he judged the time to be right for the venture northward. The path from the Tongas to his destination lead him straight to the Hawaiian Islands.

William Bligh of Bounty fame, then a lieutenant under Cook, later charted the islands and called Kauai "Atooi", which seems strange to us. However, if we bear in mind that the Kauaians at that time retained the Tahitian "t" instead of the "k", and we substitute a "k" for the "t", the sound comes closer: "a-koh-oy." The "i" should be pronounced as it is in English, not Hawaiian, which gives us "a-koh-eye." The "a" occurred because Hawaiians invariably listed their islands from windward to leeward. The recitation would end with the island of Kauai, "a" means "and", so they were saying "and Kauai." If we subtract the "a" we are left with "koh-eye", which is remarkably close to our pronunciation today.

In 1796 and again eight years later, King Kamehameha, who had united all the other islands under his rule, attempted to conquer Kauai. He failed the first time because of a storm in the channel, and the second time when an illness – probably cholera – decimated his troops. Kaumualii, the ruling chief of Kauai, saw the writing on the wall. He went to Oahu in 1810 and offered Kauai and Niihau to Kamehameha. He was told to "return and rule", and promised allegiance to Kamehameha from that day forth.

When King Kamehameha died in 1819, his wayward son, Liholiho, became king and took the title of Kamehameha II. King Kamehameha's widow, Kaahumanu, held most of the power, however. She sent Liholiho to Kauai in 1821 to kidnap Kaumualii and bring him to Oahu. Upon Kaumualii's arrival on Oahu, Kaahumanu made him marry her to strengthen the ties between Kauai and the other islands. Kauai never saw its last chief again. He died on Oahu three years later.

18

Another important event in the history of Kauai took place in 1835, when Ladd and Company leased a tract of land in the Koloa area from Kamehameha III to grow cane and produce sugar. Cane had been brought here by both major Polynesian migrations. The sugar made in Koloa was not the first sugar produced in Hawaii, as the guidebooks say, but was the first sugar produced commercially for *export*. Many Chinese immigrants to Hawaii knew the process of making sugar from cane – in fact, Marco Polo reported tasting sugar in China in 1270. In the Hawaiian Islands, the first sugar was produced by Chinese on Lanai in 1802. On Kauai, Samuel Whitney produced sugar commercially in Waimea in 1820, as did others near Lawai from 1825 to 1832.

The first sugar mill in Koloa was built at Maulili Pond in 1837 using koa wood rollers. This site is along Waikomo Stream just outside of Koloa. Wood rollers proved unsatisfactory, so a second mill was built just downstream with iron rollers. The truncated stone stack in the heart of Koloa is the remnant of the *third* mill in Koloa built in 1841. The real importance of the sugar plantation of Ladd and Company is that it established the plantation pattern that was to be followed by others throughout all of the Hawaiian Islands.

Although Wailua had been the ancient religious capital of Kauai, with Waimea an alternate capital, this was to change. In order to ship equipment into the sugar mill at Koloa and to ship the sugar out, the small Koloa Landing became the major port of Kauai for nearly a hundred years. As the town of Koloa developed around its mill, it became a major population center.

The whaling industry had its effect on Kauai, although it had more impact on Lahaina and Honolulu. This industry became significant on Kauai about 1830, reached its peak around 1840, and declined after 1859. Once again, it was at Koloa Landing that the whalers rowed ashore for their recreation and to obtain supplies. Because of this, some refer to it as "Whaler's Cove."

After Kaumualii's death, a period of restlessness ensued with no clear-cut chief system on Kauai. During this time, the descendants of missionaries, plantation owners and managers became, in a sense, the new alii. Valdemar Knudsen, Duncan McBryde, Mary Sophia Rice and Eliza Sinclair were foremost of the first generation, and some of their sons, Eric Knudsen, George N. Wilcox, Albert Wilcox, William Hyde Rice, Francis Gay, and Aubrey Robinson, continued in the next.

Lihue did not even exist until the late 1830's. The main Hawaiian trail from Waimea to Wailua passed inland of Kilohana Crater and bypassed the area completely. Lihue is first mentioned in history in 1837 when High Chief Kaikioewa, the governor of Kauai appointed by Kamehameha III, chose it as his home. He was instructed by his king to plant cane and chose this area because of its rainfall and soil. Lihue had been the name of Kaikioewa's former home on Oahu. It means "cold chill", which was appropriate there. From 1837 on, this name began to replace Puna, the former name for the area. The next appointed governor, Kanoa, also built his home in Lihue in 1846.

The principle impetus for Lihue's prominence began in 1854, when William Harrison Rice took over as manager of the Lihue Plantation located near there. He built the first sugar irrigation system on Kauai, bringing water from Hanamaulu Stream to the fields of Lihue Plantation, which increased production dramatically. George N. Wilcox also built irrigation systems for Grove Farm nearby. Both plantations and their camp towns then grew in size from 1864 on.

The sugar from both plantations was originally shipped from Ahukini Landing at the edge of Hanamaulu Bay, but under Rice's influence and later that of Wilcox, Nawiliwili went through a series of improvements to become the principal port of Kauai early in this century. Lihue, as the closest population center, then became the seat of government.

Another major result of the sugar industry was the succession of immigrants brought to Kauai for labor. By 1872, the total number of Hawaiians on Kauai had dwindled to 5,200. There simply were not enough workers for the burgeoning sugar industry. The first tentative experiment in importing labor was in 1852. A few Chinese were brought in, but when they completed their contracts with the plantations, some turned to raising rice and many moved into the various centers of population where they opened up shops in competition with the plantation stores. Nonetheless, they were excellent workers, so in two major periods – 1876-1885 and 1890-1897, more were brought to Kauai. Also in two periods, 1878-1887 and 1906-1913, a large number of Portuguese immigrated under contract, many of them with their families. From 1886-1900, an even larger number of Japanese arrived. Then groups of Puerto Ricans, Koreans, Spanish, Germans, and a large number of Filipinos followed. It is this immigration that has given Kauai its fascinating ethnic diversity.

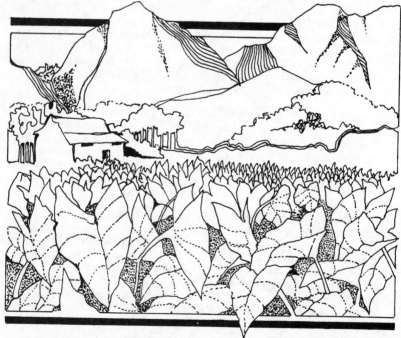

This brief history of Kauai will close with the tale of Niihau.

As the trade winds sweep up and over Waialeale, they not only leave the western plains of the island dry, but the small island of Niihau off that coast even drier. This island, which is only eighteen miles long and six miles wide, has only about one inch of rainfall per year. It does have three lakes, but they are dry lakebeds except after a heavy rain. Approximately 600 Hawaiians managed to eke out a living on this barren island over the centuries until it comes into our history.

The event that was to bring a change to their lives occurred in far-away Scotland in 1820. It was then that Elizabeth McHutchinson married a sea captain named Francis Sinclair. By 1839, they had three sons and three daughters and an unsatisfied sense of adventure. They decided to go to New Zealand, which was then being opened up for colonization by England. They sailed there in 1840 and settled on South Island to farm and raise sheep and cattle. In 1846, Captain Sinclair left for Wellington with his oldest son, and both were lost at sea, leaving Eliza a widow at age forty-six. In 1848, the oldest daughter, Jean, married Captain Thomas Gay. Two years later the second daughter, Helen, married Charles Barrington Robinson. Less than two years after that, Helen left her husband carrying their only son, Aubrey, and returned to the family without explanation.

Although the family prospered, their sense of adventure prevailed. In 1863, they sold their property, bought the ship "Bessie", and set forth for Honolulu with Thomas Gay as captain. They looked at several properties in Hawaii, among which was Niihau which King Kamehameha IV offered to sell them. They happened to visit Niihau after a season of heavy rains, were enthusiastic, and bought the island in 1864 for $10,000. The Sinclairs set up the three pre-cut houses they had brought with them and tried to make a living. Soon afterward, Captain Gay took the "Bessie" to Australia to sell her, and died there of pneumonia.

In 1867, Anne Sinclair, the youngest of the Sinclair girls, married Valdemar Knudsen, who raised cattle between Kekaha and Mana on Kauai, and left Niihau to live with him. At this point, the doughty Eliza Sinclair decided to move to Kauai to be near them and purchased a large tract of land in Makaweli. She later added adjoining lands, and in the early 1870's constructed a beautiful house on the upper slopes of Makaweli, which is still there today.

Eliza Sinclair continued to be the matriarch of the Sinclair-Robinson-Gay clan, with Makaweli as the headquarters and Niihau the colony, until October, 1892, when she died quietly at the age of ninety-three at Makaweli. Her descendants, the Robinsons, continue to own and operate Niihau. Today, approximately 225 Hawaiians live there under conditions similar to those that have always prevailed. They speak Hawaiian and retain much of their Hawaiian culture. Thus, Niihau is an island in this sense as well as a geographic one.

THE HAWAIIAN LANGUAGE

The Hawaiian language traces its origins to Austronesian roots, with elements from Madagascar, the Philippines, Indonesia and Melanesia. Each island group in Polynesia, and even some single islands such as Kauai, tended to develop differentiation due to the distances between them. It is a poetic language and contains some 20,000 words whose meanings sometimes shift with the context in which they are used. Every syllable and every word ends with a vowel, giving the language a musical sound. The accent in each word usually falls on the next-to-last syllable.

The alphabet consists of five vowels (a, e, i, o, u) and seven consonants (h, k, l, m, n, p, w), to which must be added the glottal stop. This is a "catch" in the voice, similar to the sound in the middle of "oh-oh" in English, and represents the omission of a hard consonant. In print it is indicated by a hamzah, or reversed apostrophe. Purists today also add the macron, a horizontal line over a vowel, indicating that the vowel should be stressed.

Consonants are pronounced much like they are in English, and the vowels as follows:

	Unstressed		*Stressed*
A	as in above	A	as in car
E	as in bet	E	as in play
I	as in marine	I	as in see
O	as in no	O	as in pole
U	as in the double o in moon	U	same, but longer

The "w" gives visitors the most trouble. It has a "v" sound almost always after e and i, a "w" sound after u and o, and is variable after a or when it is the initial letter. There is no "t" in Hawaiian, but there is in Tahitian. Kauai retained this for centuries while it was being lost on the other Hawaiian Islands. Thus you sometimes hear "tapu" for kapu, or "tapa" for kapa, but these are not correct.

The diphthongs, ei, eu, oi, ou, ai, ae, ao, and au, are all stressed on the first letter. The one exception is iu, in which the stress is even.

Always bear in mind that there is a tendency for us to anglicize the pronunciation. For example, you often hear POY-poo and rarely hear the correct Poh-EE-poo, or Why-POH-lee instead of the correct Why-po-OO-lee.

Tradition has passed down to us Hawaiian place names on Kauai, and the law requires that streets bear Hawaiian names. But it is surprising how little you hear the language otherwise, except in song and ceremony. Today, fewer than 10,000 people in the Hawaiian Islands are fluent in Hawaiian.

Here is a brief glossary of the most commonly used Hawaiian words – ones that are frequently added to English to give it flavor:

a'a (ah-AH)   rough, crumbling lava as distinguished from pahoehoe, which is smooth; both terms are now used worldwide by geologists.

akamai (ah-kah-MY)   smart, clever, possessing savoir faire.

ali'i (ah-LEE-ee)   a Hawaiian chief, a member of the chiefly class; also plural.

aloha (ah-LO-ha)   love, affection, kindness; also a salutation meaning both greetings and farewell.

auwe (ow-WAY)   alas, woe is me!

hala (HAH-lah)   the pandanus tree, whose leaves (lauhala) are used to make baskets and plaited mats. Don't call the *tree* lauhala.

hale (HAH-leh)   house

hana (HAH-nah)   work

haole (HOW-leh)   originally a stranger or foreigner, now a white man.

hapa (HAH-pah)   a part, usually a half.

heiau (HAY-ow)   an ancient Hawaiian temple.

hoomalimali (hoh-oh-mah-lee-MAH-lee)   flattery

huhu (hoo-HOO)   angry

hui (HOO-ee)   a group or club, most commonly an investment group.

hukilau (HOO-kee-lau)   a communal fishing party in which everyone helps to net the fish.

hula (HOO-lah)   the dance of Hawaii.

imu (EE-moo)   a pit lined with banana leaves & lava rocks on which the food is placed, covered, and allowed to cook for several hours.

kahuna (kah-HOO-nah)   a teacher, priest or other trained person of old Hawaii endowed with skills which often included supernatural powers.

kalo (KAH-low)   The correct Hawaiian pronunciation of the taro plant from whose corm or root poi is made.

kalua (KAH-loo-ah)   to bake underground; a kalua pig is a pig that has been roasted this way.

kama'aina (kah-mah-EYE-nah) literally, a child of the land, it refers to people who were born in Hawaii or have lived here for a long time.

kane (KAH-neh) a man or husband; if this word is on a door, it's the men's room.

kapa (KAH-pah) also called tapa, a cloth made of beaten bark and dyed with a geometric design.

kapakahi (kah-pah-KAH-hee) crooked, cockeyed, uneven

kapu (KAH-poo) keep out, prohibited

keiki (KAY-kee) a child; keikikane is a boy child, keikiwahine a girl.

kokua (KOH-koo-ah) help, as to give help to someone.

kona (KOH-nah) the leeward side of the islands, the direction from which comes the kona wind.

kuleana (koo-leh-AH-nah) originally "right" or "privilege", as applied to a homestead or small plot of ground which a family has farmed for generations; by extension, kuleana denotes any area in which one has a special interest.

lanai (LAH-nye) a porch or covered pavilion. Pronounced (lah-NAH-ee), it is the island of Lana'i.

lani (LAH-nee) heaven, the sky

laulau (as it appears) literally, a bundle; in everyday usage, pieces of pork and butterfish are wrapped with young taro shoots in ti leaves, then steamed.

lei (LAY) a garland of flowers

lomilomi (loh-mee-LOH-mee) to rub or massage. Lomilomi salmon is salmon which has been rubbed with onions and herbs.

luau (LOO-au) taro leaves. The real word for a Hawaiian feast is aha'aina, but for reasons of modesty, the word luau has taken is place; e.g., "Come have some taro leaves with me."

mahalo (mah-HAH-loh) thank you

makai (mah-KYE) toward the sea

malihini (mah-lee-HEE-nee) a newcomer to Hawaii.

mana (mah-nah) if both syllables are unstressed, it is the spiritual power which the Hawaiians believed to inhabit all things. If both are emphasized, MAH-NAH, it means dry or arid.

mauka (MOU-kah) toward the mountains

mauna (MAU-nah) mountain

mele (MAY-leh) a Hawaiian song or chant

moana (moh-AH-nah) the ocean

mu'umu'u (moo-oo-MOO-oo) the dress in which the missionaries first enveloped bare-bosomed Hawaiian women, now a garment in every Island woman's wardrobe.

nani (NAH-nee) beautiful

nui (NOO-ee) big

'ono (OH-noh) delicious; start this word with a glottal stop or it will sound like ono, the fish.

opu (oh-POO) abdomen

pali (PAH-lee) a cliff, precipice

paniolo (pah-nee-OH-lo) a Hawaiian cowboy, from "Espanol." The Hawaiians first learned from California and Mexican cowboys.

pau (POW) finished, done

pilikia (pee-lee-KEE-ah) trouble

pua (POO-ah) flower

puka (POO-ka) a hole

pupule (poo-POO-leh) crazy

ukulele (oo-koo-LAY-leh) literally, "jumping flea"; the stringed instrument introduced by Portuguese. The word probably came from the way it is played, which resembles a dog scratching.

wahine (wah-HEE-neh) a female, a wife, and a sign on the ladies' room door.

wai (y) fresh water as opposed to salt water, which is kai.

wikiwiki (wee-kee-WEE-kee) to hurry, hurry up

The following are a few of the phrases you might hear.

Aloha kakahiaka   (ah-LO-ha kah-kah-he-AH-kah)   Good morning.

Aloha nui loa   (ah-LO-ha noo-ee LO-ah)   Much love.

Aloha wau ia oe   (ah-lO-ha vow ee-ah OH-eh)   I love you.

Hauoli makahiki hou   (how-OH-lee mah-kah-hee-kee ho-oo)   Happy new year.

Hele mai ai   (HEH-leh my eye)   Come and eat.

Mahalo nui loa   (mah-HAH-low noo-ee LO-ah)   Many thanks.

Mai ka'i   (MY KAH-ee)   I am fine. Literally, "good."

Mele Kalikimaka   (MAY-leh kah-lee-kee-MAH-kah)   Merry Christmas.

Okole maluna   (oh-KO-leh mah-LOO-nah)ah)   Bottoms up – a relatively recent, humorous toast. The true Hawaiian toast is simply "aloha."

Pehea oe?   (peh-HAY-ah oh-eh)   How are you?

Otherwise, what you will hear most is Pidgin. This started as a means of communication between fur traders of the northwest and the Chinese to whom they sold the furs. The word "Pidgin" itself is a Cantonese distortion of the word "business." The fur traders stopped off in Hawaii to and from China, and used the same words and phrases to communicate with the Hawaiians. You still hear direct descendants of this early phase – "can do", "no can do", "bymbye", and "savvy." The Pidgin word "chowchow" was taken over by the Hawaiians and pronounced "kaukau." Many today believe it to be an authentic Hawaiian word.

Each group of immigrants added its own words and expressions while borrowing others. Remember that in 1900, only 5% of the people here spoke English as a native language. Even now, descendants of non-English speakers comprise more than half the population on Kauai.

Today there are at least three major "types" of Pidgin, all with a Hawaiian base – one with a Chinese flavor (not heard much on Kauai), Japanese, and Filipino. Each has borrowed from the others and the commonality is such that there is no difficulty when a member of one group talks to a person from another.

There are levels of Pidgin, too. This ranges from perfectly pronounced English having only a slight alteration of syntax, through a distinct rhythm and intonation using frequent "local" words, to a level that is almost incomprehensible to a mainland visitor.

You should be aware that Pidgin is much more than a way of speaking. It is an expression of the bond that binds together those who are born and raised here. Most non-haoles in Hawaii today, especially those who are younger, are perfectly capable of speaking good English. However, they tend to shift to a mild Pidgin with each other as an expression of this bond, and further to the incomprehensible when they want to exclude haoles.

Don't make the mistake of trying to speak it yourself. Only those who have been born and raised here should do that. Here are, however, a few words you should be able to understand:

bumby – from "bye and bye"; after a while.

brah, blah, or blahlah – brother

broke da mouf – delicious

bummahs – an expression of disappointment, suitable for any occasion.

calabash cousin – close friend, or related by marriage.

coast haole – anyone recently arrived from anywhere in the U.S.

da kine – watchamacallit

go fo' broke – originally a betting statement: "This time I'll gamble everything." Now, to go all out in any activity.

grines – grinds, food

hana hou – do it again

haole koa – a shrub whose leaves resemble those of the koa tree.

howzit? – how's everything; what's going on?

mek ass – to make a fool of yourself.

o wot? – or what? Added at the end of any and almost every question.

pau hana – quit work

plenny mongoose – the plural form of the word mongoose.

shaka! – great!

to da max – all the way

tanks, eh? – thank you

tutu – "granny" in an affectionate sense, not necessarily a relation.

Some of the Pidgin we hear is absolutely marvelous. Just the other day: "Wheah she stay da sponge? Befoh heah was!"

Wiggling your hand while extending your thumb and little finger could be called a "body language" form of Pidgin. It is simply a local greeting.

PLACE NAMES OF KAUAI

Anahola   (Ah-nah-HO-lah)   no known meaning

'Anini   (Ah-NEE-nee)   stunted, dwarfed

'Ele'ele   (Eh-leh-EH-leh)   black

Ha'ena   (Hah-EH-nah)   red hot

Hanalei   (Hah-nah-LEH-ee)   crescent bay

Hanama'ulu   (Hah-nah-mah-OO-loo)   tired (from walking) bay

Hanapepe   (Hah-nah-PEH-PEH)   crushed (from landslides) bay

Kalaheo   (Kah-lah-HAY-oh)   proud day

Kalihiwai   (Kah-LEE-hee-why)   edge (with a) stream

Kapa'a   (Kah-PA-ah)   the solid (as closed up)

Kaua'i   (Cow-AH-ee)   no known meaning

Kealia   (Keh-AH-lee-ah)   the salt encrustation

Ke'e   (Keh-EH)   avoidance, as too far off

Kekaha   (Keh-KAH-hah)   the place

Kilauea   (Kee-LOW-eh-ah)   spreading (lava)

Koke'e   (KO-keh-eh)   to wind or bend

Koloa   (KO-lo-ah)   long (tall) cane

Lihu'e   (LEE-who-eh)   cold chill (place)

Mana   (MAH-NAH)   dry

Moloa'a   (Mo-lo-AH-ah)   matted roots

Nawiliwili   (Nah-wee-lee-WEE-lee)   the wiliwili trees

Po'ipu   (Poh-EE-poo)   no known meaning

Wai'ale'ale   (Why-ah-leh-AH-leh)   rippling or overflowing water

Wailua   (Why-LOO-ah)   two waters

Waimea   (Why-MAY-ah)   reddish water

Wai'oli   (Why-OH-lee)   water (of) happiness

Waipouli   (Why-poh-OO-lee)   dark water

TRAVELING WITH CHILDREN

Young children find Kauai fascinating and a lot of fun. There is always something for them to do and they love running around in just their bathing suits; therefore, packing lots of clothing for them is not a necessity.

However, for parents, even getting here may be a trial. The first tip is to get your airline seating assignment and boarding passes ahead of time. Second, try to book a direct flight to Lihue, which avoids a two-hour stopover and long walk between terminals in Honolulu. At the present time, only United Airlines has direct flights to Lihue from San Francisco and Los Angeles. Those who are coming from farther inland or the east coast will have to contend with at least one transfer. To rest up and reduce jet lag, you may want to spend the night on the west coast. A third tip if traveling with infants: Find out the configuration of your particular airplane and try to obtain the seats with the most legroom in order to provide an area for your child to play on the floor. One last tip: If you can't get a direct flight to Lihue from the west coast, cut down the required layover time in Honolulu by going immediately to the inter-island terminal and take the first flight out – there is usually room. On arrival in Lihue, arrange for your rental car and buy groceries to use up the spare time until the flight you would have been on arrives. Then pick up your luggage and you're all set.

Pack a bag full of surprises appropriate for each child. Let each one open a surprise hourly if they behave. These can be picture-story books, coloring books, or toys they can play with on the airplane. Now and then one can be a snack or a box of juice that comes with its own straw. Ask the attendant for "kiddie packs" and decks of cards to supplement your own surprises.

Chewing gum is a good idea if a child has difficulty equalizing air pressure. Many people think that the newer jet aircraft are pressurized at sea level, but they are usually at an equivalent of 7,000 feet altitude.

Pack essential items, toilet articles, medicines, and bathing suits in your carry-on bag in case your luggage is delayed or lost. Distribute other important items in all bags so the loss or delay of one bag will not be catastrophic.

Be sure to ask your travel agent about the place where you will be staying and its suitability for children. Confer with your pediatrician ahead of time about any health problems your children may have.

State law requires that all children age three and under must be in an approved infant restraint seat at all times when the car is in motion on public roads. These are available from automobile rental companies, but most charge from $3-$5 per day and the cost can mount up. During peak season on Kauai, most infant restraints available from car rental agencies are taken. Reservations for them are not completely reliable, either. For these reasons, you may want to bring your own. Some carseats are approved for use on the airplane. Inquire at the F.A.A. (202/426-8374) weekdays 8:30 a.m. to 4:30 p.m. EST. If you check carseats as baggage, protect them with a large plastic garbage bag with your name and address on both the seat and bag.

Cribs can be rented at all major hotels and condominium complexes. If you plan on bringing your own, check out a new product from Fischer-Price. The Travel Tender Portable Crib and Playpen fits neatly into a totebag and weighs about twenty-two pounds. It costs about $70 and is geared for children under thirty-four inches tall weighing less than thirty pounds.

Most places to stay have lists of babysitters. The sitters have been screened informally by a responsible representative of the staff. There are no "licensed" babysitters on Kauai. The best ones may be spoken for during peak season, so make arrangements ahead of time. The charge is around $5 per hour.

For medical emergencies, pediatricians are available in all areas. One note regarding the hospitals: Kauai Veterans Memorial Hospital (not a Veteran's Administration hospital), a general service hospital operated by the State Department of Health, is in Waimea on the west side. It is staffed by the Garden Island Medical Group. However, few visitors stay in that area. Most visitors call a pediatrician of the Kauai Medical Group or an independent practitioner. Most practice in the vicinity of Lihue and use the G.N. Wilcox Memorial Hospital there. The Samuel Mahelona Memorial Hospital in Kapaa is for tuberculosis and psychiatric care only and has no emergency services.

The safest beaches for young children are described in the chapter "What to See." Few hotels or condominium complexes have shallow pools suitable for young children, nor are most pools fenced, so you will have to be watchful. Inflatable water wings are available here, as are small inflatable pools to splash in.

The three movie theatres often have films suitable for children. Most hotels and condos have cable television with cartoons. Videos are available for rent at various locations. But the major entertainment for children is outside. They will find a small plant (hilahila) in the lawn that collapses at a touch. They will be fascinated exploring tidepools along the shore at low tide. With nets, they can try to catch the small fish and tadpoles. If your child is old enough, he or she can learn to snorkel and see the fascinating underwater sealife. Feeding the fish is an experience any child will remember. Shell hunting is something all like to do. The small zoo behind the Coco Palms Hotel is worth a visit. And children love a luau. The best for them is at Smith's Tropical Paradise, where they can feed the ducks, geese and peacocks.

Ask at restaurants if they have a "keiki", or children's, menu. Meals from this menu are at a reduced price. There are fast food outlets almost everywhere. Some offer yogurt, fresh fruits, and interesting island foods. A "shave ice" is one thing your child will have to try, messy as it may be.

Local bookstores have wonderful Hawaiian books for children. Young snorkelers will enjoy *Hawaiian Reef Fishes*, a coloring book by Lori Randall featuring forty reef fish with background information on each. The *Hawaiian Animal Life* coloring book, by Sean McKeown, has more than just pictures to color. The text presents interesting factual information designed to stimulate a child to acquire a fundamental knowledge of Hawaii's birds, reptiles, amphibians and mammals. Colorful books on Hawaiian legends are also available.

TRAVEL TIPS FOR THE

PHYSICALLY IMPAIRED

Persons with disabilities, and those caring for them, should make arrangements through a travel agent who has experience in this field. All of the information you will need yourself can be obtained from the Commission on the Handicapped, P.O. Box 671, Lihue, Kauai, HI 96766. This office is open only in the afternoons on weekdays, so if you want to call, calculate the time and dial 808-245-4308. A very pleasant person, Joan Moody, is thoroughly trained, and will answer your questions. Ask her to send you: *A Key to Resources Serving the Handicapped on Kauai, Kauai Traveler's Guide for Physically Handicapped Persons*, and *A Summary of Architectural Barriers, Laws and Standards in the State of Hawaii.*

The next step is to notify the airline and the place where you are going to stay of the nature of your handicap. If you think you may require medical assistance, have your physician prepare a summary of your medical records and recommend a physician on Kauai for you. Those who have wheelchairs should bring their own, because there is a limited number for rent on Kauai and a suitable selection may not be available. Inform the airlines that you will be in or bringing a wheelchair, and tell them if it is battery powered. Airlines do not allow a battery pack – you must leave it at home and arrange ahead of time to rent one that fits your chair while you are here.

Although the older Lihue Airport did not have covered passageways to the planes, the new airport does, at least for jets (they don't fit prop planes). All facilities at the new airport are accessible to the handicapped, and assistance is available on request.

Only a few hotels on Kauai have accessible features. The Sheraton Kauai has fifteen rooms adapted for handicapped persons, the Waiohai sixteen, and the Kauai Hilton and Beach Villas sixteen.

Transportation for the handicapped is limited on Kauai. There are a few vans with a lift that are used for the programs serviced by the Office of Elderly Affairs (808-245-7230), but these are only available on a limited basis with advance notice. Avis Rent-a-Car (1-800-331-1212) will equip cars with hand controls, but the controls have to be flown over from Honolulu so they appreciate at least two or three days advance notice. Akita Enterprises, Ltd. (808-245-5344) has a few chauffeured vans designed for the handicapped available by advance arrangements. The parking permit from your home state, city or county is recognized on Kauai, and you will find that designated parking spaces are widely available on the island.

Because most of the construction on Kauai antedates legislation requiring accessibility, only the buildings constructed within the last ten or fifteen years follow the provisions in the uniform building code.

Sidewalks are in short supply on Kauai, even in downtown Lihue. There are very few curb cuts on these – in Lihue there is not a single block with continuous curb cuts.

Medical equipment and wheelchair repair are both available on the island, although you would be wise to make advance arrangements. A directory is in the *Kauai Traveler's Guide for Physically Handicapped Persons.*

WEDDINGS AND HONEYMOONS

A honeymoon on Kauai is a wondrous experience, but you can get married here, too, if you wish!

Couples often choose sites such as a beautiful private estate, a beach at sunset, a lush tropical garden by a waterfall, a yacht at sea, or the Fern Grotto. Some have a Hawaiian minister conduct the service in Hawaiian, with chanting, songs and hula. Churches of almost all denominations are on Kauai, and many are both historical and quaint. The Coco Palms Resort has a rustic chapel that was used in the movie "Sadie Thompson", and the new Westin Kauai Resort has a beautiful chapel.

Here is what you need to know to obtain a marriage license. The legal age is eighteen for both, and proof of age such as a birth certificate is required for those nineteen and under. The bride-to-be must have a premarital health certificate for rubella screening, signed by both a licensed physician and the director of the laboratory or his representative on the form prescribed by the State of Hawaii Department of Health.

This form, along with an information packet, can be obtained from the Marriage License Office, State of Hawaii Department of Health, P.O. Box 3378, Honolulu, HI 96801. Providing the proper form is used, the rubella test may be done by any government-approved laboratory on the mainland and signed by a physician licensed in any state. Allow two or three days for the results of the test to return from the laboratory.

Once you have the certificate, a marriage license can be obtained from a number of authorized agents on Kauai. Inquire of Mrs. Marsha Wong, the Registrar of Kauai, 245-4495. The most central agent is at 3016 Umi Street in Lihue, 245-5338. This procedure takes just a few minutes, the fee is $8.00, both parties must appear in person, there is no waiting period, and the license is valid for thirty days anywhere in Hawaii.

Although all arrangements for the wedding can be made here, as anywhere, by use of the telephone book and the recommendations of friends, visitors find it much more convenient to have one service arrange everything. The location, minister, priest or judge, music, flowers, limousine, cake, photography and video, reception and catering, even the rental of tuxedos and gowns can be handled by one of the three services on Kauai.

Helpful Information

The best is Wedding in Paradise, P.O. Box 340, Waimea, Kauai, HI 96796, 808-335-3502. The next choice in our opinion is The Wedding Place, P.O. Box 1469, Kapaa, Kauai, HI 96746, 808-822-7759 or 1-800-331-8071. A distant third is A Hawaiian Wedding Experience headquartered on Maui, P.O. Box 11093, Lahaina, Maui, HI 96761, agent on Kauai 808-245-2554.

Most major resorts offer special honeymoon packages, and the social director will assist you in many ways. Ask your travel agent which resorts currently offer packages, what they consist of, and the rates. It is wise to confirm this directly with the resort you choose.

OBTAINING HELPFUL INFORMATION

Before your visit, you might want to subscribe to:

The Garden Island Newspaper
3137 Kuhio Highway
Lihue, Kauai, HI 96766
808-245-3681
(5 times a week)

Kauai Magazine
P.O. Box 1811
Lihue, Kauai, HI 96766
808-245-1696
(semi-annual, Jan. & June)

Kauai Times Newspaper
3313-B Oihana Street
Lihue, Kauai, HI 96766
808-245-8825
(weekly)

Aloha, The Magazine of
Hawaii and the Pacific
P.O. Box 3260
Honolulu, HI 96801
(monthly)

Write or call:

Hawaii Visitor's Bureau (Kauai Office)
3016 Umi Street, Suite 207
Lihue, Kauai, HI 96766
808-245-3971

Ask for their 56-page "Kauai Vacation Planner" for $5 plus $1.10 postage. NOTE: You should be forewarned that this office is famous – or infamous – for its unhelpful and ungracious attitude towards tourists. Why, we don't know. Just don't get your hopes up. Some information about Kauai can be obtained from the Honolulu and mainland HVB offices, however.

Specific questions can be directed to:

Hawaii State Division of Parks
P.O. Box 1671
Lihue, Kauai, HI 96766
808-245-4444

Chamber of Commerce of Kauai
297 Kele Street, Room 201
Lihue, Kauai, HI 96766
808-245-7363

Kauai County Division
of Parks & Recreation
4193 Hardy Street
Lihue, HI 96766
808-245-1881

The Lihue Office of the
Commission on the Handicapped
3040 Umi Street
Lihue, Kauai, HI 96766
808-245-4308

Once you are here, the hotel or condominium front desk or travel desk can provide additional information.

The four free publications available to visitors were described in the "Introduction", as were guide books to all of the Hawaiian Islands.

There are three cable television services on Kauai. Each has an information channel.

KAUAI CABLE TELEVISION provides service to the entire west side, Poipu, and also to Anahola and Hanalei.

CHANNEL	CHANNEL
2 - KHON (NBC) Honolulu	12 - LIF
3 - Kauai TV Three	13 - KHNL (Ind.) Honolulu
4 - KITV (ABC) Honolulu	25 - HBO Home Box Office
5 - WTBS Atlanta	26 - DIS Disney
6 - Information Channel	27 - SHOW Showtime
7 - CNN Cable News Network	28 - Nippon Golden Network
8 - Nickelodeon (Children's	(All Japanese program)
programming)	29 - TMC The Movie Channel
9 - KGMB (CBS) Honolulu	34 - USA Sports & Family
10 - ESPN Satellite	35 - TMPO Tempo
11 - KHET (PBS) Honolulu	36 - DISC Discovery

Visitor information is on Channel 6.

GARDEN ISLAND CABLEVISION provides service from Puhi through Lihue, Nawiliwili to the Waipouli/Kapaa area.

CHANNEL	CHANNEL
2 - KHON (NBC) Honolulu	8 - WTBS Atlanta
3 - Information Center	9 - KGMB (CBS) Honolulu
4 - KITV (ABC) Honolulu	10 - CNN Cable News Network
5 - HBO Home Box Office	11 - KHET (PBS) Honolulu
6 - SHOW Showtime	12 - USA Sports & Family
7 - FUJI (All Japanese)	13 - KHNL (Ind.) Honolulu

Visitor information is on Channel 3.

PRINCEVILLE CABLE TELEVISION provided service in the Princeville area.

CHANNEL	CHANNEL
2 – KHON (NBC) Honolulu	18 – The Nashville Network
3 – Information Channel	19 – The Inspirational Network
4 – KITV (ABC) Honolulu	20 – CBN – Christian Network
5 – WTBS Atlanta	21 – WGN Chicago
6 – USA Sports & Family	22 – CNN Headline News
7 – CNN Cable News Network	23 – TEMPO
8 – Nickelodeon (Children's	24 – ESPN Satellite
Programming)	25 – WOR
9 – KGMB (CBS) Honolulu	26 – DISCOVERY
10 – PCC Bulletin Board	27 – FNN
11 – Kauai (PBS)	28 – NBC Live Feed
12 – Lifetime	29 – ABC Live Feed
13 – KHNL (Ind.) Honolulu	30 – CBS Live Feed
14 – DIS Disney Channel	35 – C-SPAN
16 – TMC The Movie Channel	36 – WeatherChannel
17 – SHOW Showtime	

Visitor information is on Channel 3.

You will find that on Kauai, both a main-frame computer and crystal ball are necessary to use the television schedules in the Honolulu newspapers or the *TV Guide*. Every Friday, *The Garden Island* has a schedule for the week which is a little better – it only requires a hand calculator. The trick with any schedule is to figure out which time is listed – EST, PST, or a daytime savings variant thereof – then convert that time to Hawaiian time. Those who get Kauai Cable Television will find electronic help for this on Channel 33.

We do not receive the Honolulu FM stations very well. On our eastern and central shores they can be heard, but are often distorted. Several are available through the television cables, however. Easy listening and the only classical music is available this way.

KUAI (720 AM) is the principal Kauai AM radio station. Every morning at 6:30 there is local news, weather and announcements of community events until about 7:15 a.m. Sunday nights features Hawaiian music from 6:00 to 11:00 p.m.

KQNG (93.5 FM), referred to as KONG locally, is Kauai's only FM station and is for younger listeners. KQNG also has an AM station (570 AM) which has almost identical programming.

The stronger AM stations in Honolulu can be heard on Kauai. KCCN (1420 AM) plays Hawaiian music constantly – the good right along with the bad. Your favorite talk station can be heard, too – KGU (760 AM). Easy listening and "golden oldies" stations are also on the AM dial.

If your interest in acquiring information goes deeper in any subject, see "Recommended Reading" at the back of this guide. A bibliography in brochure form, *What to Read about Hawaii*, can also be obtained without cost from the Hawaii State Library, 478 South King Street, Honolulu, HI 96813.

IMPORTANT TELEPHONE NUMBERS

Police – Ambulance – Fire.....................................911
Aloha Airlines..245-3691
Better Business Bureau – Honolulu.......................1-531-8131
Chamber of Commerce....................................245-7363
Civil Defense Agency....................................245-4001
Coast Guard Search & Rescue............................245-4521
Commission on the Handicapped.........................245-4308
County of Kauai Information.............................245-3213
County Parks (Camping Permits).........................245-1881
Crisis Intervention......................................245-3411
Directory Assistance for Kauai.............................1-411
Inter-island Directory Assistance.......................1-555-1212
Hawaiian Airlines.......................................245-3671
Hawaiian Telephone (Repair)................................611
Hospitals:
    Wilcox Memorial, Lihue.............................245-1100
    Kauai Veteran's Memorial, Waimea...................338-9431
Kauai Electric Company.................................335-6236
Marine Weather...245-3564
Mayor's Office (For Complaints).........................245-3385
Mid Pacific Airlines.....................................245-7775
Pacific Missile Range Facility...........................335-4229
Physicians:
    Kauai Medical Group.................245-1500, 245-6810
    Garden Island Medical Group.......................338-9431
Poison Control Center – Honolulu....................1-800-326-3585
Red Cross...245-4919
Sexual Assault Services.................................245-4144
Surf Report...335-3611
State Parks (Camping Permits).........................245-4444
Tel-Med (Taped Information)............................245-9011
Time 245-0212
United Airlines..245-9533
Visitor's Bureau.......................................245-3971
Visitor Information Office, Hawaii......................246-1440
Weather..245-6001

Note that the first three digits in telephone numbers give the location you are calling on the island:

826 – Princeville	742 – Koloa
828 – Kilauea	332 – Kalaheo
822 – Kapaa	335 – Hanapepe
245 – Lihue	337 – Kekaha
246 – Lihue	338 – Waimea

All numbers in the Hawaiian Islands are within the area code 808. Inter-island calls require a "1" first and are toll calls. This guide will give the Hawaii area code only when a number is likely to be called from the mainland.

You can dial Wide Area Telephone Service (WATS) numbers toll-free from the mainland by using the code "800" with a "1" first. This is *not* to be confused with the area code of Hawaii. Some "800" numbers listed in this guidebook cannot be dialed from Kauai. Unfortunately, there is no good system to know which these are ahead of time. The only thing to do is try, and if a funny tone comes on followed by "Code 808 512", that's one you can't.

GROCERY SHOPPING

Grocery shopping on Kauai is a little different from what you may be used to at home. Most of what we consume here comes from the mainland to Honolulu, and then by barge behind a tow boat to Kauai. The barges may come as frequently as twice a week in good weather, but sometimes the stormy channel stops them for two or three weeks at a time. So when you go into one of our grocery stores they may be out of what you want for a few days, and what they do have is a little older than the items in your store at home. Although the climate of Kauai favors the growing of fresh fruits and vegetables, it is good for fungus and little pests, too. And traditionally, most of what we produce here is by small farmers. They resist forming more efficient cooperatives, so only a limited amount is grown here for local consumption. As sugar declines, the large plantations are starting to experiment with various other crops, but their production has not yet reached the market.

As a result of all this, Kauai doesn't have many major supermarkets with an abundance of everything. The closest is the Star Supermarket in the Kukui Grove Shopping Center. The Foodland stores in the Waipouli Town Center and Princeville are also good. The Big Save markets are smaller but very adequate. Because of the price of land, shipping costs and "middlemen", prices tend to average 25% higher than on the mainland. Big Save stores price a bit lower and have a wider selection of oriental and ethnic foods. Clockwise around the island, they are located in Hanalei, Kapaa, Lihue, Koloa, Eleele, Waimea and Kekaha.

Of course, each population center has its local store of the "mom and pop" type. Some of these have considerable charm and character and *may* have what you want. Then there are mini-marts scattered along the major highways just like the ones at home. Military personnel (active, retired or reserve) can shop at the small PX-commissary at the Pacific Missile Range Facility, Barking Sands, and save about one-third.

The best sources for fresh fruit are the fruit stands that are just about everywhere. There are also four "Sunshine Markets", where producers bring what they have grown and you buy from them directly. The one in Lihue is at 3:30 p.m. on Fridays at Vidinha Stadium off Route 51. A second is in Kapaa on Wednesdays at 3 p.m. in the new ballpark across from the Armory. The third is in Koloa at the ballpark on Mondays at noon. The fourth is 3 p.m. on Tuesdays in Hanalei at Waipa. The Sunshine Markets are only active for a short time so arrive early, pick out what you'd like, and stand close to what you want until the market opens.

The only retail outlet for mainland aged beef is Ray's Special Meats at 1-3959 Kaumualii Highway in Hanapepe (335-6150). Major restaurants have their meat flown in from the mainland.

The freshest fish is found at Seafoods of the Pacific in Port Allen (335-3505). J & R Seafoods, at 4361 Rice Street in Lihue (245-9946), is another reliable source. If you inquire by phone about deliveries of fresh fish and time your shopping accordingly, you can also get fresh fish at many markets around Kauai.

ANNUAL EVENTS ON KAUAI

FEBRUARY
Hanapepe Raft/Run – Includes a raft-making contest and race, along with a fun run.

Waimea's "Main Street" Celebration – Cultural displays of the town's historic past.

Captain Cook Celebration in Waimea – Includes entertainment, food, games and craft booths. There are also cultural exhibits, a canoe race and Caper Fun Run 10K. The weekend activities culminate with a luau.

Women's Kemper Open – Princeville Makai Golf Course.

MARCH
Japanese Girl's Day on the 3rd – Small girls in traditional garb everywhere on the island.

Prince Kuhio Festival – Includes pageantry, songs and dances from the era of Prince Kuhio. There are canoe races and many festivities in Lihue and other towns.

Prince Kuhio Day on the 26th – A State holiday.

APRIL
Polo Season – Runs throughout spring and summer at the polo field at Anini Beach, just past the pavilion.

Kokee Wilderness Festival – A run in Kokee State Park. Also a mountain bike race, a music festival and a fair.

Buddha Day – At all island temples in celebration of the birth of Buddha.

MAY
May Day on Kauai – The first day of May (called Lei Day locally). Don't miss the lei-making contest, displays and other events at the Kauai Museum.

Japanese Boy's Day on the 5th – Colorful carp flown from bamboo poles everywhere.

Ke Ola Hou – Spring festival with games, crafts and dance in Hanapepe.

Fiesta Filipina – Colorful Filipino ceremonies at various places on the island.

Fitness Fair – A multi-sports event to select best all-around athlete, includes a 5 km and 10 km run, a roughwater swim, weightlifting and more. Entertainment and party. Poipu.

JUNE
King Kamehameha Day (June 11) – Island-wide festivities include a parade, hoolaulea, and arts and crafts booths.

Bougainvillaea Festival – Hanapepe.

JULY
Kekaha 4th of July Celebration – Entertainment, food booths, festivities and fireworks. Other festivities elsewhere.

Koloa Plantation Days – A parade in Koloa and festivities celebrating the opening of the "first" sugar mill in Koloa. Daily events include tours of the mill, lectures and films.

Obon Season (Late June through August) – Bon Odori festivals are held in rotation at each Buddhist Mission around the island at 8 p.m. Fridays and Saturdays during this period. American Buddhists of Japanese ancestry perform colorful folk dances honoring departed ancestral spirits. On Sunday, the toro, or floating lantern, ceremony is held at the seashore near each Mission. A white boat tows hundreds of floating lanterns out to sea as their way of bidding farewell to departed ancestors. You can participate if you wish.

AUGUST
Hanalei Stampede – The biggest rodeo event of the season, drawing cowboys from outer islands for bronco-busting.

Sela Moku – Pants dance, a time for young and old to come out dancing under the stars around the County Building in Lihue.

Admission Day (August 21) – A State holiday.

West Kauai Summer Festival – Old fashioned, end-of-summer beach party. Games, races, Hawaiian crafts, luau and cookout, beauty pageant, hula, street dancing and a concert. Waimea.

SEPTEMBER

Aloha Week – Festivals, keiki hula, canoe races and a variety of other events including a parade.

Kauai County Fair – Exhibits, produce, flowers, 4-H livestock and entertainment. Kauai War Memorial Convention Hall, Lihue.

Century Bike Rides – 25, 50 and 100 miles through Kauai's countryside.

OCTOBER

Kauai Loves You Triathlon – A world championship super-series event. A 1.5 mile swim, 54-mile bike ride and 12.4 mile run. Begins and ends at Hanalei.

NOVEMBER

Thanksgiving Day on Kauai. Attend service of your choice and hear beautiful hymns sung in Hawaiian.

DECEMBER

International Film Festival

Bodhi Day – Buddhist temples commemorate "Day of Enlightenment."

Christmas in Waimea – Candlelight tour of missions and churches, caroling in the streets, and displays of "Twelve Days of Christmas" Hawaiian-style.

★ For dates and details on any of these events, try calling the Lihue Office of the Hawaii Visitor's Bureau, (808) 245-3971, or better yet, watch the local papers.

★ Smaller local events take place all the time. The television information channels and "The Garden Island" newspaper are two good sources of information, but the best is KUAI-720 AM radio from 6:30 to 7:15 a.m. daily.

WEATHER

The weather on Kauai affects almost everything you do here. So we'll go into some detail, but stick to the coastal areas because it can be extremely variable in the mountains.

In Hawaii we have only two seasons, not four as on the mainland. Summer, in Hawaiian "kau", is five months in length from May through September. Winter, "hooilo", is seven months in duration from October to April.

During the winter, the temperature on Kauai ranges from the low to the mid-seventies during the day, and in summer from the mid-seventies to the mid-eighties, which is about two degrees lower than Honolulu. Temperatures at night are ten to twelve degrees below that. This relative stability occurs because the islands are small land masses surrounded by thousands of miles of ocean. The average temperature of the surrounding water in the coolest month of February is seventy-four degrees, and in the warmest month of August, eighty degrees. Another factor adding stability is that the days and nights are nearly equal in length all year. In the summer, the longest day is thirteen hours, twenty minutes, and in the winter the shortest day is ten hours, fifty minutes. This is also the reason there is no Daylight Savings Time in Hawaii.

In the summer, the trade winds blow about 90-95% of the time from a relatively fixed high about 1,000 miles to the northeast called the Pacific Anticyclone at an average velocity of twelve to fourteen knots, which makes the warmer temperatures then much more pleasant. The trades are weaker, averaging six to ten knots, more from the east, and less constant during the winter. When the trade winds are blowing, the relative humidity is usually in the eighties on the northeast or windward coast, and in the sixties or seventies along the leeward (southwest) shores.

Rain is less frequent and briefer in duration in the summer than winter, and more falls on the north and east (average sixty to eighty inches) than southern coasts (average twenty to thirty inches) in both seasons. As the trade winds rise up over the northeast coast and ascend into the mountains, the moisture in them condenses and precipitates. This is called the orographic effect. At the top of our main mountain range is Mt. Waialeale, which has an average rainfall of 486" per year, and it rains there almost constantly. Annual rainfalls exceeding 600" (fifty feet) are on record! On the southwest shore at Mana rainfall is scant, rarely reaching a dozen inches per year. During both winter and summer, there is a tendency for rain to occur mostly during the night and early mornings, except when storms occur. Because the afternoons are often clear, you shouldn't cancel your plans when you wake up to the sound of rain.

Overcast skies follow this same pattern. When the trade winds are blowing, the leeward or southern shore is overcast only 5-10% of the time, but the windward (or northern) shores are cloudy 30-60% of the time. The upper figures are more frequent in the summer, and the lower figures in the winter.

Most visitors don't pay much attention to the season in Hawaii when they pick the date for their vacation. Rather, it is the season back home, usually the coldest part of the winter, that determines the date. But even the summer weather here is more pleasant than at most places on the mainland.

Experienced visitors select the south shore as their base of operations. Hawaiian kings, who could live anywhere they wanted to, invariably picked the lee shores of the islands. Waikiki on Oahu, the Kona and Kohala areas on the Island of Hawaii, Kaanapali and Wailea on Maui, and the Waimea area on Kauai were their traditional places of residence for centuries.

Storms are the one thing that alters the relatively constant weather on Kauai. Winter storms arising in north Pacific lows come closer to the islands, so ten to twelve of these each winter impact upon the north and northwest shores. They bring high winds, rain, and waves that often reach heights of twenty to thirty feet. This is the time that, on all the famous north shore surfing spots, the word "surf's up!" goes out and the major surfing contests are held. This is also why you will be cautioned against swimming anywhere but the southern shore in the winter. The winter storms do not affect the south shore.

It is different during the summer. Then it is winter below the equator. Equivalent south Pacific lows generate the same number of storms there, but because they are so much farther away, their effect on the south shore is much less. Perhaps four to six storms per season come close enough to affect the southern shore, usually causing waves of only six to eight feet.

Storms that occur north of the equator but south of Hawaii bring most of the Kona winds, accompanied by rain, higher humidity and high waves. Occasionally they are only strong enough to stop the trade winds. Although Kona winds can occur at any time, summer or winter, those that come in the summer are the ones that are really felt, especially on the southern shore. The summer is already warmer, and then comes an overcast sky, high humidity, and either no breeze or an onshore wind that makes the surf choppy and unpleasant. Fortunately, Kona winds occur only about 5-10% of the time in the summer. During the winter, they may be present 20-25% of the time, but residents and visitors don't mind because the temperatures are lower then.

Hurricanes do occur in Hawaii, but infrequently. These are giant whirlwinds in which the wind speed is seventy-four miles per hour or more. The proper term is "tropical cyclone", but they are commonly known as hurricanes throughout the Atlantic and most of the Pacific and as typhoons in the Far East. They are most likely to occur from July to December, with August being the peak month. Most of them form south of the Hawaiian Islands in far-off tropical seas and pass south of the Islands toward the west. Although formal meteorological records have only been kept by the National Weather Service since 1947, the memory of those living here goes back seventy-five years, and in that time six hurricanes have affected Kauai:

1950 Hiki passed north of Kauai, bringing rain to the island.

1957 Della passed to the south of Kauai, bringing high waves and rain. This was a particularly bad year because Nina also passed closer, 120 miles to the southwest, and brought high winds, rain and thirty-foot waves, but produced only minor damage on Kauai.

1959 The strongest winds (102 miles per hour with higher gusts) ever recorded on Kauai were when the eye of Hurricane Dot crossed over the island, causing $6 million in damage, mostly to sugar cane.

1978 Fico passed 190 miles southwest of Kauai, bringing only rain and high surf.

1982 The eye of Hurricane Iwa passed between Niihau and Kauai. Winds were only sixty-five miles per hour with gusts to 100 miles per hour, but Iwa produced greater destruction than Hurricane Dot because the island was more built up. It caused approximately $250 million in damages to the island.

Hurricanes wreak their havoc by four factors: high winds, rain, waves, and storm surge. The latter is a dome of higher water level under the eye of the hurricane.

Due to constant monitoring by satellites, Hawaii always receives adequate notice of the approach of a hurricane. A "warning" is issued when it appears that one may affect the Islands, and an "alert" is issued when its impact is expected within twenty-four hours. The public is advised through local radio, television and newspaper announcements.

You can find out about the tides by calling Marine Weather (245-3564). Normal tides have a range of only about two feet on Kauai, but a tsunami or seismic wave, incorrectly called a tidal wave, can cause considerable damage to certain types of shoreline. It is produced by a slippage of tectonic plates, a landslide, or a volcanic eruption on the ocean floor. Most originate around the Pacific Rim north, east and west of Hawaii and affect the corresponding shores of Kauai the most, with only "wraparound" effects on the south coast. At sea, a tsunami can scarcely be detected. From crest to trough it will measure a foot or less, and the crests, usually four or five, come about fifteen minutes apart and travel at speeds of four to five hundred miles per hour. The height of the crests diminishes with the distance from the originating event.

The danger is determined almost entirely by shore conditions. If the impacted shoreline drops off abruptly to great depths, there is no effect at all. However, if the ocean bottom gradually shoals, a crest of a few inches at sea can become several feet in height by the time it reaches the shoreline. Low-lying land may be inundated by this. If there is a narrowly restricted passage such as an entry to a harbor, a strong current may be formed. But the most serious condition results when a tsunami comes ashore at a wide opening of a v-shaped enclosed valley. As the valley narrows inland, the tsunami increases in both height and velocity. It may form a "bore", or rapid wave, with a height of thirty to forty feet toward the apex of the valley.

Thirty-two tsunamis have been detected in the Hawaiian Islands since 1819, but only a half dozen have caused serious damage. Because of this threat, the Pacific Tsunami Warning Center has been established at Ewa Beach on Oahu under the control of the National Weather Service. The Center receives input from a network of seismological and tide stations around the world.

If a tsunami is generated anywhere in the Pacific, an early warning is issued to the public by radio and television. If it appears that the tsunami is headed toward Hawaii, the Hawaii State Civil Defense directs evacuation of the tsunami inundation areas, maps of which can be found in the front of all island telephone directories. Civil Defense sirens sound a three-minute steady tone from the yellow sirens you see erected on poles in susceptible areas. The radio stations then switch to Emergency Broadcasting System (EBS) status and broadcast regular announcements over the appropriate frequencies. Once the estimated time of arrival of the tsunami in Hawaiian waters is determined, the same siren signal is sounded two hours ahead of the time of arrival and again a half hour before arrival.

The warning sirens are tested on the first working day of every month at 11:45 a.m., and this test is coordinated with the radio stations, so don't get upset if you hear the sirens then.

WHAT TO PACK

As you probably gathered from the foregoing, you won't need to pack much for your visit here. Kauai is a casual place. Only two or three restaurants request a jacket for men, but a long-sleeved shirt with a collar will do. None require ties. The emphasis for both sexes is on wash-and-wear summer clothes throughout the year. The newer treated cotton fabrics are best – synthetics tend to be too warm. If you are coming from the east coast in the dead of winter with a stop on the west coast, of course you should wear what will be comfortable in the airports. If you plan to stay on Oahu a while and dine at the better restaurants there, slacks and a jacket or a light-weight suit and tie for him and an appropriate dress for her should be included. Solid-color slacks go better with aloha shirts – white are favored. Shorts for both sexes will get a lot of use, but don't wear them with dark socks and street shoes or you will certainly stand out in the crowd.

Women will find having a scarf handy, and a hat in the sun is essential for both men and women. For the frequent rains here, a light nylon shell jacket (hooded for the ladies' hair) is wise – and will serve well for the trip to Kokee, where the temperatures can be ten to fifteen degrees cooler. If you chill easily, also bring along a light sweater for Kokee. Umbrellas tend to be a nuisance, but in the winter when the rains last longer, a collapsible one comes in handy.

For footwear, visitors almost live in sandals or zoris here, but they can be purchased anywhere after arrival. Loafers and comfortable white shoes are popular. Bring light-weight hiking shoes and good socks if you plan to hike. Tennis shoes will do, but lack ankle support. Two bathing suits, each in a plastic bag, are *de rigueur*. Bring tennis stuff, masks, snorkels and fins if you will be doing these things. They can all be rented here, but the cost, especially for a family, can mount up. For example, snorkeling equipment rental is $7 to $20 per day. Bring dark glasses and sunscreen – SPF 15 or 18 if possible – at least one that is water-resistant.

Your address book will come in handy for sending postcards, and some personal or business cards for friends you will make here.

Laundry can be done at several places on Kauai. Dry cleaning is a bit more difficult, so don't bring a lot of clothing that requires it. Bring or plan to buy an assortment of plastic bags for everything from wet bathing suits to seashells. Try to keep your luggage down to one bag and one carry-on per person, and leave one of them half-empty for things you will buy. Aloha shirts and muumuus find their way into almost every suitcase going back home.

Leave your portable radios and cassette players that don't have earphones at home. Kauai is a quiet island. People here are courteous, so you may never know you are offending someone near you with loud music. A radio or cassette player *with* earphones, however, is pleasant while sunning.

Carry your film in a film-shield bag – x-rays *do* harm it, especially with multiple exposures. Or better yet, carry it in your hand through the metal-detecting device, which is magnetic and does not harm film. The quality of film development on Kauai is equal to that of any place on the mainland.

Small binoculars will come in handy to see whales and porpoises or birds and flowers when you can't get near them – or just to check bikinis on the beach!

GETTING THERE

First, a word or two about travel agents. The ideal one should take the time to sit down with you, discuss your personal preferences and arrange an itinerary to suit you individually. Try to avoid one who rushes you through or attempts to sell you something they arranged previously for someone else. If you have dealt with a travel agent before, and found him or her satisfactory, by all means stay with the one you have chosen. But if you have to select one, he or she should be a member of the American Society of Travel Agents and licensed by the Airlines Reporting Corporation. These are minimum qualifications. Beyond this, the most competent ones have the initials C.T.C. after their names, standing for Certified Travel Counselor. This means that the agent has completed a two-year course conducted by the Institute of Certified Travel Agents.

Your trip will be much more rewarding if, before you consult with your agent, you have made some decisions on what you would like to see, how much time you can spare, and what you would like to spend. With a little research and this guide book, you can help your agent do a much better job for you – and they don't necessarily have to have extensive experience booking people to Kauai.

This guide book is for independent travelers and will not say much about pre-packaged tours. If these interest you, contact American Express, Cartan, Maupintour, Tauck, or let your travel agent advise you. If you decide on a package tour after you arrive in Hawaii, try Trade Wind Tours, Hawaiian Holidays, Aloha Hawaii, Island Holidays, Roberts Hawaii or Mackenzie.

Of course, most people come to Hawaii by air. But it is still possible to take that leisurely cruise, anticipate the Islands during passage, and luxuriate in the arrival ceremony. American Hawaii Cruises makes a few trips from San Francisco each year that connect with its week-long tour of the neighbor islands in the *Independence* and *Constitution*. Occasionally, one or the other leaves from Seattle or Los Angeles. The P & O Lines (originating in Europe) sometimes stop at Honolulu during its world tours in either the *Oriana* or *Canberra*. Their *Pacific Princess* regularly departs from the mainland west coast and stops off in Hawaii on its way to New Zealand and Australia. The Royal Viking Line's *Sagafjord* and *Vistafjord*, and Cunard's *Queen Elizabeth 2* occasionally call in Honolulu. Rarely there are others. And don't overlook freighters! If these or any other ocean cruise interest you, ask your travel agent.

Now for the airlines. There are about a dozen foreign carriers that fly to Hawaii, but the Jones Act prevents their taking passengers from one U.S. city to another – and that includes Honolulu. This Act also applies to the ships described above. But you can take a foreign carrier if you are only stopping over in Hawaii before going on to a foreign destination.

There are presently eight major American carriers that fly from several mainland cities to Honolulu:

AIR AMERICA – Their 800 number is 1-800-247-2475; in Honolulu, 808-833-4433. One note: This newest arrival on the scene has only one L-1011 for their San Francisco-Honolulu route, so any mechanical difficulty will delay your flight.

AMERICAN AIRLINES – Their 800 number is 1-800-433-7300; in Los Angeles, 213-568-8999; in Honolulu, 808-526-0044.

CONTINENTAL – Their 800 number is 1-800-525-0280; in Honolulu, 808-836-7730.

DELTA AIR LINES – They fly out of Atlanta, stopping on the west coast. Their 800 number is 1-800-221-1212.

HAWAIIAN AIRLINES – Their 800 number is 1-800-367-5320; in Honolulu, 808-537-5100.

NORTHWEST AIRLINES – Their 800 number is 1-800-225-2525; in Honolulu, 808-955-2255.

TWA – Their 800 number is 1-800-321-2000; in Honolulu, 808-241-6522.

UNITED AIRLINES – United has more flights to Hawaii from more U.S. cities than any other airline. They have no central 800 number, but do have one for each area in the United States. See your telephone directory. Their Honolulu number is 808-547-2211.

United is the only airline that flies directly to Lihue. Their smaller DC-8's can land here, but the length of the runway is not sufficient for a takeoff with a full load of fuel. Their return flights stop on another island where there is a longer runway, usually Maui, top off their fuel, and then go on to the mainland.

Most of these airlines allow two bags per person plus a carry-on. The carry-on must be of such a size as to fit under the seat in front of you or in the overhead rack. Although each bag should weigh less than seventy pounds, it is a rare airline today that weighs your bags. They do require, however, that you have a name tag with your address and telephone number affixed to each bag. The usual restriction on dimensions pertain; that is, the height, width and length of each bag should not exceed a sum of 62 inches. Ask about unusually bulky items such as surfboards – the extra charge for them is substantial.

Once you are in Honolulu, you have a choice of three airlines for your flight to Lihue. Try to arrive at the check-in counter at least a half hour before your flight because some tend to give away your reservations to standbys about fifteen minutes before each flight. There is intense competition between Aloha and Hawaiian, so you'll find the fares are competitive. Mid Pacific flies prop-jets, takes approximately ten minutes longer, and their fares are a bit lower.

One tip that was already mentioned in "Traveling With Children", but that might not be read by those who are not bringing children with them, and deserves repeating here. If you are not stopping off for a while on Oahu, but are coming straight to Kauai, check your bags all the way through to Lihue Airport. Your travel agent will inform you that at least a seventy-minute interval must be scheduled between your carrier's arrival in Honolulu and the takeoff time to Lihue of your inter-island carrier to permit the transfer of baggage. However, after disembarking from your major carrier, you can walk or take the Wikiwiki Shuttle to the inter-island terminal and catch the next flight on any inter-island carrier to Lihue. Each honors the tickets of the others. The aircraft are rarely full, so you can almost always do this. Then, when you arrive in Lihue, you will have an hour or so to rent your car or do some grocery shopping. When you return to the airport, your baggage will have arrived on the flight you were scheduled on.

Your travel agent will have advised you about the special offers inter-island carriers have from time to time that include a rental car and accommodations. If you have at least three in your family or if you plan to make six or more inter-island flights, inquire about the coupons sold in blocks of six which save you approximately 15% per flight. If you came from the mainland on Hawaiian Airlines, inter-island fare was included in the price of your ticket. Ask also about the lower fares for children, senior citizens, military, and for the first and last flights each day.

The inter-island carriers that operate between Honolulu and Kauai are:

ALOHA AIRLINES - They fly only jets - mostly 737's. Their telephone number in Honolulu is 808-836-1111; in Lihue, 808-245-3691. This airline tends to have more respect for its schedule than the others, and its personnel are more courteous.

HAWAIIAN AIRLINES - They fly DC9's, Dash 7's and prop planes. Their 800 number is 1-800-367-5320; in Honolulu, 808-537-5100; in Lihue, 808-245-3671.

MID PACIFIC AIRLINES - They fly only turbo-prop airplanes. Their 800 number is 1-800-367-7010; in Honolulu, 808-836-3313; in Lihue, 808-245-7775. Flights tend to take a few minutes longer on one of their prop planes, but you see more because of the lower altitude.

PRINCEVILLE AIRWAYS - (owned by Aloha Airlines) flies Dehaviland Twin Otters only to Princeville airport. Their 800 number is 1-800-652-6541; in Princeville, 808-826-3770; in Honolulu, 808-833-9555.

Of course, charter flights in smaller aircraft can be arranged to either airport.

The Lihue Airport ocean approach runway was completed in 1985, and the new terminal facilities were opened in 1987. Although neither of the two runways permit direct flights to the mainland, they are due to be lengthened by 1990, which will permit such flights.

The new terminal facilities are approximately five times larger, having 200,000 square feet and two baggage carrousels. The covered ramps that fit jets mean that sudden showers will no longer drench you. The facilities include a snack bar, bar, visitor information booths, and parking for 500 automobiles. It is attractively landscaped and a considerable improvement over the older terminal.

One luxurious way to reach Kauai from Oahu - and to visit other islands as well - is on one of the American Hawaii Cruises ships, the *Independence* or *Constitution*. These comfortable 700 foot ships are decorated in a 1950's version of 1930 art deco, if you can conceive that. Decor aside, accommodations are adequate, the service is friendly, and about half the crews are from Hawaii.

Each week-long cruise departs from Honolulu, and then the schedules differ. The one you would want stops one day at Hilo, one at Kailua-Kona, two at Kahului, Maui, and then one at Nawiliwili, Kauai. Arrivals at all ports are early in the morning to allow shore excursions, with departures in the evenings. Ask your travel agent or contact American Hawaii Cruises, 550 Kearny Street, San Francisco, CA 94108, 1-800-227-3666.

At this writing, similar cruises are being planned by Matson Lines on the refurbished *SS Monterey* starting in 1988.

Air tours of one or more islands departing from Honolulu are sometimes scheduled by Panorama Air Tours and Hawaiian Airlines.

GETTING AROUND

TAXIS

There are no regular shuttles to hotels or condos, but one from the Princeville Airport to the Sheraton Princeville may be set up by pre-arrangement. And there is no public transportation on Kauai, so unless you are renting a car, you have to rely on a taxi to get you to where you are staying. Kauai Airport Taxi Association (KATA) has the airport concession, and a cab stand is located at each of the two carrousels at the airport. If a taxi is not there, use the direct-line phone nearby.

Other taxi companies can be called to the airport or used for transportation anywhere on the island:

Abba Taxi	245-5225
ABC Taxi	822-7641
Ace Taxi	822-7211
Akiko's Taxi	822-3613
Al's Taxi	742-1390
Dad's Taxi Service	335-3482
Garden Isle Taxi & Tours	245-6161
Hanalei-Surfside Taxi	826-6658 (North Shore Only)
Lorenzo's Taxi Service	245-6631
North Shore Cab Co.	826-6189 (North Shore Only)
Poipu Taxi Service	742-1717
Wailua Taxi	822-3671

In general, you will find the cab drivers on Kauai friendly and fair. They have standard rates, which presently are set at $1.60 at the drop and 20 cents for every 1/6th of a mile. Many of these give you impromptu tours along the way, and will also arrange more formal tours to suit your schedule.

Limousines may be rented at:

Al's Taxi	742-1390
Dad's Taxi	335-3482
Exotic Rides, Inc.	456-1939
(Headquarters on Oahu)	
Limo Limo	822-0393

Once in your hotel, one service will take you to the major shopping areas in a van. Call Shoppe Hoppers (332-7272). Shoppe Hoppers is planning to institute an island-wide shuttle service sometime in the future. As we go to press, they have set up a shuttle from the Lihue Airport to south shore hotels by reservation only.

RENTAL CARS

As tempting as it might sound, no one stakes out a bit of beach in front of their hotel or condo and stays there all the time. You will find once you are here that you will want mobility. Perhaps those who are on a package tour with all transportation provided can get by without renting a car. The car rental agencies on Kauai are extremely competitive, and this is one of the best bargains on the island. Be sure to reserve a car well in advance. During peak seasons, some of the agencies are completely out, or the cars that are available may not be what you want.

Before leaving home, check with your insurance agent concerning your automobile coverages. Most of the rental agencies here have a policy of looking to the person renting the automobile for the estimated cost of repairs (up to the full value of the car) in the event of any damage. Their position is that they will not deal with an insurance company, so even if your collision coverage is adequate, you need to ask your agent about rapidity of payment. You may find it necessary to arrange rapid access to a substantial sum of money with not more than two or three days wait in case a hitch develops with your insurance payment. Otherwise, you have to take the collision damage waiver (CDW) that costs about $9 or $10 a day. Over a week or two this mounts up.

The other "insurance" the rental agencies push is personal accident insurance (PAI). Again, your own liability coverage may be perfectly adequate. This election is a form of liability coverage for the driver and all passengers that costs $3-$4 per day.

On Kauai, the major national and international car rental agencies are in competition with those that only do business in the Hawaiian Islands or on Kauai, so all rates tend to be about the same. Hertz manages to keep theirs a little higher than the average, and Rent-a-Wreck's are a little lower because they have cars two or three years old. All offer flat rates – that is, unlimited mileage – at so much per day plus gas and tax. Gas is about ten cents more per gallon here than on the mainland, and the tax is 4%. These rates vary with the season, which may not be mentioned in their literature. Ask for the rate for the days you want to rent the car. Also, some agencies have packages with airlines and/or hotels that you can inquire about.

Those agencies that have a booth at the airport run slightly higher because of the convenience of being able to walk to the desks and drive the car away from a nearby parking lot. You may also return the car to the airport parking lot on your departure. The other agencies have a shuttle service to offices in Lihue. This means going to the call board near the carrousel in the airport where, with the touch of a button, you are connected to the Lihue office. The shuttle vans usually take about as long to arrive as your baggage does, but on occasion the wait at the airport can be a distraction.

The rate for a subcompact with manual shift and no air conditioning is about $20 per day, plus gas and tax. Jeeps are $30 – $35 per day. Vans and convertibles are about $50 per day. Luxury cars may range up to $200 a day. Three-day, seven-day, and monthly rates are available, so ask about these. All agencies require a major credit card in your name or a substantial cash deposit. Most accept Master Charge and Visa, but some no longer accept American Express or Diners Club.

Two things other than the CDW and PAI coverage may raise your rental car expense. Approved infant seats for those three and under are required under Hawaii State law, and most agencies charge $3 to $5 per day to rent one. You may also be charged for any additional drivers.

There are a couple of catches you have to watch out for. You might be offered a low flat rate, and then discover on turning the car in that the fine print specified a mileage minimum that you didn't use. The other is the drop-off charge. This is minimal if you pick up the car at the agency's office in downtown Lihue and drop it off at the airport, about $10. However, if you choose to leave your car at a hotel, this can be $25 or more.

The car rental agencies on Kauai have various restrictions as to age. Most will not rent to any driver under twenty-five or over seventy. Those that do rent to persons under twenty-five charge much higher rates for those twenty-one to twenty-five. None rent to those under twenty-one. All have restrictions about driving their automobiles off paved roads, so if you plan to do some adventuring on cane roads, clarify this ahead of time. Most of the interesting out-of-the-way places on Kauai are reached only on cane roads, and some of these require a four-wheel drive vehicle.

Although it is cheaper to get a car without air conditioning, during the summer months the inside of a car can turn into an oven in slow traffic. You can get by without air conditioning during the winter, but we would advise it in the summer.

Before you drive your car away, check for body damage. One or two agencies on Kauai have been known to collect for the same damage several times. Also, make sure the lights, brakes and windshield wipers work, that the trunk locks, and that there is a spare tire and jack.

You will notice as you drive around Kauai that more courtesy is paid to pedestrians and other vehicles than is usual on the mainland. There is little or no horn tooting – this is regarded as discourteous. One thing that you should be forewarned about is that almost all our roads are two-lane and it is difficult to pass on them. Much of the time it is illegal. One slow cane truck makes cars line up for miles. Residents of Kauai have adapted to this and do not attempt any scary passing. Sooner or later the truck turns off. You would be wise to do as we do – don't attempt to pass. Most of the serious head-on accidents involve tourists who tried to pass. Another way tourists get involved in accidents is by slowing or stopping unexpectedly to get their bearings or see sights. Please pull well off the road for this. One other tip: Try to avoid the Lihue area during commuting hours on weekdays.

Here are the rental agencies on Kauai. Those agencies marked with a ★ are those from whom we have obtained the best service ourselves, or which were highly recommended by visitors.

ALAMO
1-800-327-9633
Lihue Airport booth, 808-245-8953

AMERICAN INTERNATIONAL
RENT-A-CAR
No 800 number
Lihue Airport booth, 808-245-8855

AVIS RENT-A-CAR
1-800-331-1212
Lihue Airport booth, 808-245-3512
Princeville Airport, 808-826-9773

★ BUDGET RENT-A-CAR
1-800-527-0700
Lihue Airport booth, 808-245-4021
Offices at Waiohai and Coco Palms

DOLLAR RENT-A-CAR
1-800-342-7398
Lihue Airport booth, 808-245-4708

HERTZ
1-800-654-8200
Lihue office, 808-245-3356, they
can also transfer you to their
airport booth if you wish.
Princeville Airport, 808-826-7455

HONOLULU RENT-A-CAR
No 800 number, no airport booth
Lihue office, 808-245-8726

KAUAI RENT-A-BUG
No 800 number, no airport booth
Lihue office, 808-245-7280

★ NATIONAL
1-800-342-8431
Lihue Airport booth, 808-245-3502
Princeville Airport, 808-826-6165

RAY'S RENT-A-CAR
No 800 number, no airport booth
Lihue office, 808-245-6272

RENT-A-JEEP
No 800 number, no airport booth
Lihue office, 808-245-9622

RENT-A-WRECK
No 800 number
Lihue Airport booth, 808-245-6411
Lihue office, 808-245-4755

★ ROBERTS HAWAII INC.
No 800 number
Lihue Airport booth, 808-245-4408

THRIFTY RENT-A-CAR
1-800-367-2277
Lihue office, 808-245-7388

TRAVELERS USA
No 800 number
Lihue Airport booth, 808-245-9541

★ TROPICAL
1-800-367-5140
No airport booth
Lihue office, 808-245-6988

UNITED CAR RENTAL
SYSTEMS INC.
1-800-367-8100
Lihue Airport booth, 808-245-8894

USA RENT-A-CAR
No 800 number
Lihue Airport booth, 808-245-9541

WATASE'S U-DRIVE
No 800 number, no airport booth
Lihue office, 808-245-3251

WESTSIDE U-DRIVE
No 800 number, no airport booth
Kalaheo office, 808-332-8644

It is advisable not to leave anything valuable in your car, even while parked in a hotel or condominium parking lot. Until two or three years ago valuables could be locked in the trunk, but some of the teenage vandals here, as elsewhere, have learned to open trunks.

Once again you are reminded: Hawaii State law requires that all infants three and under be restrained by a federally-approved car seat when traveling on public roads and highways on Kauai. Children three to four years of age may be secured by either a seatbelt or car seat. Seatbelt use is required for *all* occupants of the front seat, and this law is enforced on Kauai.

On Kauai, driving is not measured as much in miles as in minutes to get there. This, of course, leaves out certain variables such as large trucks on the road, but the average driving time from Lihue to the following points is:

Poipu – Twenty minutes
Waimea – One hour
Waimea Canyon – Two hours
Wailua River – Fifteen minutes
Hanalei – One hour, fifteen minutes
Haena – One hour, thirty minutes

Hitchhiking is legal on Kauai if the hitcher stays on the shoulder of the road. As far as a driver is concerned, there must be room to pull completely off the road and stop. Such shoulders are rather rare around Kauai, so hitchhiking is discouraged. On most of the belt road, it is not only hazardous to the motorist, but to the hitchhiker as well.

TOURS

If after your arrival you wish to take a sightseeing tour around Kauai, five firms currently handle these:

Chandler's Kauai Tours	245-5675
Gray Line Kauai	245-3344
Kauai Island Tours, Inc.	245-4777
Robert's Hawaii, Inc.	245-9558
Trans-Hawaiian Kauai	245-5108

The prices and routes of the tours are competitive and comparable. A half-day tour is around $25 and a full day $40. All of these firms will pick you up at your hotel. Be sure you get an English-speaking guide, because a lot of tours are for Japanese.

The company we recommend is Trans-Hawaiian Kauai. They only use vans, so you will never get stuck on a large bus. With a smaller group of people, your questions will be answered and you may be able to talk your guide into stopping for occasional pictures if the remaining passengers do not object.

We have an extensive chapter "What to See" to use for a self-guided tour in a rented car or jeep, and of course suggest this way of seeing Kauai. The tour companies do not visit many of the most interesting places, may just zip by some of those listed on their schedule, and too often stop over-long at certain places to shop. So, unless you prefer to "zip-and-tip", we suggest you tour Kauai on your own.

MISCELLANEOUS INFORMATION

Now some miscellaneous information. A "local" is usually a non-haole who was born and raised here. Haoles who were raised here, especially those of old-time families, sometimes have honorary "local" status. A term just coming into use for anyone other than the above who lives here is "islander." You are visitors from the continental United States – "mainlanders." You do not come from the "United States" or "America", but from the "mainland." Only use the term "Hawaiian" if the person is of Hawaiian blood. Never use "kanaka" – that is a word reserved for use by locals. Sometimes you will hear "going up to the mainland." This is a carry-over from the days of sail when departing ships headed north to get above the trade winds.

Prepare for jetlag by progressively adjusting your schedule a half-hour or so a day for a few days before getting on the plane. Take it from a physician – there is no diet, pill, secret potion or other remedy that does anything to lessen its effect.

This may be paradise, but we do have our little critters. Mosquitoes can be bothersome, especially when you are out of the trade winds. Mosquitoes have trouble coming in for a landing on your skin when the wind is more than four or five miles per hour. Bring or buy a small container of liquid or stick repellant and always have it with you – even when you go out for dinner. *They* like to have dinner, too! Mosquitoes are most avid around dusk, so close the screens where you are staying before then or you might have one buzzing around your ear all night. Mosquito coils that burn like incense are available here. They are effective, and their aroma lends a tropical atmosphere. Follow directions.

There are no poisonous spiders here, and no snakes at all. But we do have termites that give older wooden buildings that rustic sway-backed look. And cockroaches thrive here better than on the mainland.

An African snail may meander across your path after a rain. They are up to five inches in length and their sheer size may come as a shock. Then there is our *Bufo marinus*, a toad who loves to come hopping out at night. If you shuffle as you walk, he will hop out of your way. The roads often have a lot of very flat toads on them, because cars don't shuffle!

The last little critter we should mention is the gekko. He is a harmless lizard from two to four inches long that is related to the chameleon. He loves bugs and waits by lights and other likely places for them. But you will find that he is more frightened of you than you may be of him. Make any sudden move or noise and he will vanish in a flash (for a few minutes, then he'll be back). If you hear chirping noises at night, one is probably talking about you to another.

"Hawaiian Time" is sort of like being sociably late back home. But "Polynesian Paralysis" is worse. If you stay here long enough, it may be catching, and instead of arriving late, you might not get there at all – or even care!

Kauai is the least populous of the major Hawaiian Islands. We had 38,891 residents in the 1980 census – probably about 45,600 by now. Believe it or not, the outlying town of Kapaa outnumbered the capital of Lihue in 1980 – 4,491 to 4,001! The racial makeup here is: Caucasian 28.5%, Filipino 26.2%, Japanese 25%, Hawaiian 14.6%, Chinese 1.3%, and all others 4.2%. Although caucasians are the most numerous, haoles are a true minority here.

Kauai leads the state in tourism growth. On any given day there are about 12,000 tourists on the island. We had a total of 1,014,000 visitors in 1986! This was an increase of 22.2% over 1985, and represents a dramatic growth from 426,030 in 1970 and 783,164 in 1980. Our average visitor is from the coastal United States, forty years old, affluent, 60% are at the executive level or married to one, and the average stay is 11.3 days. Japanese tourists are now coming to the neighbor islands more. One-quarter of our visitors are from Japan, and each one spends $300 a day compared to the mainlander's $100. So you will understand why some menus, guidebooks and such are printed partly in Japanese.

Kauai has the lowest rate of violent crime of the four major islands. We do have crime here, but most of it is the drunk and disorderly type late at night among locals. Some teens and young twenties blast their car radios, toss beer cans and trash, and take whatever isn't tied down (and occasionally, things that *are* tied down), but violent crime is extremely rare on Kauai.

The Hawaiian Islands are remarkable in having come from the stone age to the space age in just 200 years. This may be the best place in the world for Americans to take vacations. The drinking water is safe, you don't need a phrase book, you don't have to change your money, and there has never been an incident of terrorism here.

We still have the aloha spirit on our island. If someone you meet in Waikiki wonders where it has gone, just tell him it is alive and well on Kauai.

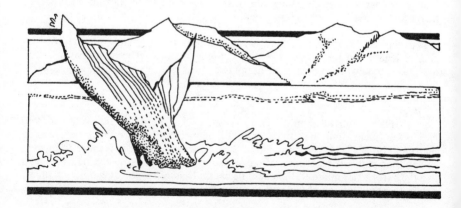

WHERE TO STAY

INTRODUCTION

Your decision on where to stay on Kauai is necessarily a personal one. It depends upon such things as what you plan to do, the amount of time you have, the type of weather you prefer, the amenities you desire, the proximity of restaurants and night life, whether or not you will have children with you, your budget, and several other factors. We will present all options and give you a brief description of each with its price range. Then you can send for brochures, check with your travel agent, and decide for yourself. It is recommended that you make reservations at least three or four months in advance, and in peak seasons six months to a year ahead. Christmas requires more than a year.

Tourism is booming here, and the accommodations are matching the pace. In 1960, Kauai had only 240 rental units for visitors. By 1970, it had 3,000 and in 1980, 6,000. These are located in four major areas, and we will try to sketch the general characteristics of each area for background information.

To the north in Princeville and Hanalei, the emphasis is on a deluxe resort atmosphere except for a few vacation rentals in Hanalei and Haena. This is the part of Kauai which receives the most rainfall. So the tradeoff for residents and visitors alike is the beauty of lush green mountains, waterfalls and valleys against the limitation on outdoor activities of overcast skies, higher humidity and rain. Ocean sports in this area are more dangerous most of the year due to the northeast trade winds and north Pacific storms. These cause high surf along the coast, especially from September through June. As a consequence, the area attracts the older, more affluent visitor who enjoys passive activities – relaxing, viewing the scenery, golf when weather permits, and dining. Most of the units are condominiums, and many are luxurious.

The east shore, now called "The Coconut Coast", including Kapaa, Waipouli and Wailua, caters to a somewhat less affluent tourist. There are more places to stay at lower rates than any other area. Shopping and restaurants follow the same trend – fewer high-quality places but more places overall. Rainfall is less than farther north, but ocean sports are still dangerous much of the time. Because expenses are lower for the visitor, this is where more than half elect to stay and they then visit other areas on Kauai from there. The tour bus industry is concentrated here, and it is where most packaged tours stay.

The central area, Hanamaulu, Lihue, Nawiliwili and Puhi, is a study in contrasts. Older motels and hotels in Lihue with "bare bones" accommodations are side-by-side with two major resorts – The Westin Kauai Resort and Kauai Hilton & Beach Villas. The latter are designed to be destination resorts in their own right, with all facilities available. The new Westin Kauai Resort is the largest resort on Kauai, in fact, in all of Hawaii, with an emphasis on opulence and ostentation. Meanwhile, the older, smaller establishments in Lihue cater to the backpack set. Shopping and restaurants (outside of the two major resorts) are mostly for the local population.

Poipu, on the south shore, is expanding rapidly with over 2,000 rental units at the present time. It leads the entire state of Hawaii in occupancy rates. Skies are usually clear and the weather sunny. The ocean is calm in winter and perfect for surfing in summer. Accordingly, it attracts travelers who are more active than their northern and eastern counterparts. More visitors are also on individual tours rather than packages and are on return trips, having first stayed elsewhere and learned about the island. Small, inexpensive restaurants for locals are in the area, along with some of the finest ones on the island. The places to stay follow the same pattern, and shopping is similar. A little more than half of the finest of each that Kauai has to offer are in Poipu.

To the west, in Waimea and up in the Kokee area, there is very little in the way of visitor accommodations, restaurants or shops. Kekaha, for example, offers the best weather and some of the most beautiful beaches on the island. The surf is safer than on the north and east shore, but this side of the island is almost totally undeveloped for tourism.

Most guide books to the Hawaiian Islands, or anywhere for that matter, tend to describe the major hotels and stop there. Many travel agents do the same. As a result, approximately 80% of the visitors to Kauai stay in hotels. Some of the other alternatives offer more space at lower rates, with equivalent locations and amenities. Therefore, we will list the alternatives first and hotels last.

The low season is generally from mid-April to mid-December, when rates may be 15%-25% less than the rest of the year. Premium prices are often asked for the Christmas and Easter holidays. The range of rates given is from the lowest in the low season to the highest in the high season for two persons. Additional persons may run from $10 to $25 each – more at luxury hotels. Children under three are usually free. Remember that the rates quoted do not include the State Excise Tax of 4% or the Transient Accommodations Tax of 5%.

ACCOMMODATIONS INDEX

HOME EXCHANGE

If you have a desirable home or vacation condominium and are willing to take the risk, consider a home exchange. There are several organizations you can contact to do this. Be forewarned, however, that those who live on Kauai may not want to exchange unless your home or condo offers something they do not have. A neighbor of ours here joined one of these looking for a castle in Europe!

The principle organizations are: International Home Exchange Service, P.O. Box 3975, San Francisco, CA 94119, 415-382-0300; The Vacation Exchange Club, 12006 111th Avenue, Unit 12, Youngstown, AZ 85363, 602-972-2186; and Interservice Home Exchange, P.O. Box 87, Glen Echo, MD 20812, 301-229-7567.

CAMPING

Places that allow you to camp in a tent are described in "What to Do." Here we will mention those that offer some sort of permanent structure that is supplied with linens and utensils. One is in Kokee State Park, where there are a dozen housekeeping cabins with refrigerators, stoves, fireplaces and hot showers. The cabins vary in size, but the rate for all is $25 per cabin per night. Write to Kokee Lodge, P.O. Box 819, Waimea, Kauai, HI 96796, or phone 808-335-6061. The Lodge itself offers a restaurant, lounge and convenience store. No maid service. The one disadvantage of using this site as your base is its distance from most of the interesting areas on Kauai.

Another is Kahili Mountain Park. This facility, operated by the Seventh Day Adventist Church, has two types of accommodations: Fifteen cabinettes, which are a single room with an attached screened cooking area; and cabins with kitchens, private bathrooms and outdoor showers. The rates are $20 per night for the former and $35 for the latter. Their location near Koloa allows easy access to the rest of the island. Write to Kahili Mountain Park, P.O. Box 298, Koloa, Kauai, HI 96756, or phone 808-742-9921.

The YMCA has two places that are primarily tent-camping areas. However, the YMCA-Poipu has a small hostel and YMCA-Camp Naue in Haena has a bunkhouse. Write to The YMCA, 2080 Hoone Road, Poipu, Kauai, HI 96756, or phone 808-742-1200. Also, the YWCA-Camp Sloggett in Kokee offers similar facilities from time to time. Write to The YWCA, 3094 Elua, Lihue, Kauai, HI 96766, or phone 808-245-5959.

BED AND BREAKFAST

An alternative not available a few years ago are Bed and Breakfast accommodations. The rates range from $20 to $40 for one person and up to $80 for two. The organization that has the widest selection on Kauai is Bed & Breakfast Hawaii, P.O. Box 449, Kapaa, Kauai, HI 96746, 808-822-7771. They ask a membership fee of $5 and their directory costs another $5 plus $2.40 postage. Another with a few units on Kauai is Pacific-Hawaii Bed & Breakfast, 19 Kai Nani Place, Kailua, HI 96734, 808-262-6026. One other, that has only a single home but with four bedrooms, is K. Barker's B & B, P.O. Box 740, Kapaa, Kauai, HI 96746, 808-822-3703.

PRIVATE HOMES AND GUEST COTTAGES

Most private residences are luxurious and expensive, but some have inexpensive guest cottages which are rented separately. The principal agent for all areas is Kauai Vacation Rentals. Two agents that specialize on the north shore are Na Pali Properties and Hanalei North Shore Properties. Four that concentrate on the south shore are Grantham Resorts, Prosser Realty, Bob Lloyd Realty, and R & R Realty. For all addresses and telephone numbers, see the list of agents at the end of this section.

JANORA BAYOT

CONDOMINIUMS

The term condominium covers a variety of types: townhouses, where the land is owned rather than leased; apartments; time-share condos, and so forth. Rental arrangements for them are somewhat confusing, too. They may be handled by the owner, the front desk, a rental agency, or in many cases by several agencies with different rates and policies. The amenities also vary considerably among the condo complexes. Some resemble large resort hotels with swimming pools, tennis courts, and other features, while others are more like a large downtown apartment house in your own community. The key to all that allows us to group them together is that linens and full kitchen facilities are provided.

Most of the condos require a minimum stay, usually three days, and a deposit. Discounts for stays of a week or more are usually available. They also require full payment in advance or on the first day of occupancy. Policies for cancellation refunds vary. Most do not accept credit cards. Bear in mind that each condominium unit is privately owned so differ in decoration, furnishing and condition. Telephones are not provided in most units. If this is important to you, ask. No condos have air-conditioning, but some have ceiling fans. Because building height is limited to four stories on Kauai, few have elevators. Most provide maid service only on request. The number of units given for each complex is that presently in the vacation rental program. The total in any one complex may be several times this.

Rather than repeat the addresses of the agents after each condo, they will only be identified and a list with their addresses and telephone numbers is given at the end of the this section. If the front desk of the condominium complex handles reservations, the address and phone number are given with each listing. For the most part, the front desk is there to serve the owners and occupants and is not staffed or set up to handle inquiries from the mainland, so the addresses and phone numbers are not given.

Our preferences, indicated by a ★, are for value, location, weather, hospitality and other factors – not necessarily for luxury.

NORTH (HANALEI/PRINCEVILLE)

ALII KAI I
Princeville. 50 units. Pool, golf, tennis, television, ocean view. No telephones in units. ACCOM.: 2 bedroom units. RATES: $100 – $110. AGENTS: Blue Water Vacation Rentals, Hanalei Aloha Rental Management, Kauai Aina Enterprises, Na Pali Properties, Kauai Vacation Rentals.

ALII KAI II
Princeville. 24 units. Tennis, shop, golf, pool, television, restaurant, lounge. Most units have telephones. ACCOM.: 2 bedroom units. RATES: $70 – $80. AGENTS: Hanalei Aloha Rental Management, RHK Enterprises.

THE CLIFFS
Princeville. 200 units. Television, ocean view, pool, golf, tennis, meeting room. Some units have telephones. ACCOM.: 1 & 2 bedroom units. RATES: $100 – $130. AGENTS: Hanalei Aloha Rental Management, Hanalei North Shore Properties, Kauai Aina Enterprises.

HALE MOI
Princeville. 8 units. Near golf, tennis, pool, etc., at other resorts for small charge. No telephones in units. ACCOM.: 1 bedroom units. RATES: $80 – $85. AGENTS: Blue Water Vacation Rentals, Hanalei Aloha Rental Management, Hanalei North Shore Properties.

HANALEI BAY RESORT & VILLAS ★
Princeville. 134 units plus villas. Restaurant, pools, shuttle to beach, tennis, golf, shops, meeting room. Telephone in each unit. ACCOM.: Studio, 1, 2 & 3 bedroom units. RATES: $65 – $350. AGENTS: Blue Water Vacation Rentals, Hanalei Aloha Rental Management, Hawaiian Apartment Leasing Enterprises, Hanalei North Shore Properties, Hawaiiana Resorts, Kauai Aina Enterprises, Na Pali Properties.

HANALEI COLONY RESORT
Haena. 45 Units. On the beach. Pool, restaurant. No telephones in units. ACCOM.: 2 bedroom units. RATES: $70 – $115. AGENT: Kauai Aina Enterprises.

KA'EO KAI
Princeville. 51 units. Pool, golf, tennis, private jacuzzi, projection television, stereo. All units have telephones. ACCOM.: 2 bedroom units. RATES: $70 – $115. AGENTS: Blue Water Vacation Rentals, Hanalei Holidays, Hanalei Aloha Rental Management, Kauai Aina Enterprises.

MAUNA KAI
Princeville. 5 units. Pool, golf, television. Some units have telephones. ACCOM.: 2 & 3 bedroom units. RATES: $80 – $105. AGENTS: Hanalei Aloha Rental Management, Na Pali Properties.

PALI KE KUA ★
Princeville. 67 units. Path to small beach. Ocean view, television, pool, golf, restaurant, lounge. Telephone in each unit. ACCOM.: 1 & 2 bedroom units. RATES: $75 – $130. AGENTS: Blue Water Vacation Rentals, Hanalei Aloha Rental Management, Hanalei North Shore Properties, Hawaiian Island Resorts, Inc.

PALIULI COTTAGES
Hanalei. 8 units. Lounge, television, tennis, golf, shop. Telephone in each unit. ACCOM.: 2 bedroom cottages, each with small private pool. RATES: $75 – $90. AGENT: None. Write P.O. Box 351, Hanalei, Kauai, HI 96714, phone (808) 826-6264.

PANIOLO
Princeville. 23 units. Pool, golf. Telephone in each unit. ACCOM.: 1 bedroom units. RATES: $80 – $85. AGENTS: Hanalei Aloha Rental Management, Hanalei North Shore Properties.

PUAMANA
Princeville. 97 units. Pool, golf, television, meeting room. Telephones in some units. ACCOM.: 2 & 3 bedroom units. RATES: $95 – $110. AGENTS: Hanalei Aloha Rental Management, Kauai Aina Enterprises.

PU'U PO'A AT PRINCEVILLE
Princeville. 20 units. Ocean view, pool, television, golf, meeting room. All units have telephones. ACCOM.: 2 bedroom units. RATES: $110 – $145. AGENTS: Blue Water Vacation Rentals, Hawaiian Island Resorts, Inc., Hanalei Aloha Rental Management, Hanalei North Shore Properties, Kauai Aina Enterprises, Kauai Vacation Rentals.

SANDPIPER VILLAGE
Princeville. 35 units. Pool, jacuzzi, sauna, barbecue. No telephones in units. ACCOM.: 2 and 3 bedroom units. RATES: $85 – $100. AGENTS: Hawaiiana Resorts, Inc., Blue Water Vacation Rentals, Island Pacific Resorts.

SEALODGE
Princeville. 40 units. Ocean view, pool, television, golf. Telephone in each unit. ACCOM.: 1 & 2 bedroom units. RATES: $80 – $105. AGENTS: Blue Water Vacation Rentals, Hanalei Aloha Rental Management, Hanalei North Shore Properties, Kauai Aina Enterprises, Na Pali Properties.

EAST (KAPAA/WAIPOULI/WAILUA)

KAHA LANI ★
Next to Lydgate Park. 51 units. On the beach. Tennis, pool, television. Telephone in each unit. ACCOM.: 1, 2 & 3 bedroom units. RATES: $90 – $200. AGENTS: Aston Hotels and Resorts, Kauai Vacation Rentals.

KAPAA SANDS
Kapaa. 23 units. On the beach. Restaurant, lounge, pool, tennis, golf, shops. No telephones in units. ACCOM.: Studios & 2 bedroom units. RATES: $49 – $79. AGENT: RHK Enterprises.

KAPAA SHORE
Kapaa. 32 units. Beach, golf, tennis, television, pool. No telephones in units. ACCOM.: 1 & 2 bedroom units. $55 – $95. AGENTS: Hawaiiana Resorts, Inc., Kauai Vacation Rentals.

LAE NANI
Kapaa. 50 units. Beach, pool, tennis, television. All units have telephones. ACCOM.: 1 & 2 bedroom units. RATES: $90 – $180. AGENTS: Hawaiian Apartment Leasing Enterprises, Kauai Vacation Rentals, Colony Resorts.

LANIKAI
Kapaa. 6 units. Ocean view, beach, pool, barbecue, golf, restaurant, tennis. All units have telephones. ACCOM.: 2 bedroom units. RATES: $170 – 195. AGENTS: Colony Resorts, Kauai Vacation Rentals.

PLANTATION HALE
Kapaa. 153 units. Walk to beach. Restaurants, lounges, pool, television. All units have telephones. ACCOM.: 1 bedroom units. RATES: $75 - $85. AGENT: Colony Resorts, Inc.

PONO KAI
Kapaa. 110 units. Beach, pool, television, tennis, jacuzzi, sauna. All units have telephones. ACCOM.: 1 & 2 bedroom units. RATES: $85 - $150. AGENTS: Aston Hotels & Resorts, Kauai Vacation Rentals.

WAILUA BAYVIEW APARTMENTS
Kapaa. 44 units. Beach, pool, television, barbecue, lounge. Some units have telephones. ACCOM.: 1 bedroom units. RATES: $95. AGENTS: Island Pacific Resorts, Kauai Vacation Rentals, RHK Enterprises.

CENTRAL (HANAMAULU/LIHUE/NAWILIWILI)

There is only one condominium complex in the Lihue area, although some "villas" are available at the Kauai Hilton:

BANYAN HARBOR
Lihue. 10 units. Tennis, pool, near Kalapaki beach. No telephones in units. ACCOM.: 2 bedroom units. RATES: $85 - $100. AGENTS: Kauai Vacation Rentals, RHK Enterprises.

SOUTH (POIPU)

Most accommodations in this area are in Poipu:

GARDEN ISLE COTTAGES ★
Poipu. 13 units. Some have ocean view. Small pool. No telephones in units. ACCOM.: Studio, 1 & 2 bedroom units. RATES: $36 - $140. AGENT: None. Write Bob and Sharon Flynn, Garden Isle Cottages, R.R. 1, Box 355, Koloa, Kauai, HI 96756, 808-742-6717.

KIAHUNA ★ ★
Poipu. 325 units. On beautiful beach. Shops, restaurant, lounge, pool, tennis, golf. Telephones in most units. ACCOM.: 1 & 2 bedroom units. RATES: $95 - $300. AGENTS: Hawaiiana Resorts, Inc., Village Resorts, Inc. One comment should be added: considered from all aspects, this is the best place to stay on Kauai. The premier units on the beachfront are handled by Hawaiiana Resorts, and most of the rest by Village Resorts.

KOLOA LANDING COTTAGES ★
Poipu. 4 units. Garden setting. No telephones in units. ACCOM.: 2 bedroom cottages. RATES: $40 - $60. AGENT: None. Write Hans & Sylvia Zeevat, R.R. 1, Box 70, Koloa, Kauai, HI 96756, 808-742-1470. Hospitality is the keynote here. Excellent value, also.

KUHIO SHORES
Poipu. 34 units. Ocean view, beach, restaurant. Telephones in all units. ACCOM.: 1 & 2 bedroom units. RATES: $80 - $100. AGENTS: Kauai Vacation Rentals, Prosser Realty, R & R Realty.

LAWAI BEACH RESORT
Poipu. 104 units. Ocean view, beach. Telephones in all units. ACCOM.: 1 & 2 bedroom units. RATES: $80 - $100. AGENT: Colony Resorts, Inc.

MAKAHUENA AT POIPU
Poipu. 35 units. Pool, tennis, television, paddle tennis. No telephones in units. ACCOM.: 1, 2 & 3 bedroom units. RATES: $95 - $215. AGENTS: Aston Hotels & Resorts, Kauai Vacation Rentals, Prosser Realty, R & R Realty.

NIHI KAI VILLAS
Poipu. 60 units. Near beach. Pool, television, tennis. No telephones in units. ACCOM.: 2 bedroom units. RATES: $115 - $145. AGENTS: Grantham Resorts, Great American Management Co., Kauai Vacation Rentals, Prosser Realty, R & R Realty.

POIPU CRATER RESORT
Poipu. 30 units. Inside extinct crater (warm in summer). Near beach. Tennis, pool, paddleball. Telephone in each unit. ACCOM.: 2 bedroom units. RATES: $80 - $150. AGENTS: Grantham Resorts, Suite Paradise.

POIPU KAI ★
Poipu. 125 units. Some near beach, some have ocean view. Television, pool, tennis, meeting room, restaurant, lounge. Telephone in each unit. ACCOM.: 1, 2 & 3 bedroom units. RATES: $64 - $250. AGENTS: Colony Resorts, Inc., Kauai Vacation Rentals, Prosser Realty, R & R Realty, Suite Paradise.

POIPU KAPILI ★
Poipu. 59 units. Ocean view, pool, tennis, television. Telephone in each unit. ACCOM.: 1 & 2 bedroom units. RATES: $110 - $145. AGENT: None. Write Mike Hill, Poipu Kapili, R.R. 1, Box 272, Koloa, Kauai, HI 96756, 1-800-367-8047, Ext. 105, or 808-742-6449.

POIPU MAKAI
Poipu. 4 units. Near beach. Ocean view, small pool, barbecue. Telephone in each unit. ACCOM.: 2 & 3 bedroom units. RATES: $100 - $110. AGENTS: Kauai Vacation Rentals, Prosser Realty, R & R Realty.

POIPU PALMS
Poipu. 4 units. Some have ocean view. Pool. Telephones in some units. ACCOM.: 2 bedroom units. RATES: $80 - $100. AGENTS: Prosser Realty, R & R Realty.

POIPU PLANTATION
Poipu. 6 units. Beach, ocean view. No telephones in units. ACCOM.: 1 & 2 bedroom cottages. RATES: $50 - $100. AGENT: Bed & Breakfast Hawaii, P.O. Box 449, Kapaa, Kauai, HI 96746, 808-822-7771.

POIPU SHORES
Poipu. 34 units. Ocean view, near beach. Television, pool, tennis. Telephone in each unit. ACCOM.: 1, 2 & 3 bedroom units. RATES: $100 - $140. AGENT: None. Write Poipu Shores, R.R. 1, Box 95, Koloa, Kauai, HI 96756, 1-800-367-5686, 808-742-6522.

PRINCE KUHIO RESORT
Poipu. 40 units. Pool, beach, television, barbecue, restaurant. No telephones in units. ACCOM.: Studios & 1 bedroom units. RATES: $39 - $69. AGENT: Kauai Vacation Rentals and direct - Prince Kuhio Rentals, P.O. Box 1060, Koloa, Kauai, HI 96756, 808-742-1670.

SUNSET KAHILI CONDOMINIUMS
Poipu. 28 units. Some have ocean view. Pool, meeting room. Telephone in each unit. ACCOM.: 1 & 2 bedroom units. RATES: $44 - $63. AGENT: Kauai Vacation Rentals and direct - Sunset Kahili Rentals, P.O. Box 100, Koloa, Kauai, HI 96756, 808-742-1691.

WAIKOMO STREAM VILLAS
Poipu. 40 units. Garden setting, tennis, pool. Telephones in some units. ACCOM.: 1 & 2 bedroom units. RATES: $75 - $85. AGENT: Grantham Resorts, Aston Hotels & Resorts.

WHALER'S COVE
Overlooking Koloa Landing, Poipu. 38 units. Snorkeling, scuba diving, pool. AC-COM.: 2 bedroom units. RATES: Not yet known. This property has just been completed and the units are presently being sold. When a sufficient number of new owners are achieved to form a Homeowners Association, some units will be placed on the rental market. Perhaps they will be available by the summer of 1988. AGENT: Aston Hotels & Resorts.

WEST (WAIMEA)

The only condo on the west side is:

WAIMEA PLANTATION COTTAGES
Waimea. 14 units. Beach (dark gray sand). Telephone in each unit. ACCOM.: Individual cottages, 1, 2, 3 & 4 bedroom units. RATES: $70 - $90. AGENT: None. Write Waimea Plantation Cottages, P.O. Box 367, Waimea, Kauai, HI 96796, 808-338-1625, 1-800-9-WAIMEA.

HOTELS

NORTH (HANALEI/PRINCEVILLE)

SHERATON PRINCEVILLE HOTEL
Princeville. P.O. Box 3069, Princeville, Kauai, HI 96722, 1-800-325-3535, 808-826-9644. 300 units. Ocean view, beach, restaurants, television, pools, shops, tennis, golf, meeting rooms. All units air-conditioned. ACCOM.: 1 bedroom units & suites. RATES: $160 – $1,000. Luxurious. Spectacular view.

EAST (KAPAA/WAIPOULI/WAILUA)

COCO PALMS RESORT HOTEL
Wailua. P.O. Box 631, Lihue, Kauai, HI 96766, 1-800-542-2626, 808-822-4921. 392 units. Beach, restaurants, lounges, shops, meeting rooms, three pools, tennis, television. All units air-conditioned. ACCOM.: 1 & 2 bedroom units, suites, cottages. RATES: $85 – $355. Huge and rambling on 45 acres. A bit worn, but being reconditioned. Beach often unsafe.

HOTEL CORAL REEF
Kapaa. 1516 Kuhio Highway, Kapaa, 1-800-843-4569, 808-822-4481. 26 units. Pool, restaurant, lounge, shops. ACCOM.: Studio & 1 bedroom units. RATES: $25 – $35. A bargain for budgeteers. Beach for this and all hotels near the Coconut Plantation Market Place is narrow with rough water.

ISLANDER ON THE BEACH HOTEL
Wailua. At the Coconut Plantation, 808-822-7417. 199 units. Beach, pool, television, shops, restaurant. Refrigerator in each room. All units air-conditioned. AC-COM.: 1 bedroom units. RATES: $79 – $99. AGENTS: Village Resorts. Good value.

KAUAI BEACHBOY HOTEL
Wailua. At the Coconut Plantation, 484 Kuhio Highway, Kapaa, Kauai, HI 96746, 1-800-227-4700, 808-822-3441. 243 units. Beach, restaurant, television, lounge, pool, meeting room, tennis, shops. All units air-conditioned. ACCOM.: 1 bedroom units. RATES: $65 – $78. Good value. No room service.

KAUAI RESORT HOTEL ★
Wailua. Near Lydgate Park and Beach, 3-5920 Kuhio Highway, Kapaa, Kauai, HI 96746, 1-800-367-5004, 808-245-3931. 242 units. Safe beach, restaurant, television, lounge, pool, shops, meeting rooms. All units air-conditioned. ACCOM.: 1 bedroom units and cabanas. RATES: $57 – $190. Sterile, pseudo-Polynesian structure, but excellent location. Rooms are large.

KAUAI SANDS HOTEL ★
Wailua. At the Coconut Plantation, 808-822-4951. 200 units. Restaurant, lounge, television, pools, shop, meeting room. All units air-conditioned. ACCOM.: 1 bedroom units. RATES: $46 – $72. Good value. Hotel itself lacks luster, but staff is friendly.

SHERATON COCONUT BEACH HOTEL
Wailua. At the Coconut Plantation, 1-800-325-3535, 808-822-3455. 309 units. Beach, restaurant, pool, television, tennis, shops, lounge, putting green. All units air-conditioned. ACCOM.: 1 bedroom units & suites. RATES: $100 – $275. Four-story rambling structure on attractive grounds, eleven acres. Most units have ocean view, all have lanais. Waterfall in the lobby!

CENTRAL (HANAMAULU/LIHUE/NAWILIWILI)

Most of the hotels and motels in the Lihue area are inexpensive ($20 – $25) and spartan. The Kauai Hilton & Beach Villas and the new Westin Kauai Resort (built on the site of the old Kauai Surf) are two exceptions.

AHANA MOTEL
Lihue. 3115 Akahi Street, Lihue, Kauai, HI 96766, 808-245-2206. 17 units. Clean, some kitchenettes. No air-conditioning. ACCOM.: 1 bedroom units. RATES: $16 – $22.

HALE LIHUE HOTEL
Lihue. 2931 Kalena Street, Lihue, Kauai, HI 96766, 808-245-3151. 22 units. Some kitchenettes. Some units have air-conditioning. ACCOM.: 1 bedroom units. RATES: $17 – $24.

HALE PUMEHANA MOTEL
Lihue. P.O. Box 1828, Lihue, Kauai, HI 96766, 808-245-2106. 17 units. No air-conditioning, but ceiling fans. ACCOM.: 1 bedroom units. RATES: $20 – $25. Small, noisy.

KAUAI HILTON & BEACH VILLAS
Three miles north of Lihue on the beach. 4331 Kauai Beach Drive, Lihue, Kauai, HI 96766, 808-245-1955. 350 units and 138 villas. Beach, pool, restaurant, shop, television, tennis. All units air-conditioned. ACCOM.: Standard-Super-Deluxe 1 & 2 bedroom units. RATES: $105 – $185. Large, with landscaped grounds. Lacks personality.

KAUAI INN (Formerly Hale Niumalu)
Nawiliwili. 3100-9 Kuhio Highway, Lihue, Kauai, HI 96766, 1-800-367-8047, ext. 243, 808-245-3316. 32 units. Pool. ACCOM.: 1 bedroom units. RATES: $40 – $60. Near Niumalu Park, recently renovated. South seas atmosphere.

OCEAN VIEW MOTEL
One mile out of Lihue at 3445 Wilcox Road, Lihue, Kauai, HI 96766, 808-245-6345. 16 units. Two blocks from Kalapaki Beach. Refrigerator in each room. No air-conditioning. ACCOM.: 1 bedroom units. RATES: $17 – $18.

TIP TOP MOTEL
Lihue. 3173 Akahi Street, Lihue, Kauai, HI 96766, 808-245-2333. 30 units. Restaurant, lounge, meeting room. All units air-conditioned. ACCOM.: 1 bedroom units. RATES: $20 – $28. Plain, but pleasant for the price. Popular with salesmen and construction workers.

WESTIN KAUAI RESORT ★
Nawiliwili. On Kalapaki Beach. 1-800-228-3000, 808-245-5050. 850 units. Second hotel in 1990 will add 750 units. Meeting rooms, health spa, jacuzzis, two shopping villages, restaurants, lounges, pools, tennis, golf. With 580 landscaped acres and botanical gardens, the most luxurious resort in Hawaii. All units air-conditioned. ACCOM.: 1 bedroom units, suites, penthouses. RATES: Most $180 – $350; suites to $1500. COMMENTS: Reactions are varied on this new "mega" resort. While most impressive, some feel that the renovations and decorations are extreme, over-done or ostentacious. However, it is for each to judge and we invite you to be sure and include a tour, if not a stay, at this incredible new hotel.

SOUTH (POIPU)

There are currently no hotels on the western side of the island. There are three on the south shore in Poipu, with beautiful beaches in front of them. In the planning stage for the south shore is the Hyatt Regency Hotel. This 605-bed luxury resort will have two separate buildings, one will be two story, the other four story in a tropical architectural style. Public access to the beach will be maintained as well as a one acre public park. Completion of this project at Keoneloa Bay is scheduled for 1990.

POIPU BEACH HOTEL
Poipu. R.R. 1, Box 174, Koloa, Kauai, HI 96756, 1-800-227-4700, 808-742-1681. 139 units. On the beach. Restaurants, pool, television, tennis, lounges, shops. All units have air-conditioning. ACCOM.: Standard-Super-Deluxe 1 bedroom units, cottages. RATES: $79 – $600. Adjacent to the Waiohai Resort Hotel. Good value for the location.

SHERATON KAUAI HOTEL ★
Poipu. Rt. 1, Box 303, Koloa, Kauai, HI 96756, 1-800-325-3535, 808-742-1661. 340 units, in process of adding 120-bed wing. On the beach. Restaurants, lounges, pool, television, tennis, meeting rooms. All units air-conditioned. ACCOM.: Standard-Super-Deluxe 1 bedroom units. RATES: $100 – $255. Comfortable and satisfactory all-around. Beautiful grounds.

WAIOHAI RESORT HOTEL
Poipu. R.R. 1, Box 174, Koloa, Kauai, HI 96756, 1-800-227-4700, 808-742-9511. 434 units. On the beach. Restaurants, lounges, shops, pools, television, tennis, meeting rooms, fitness center. All units air-conditioned. ACCOM.: Standard-Super-Deluxe 1 bedroom units. RATES: $125 – $720. A bit glitzy, perhaps. Attractive grounds.

RENTAL AGENTS

ASTON HOTELS & RESORTS
2255 Kuhio Ave.
Honolulu, HI 96815
800-342-1551, 808-922-3368

BOB LLOYD REALTY
P.O. Box 99
Koloa, Kauai, HI 96756
800-635-2824, 808-742-1243

BLUE WATER
VACATION RENTALS
P.O. Box 366
Princeville, Kauai, HI 96714
800-367-8047, Ext. 311
808-826-9229

COLONY RESORTS, INC.
32 Merchant St.
Honolulu, HI 96813
800-367-6046, 808-523-0411

GRANTHAM RESORTS
P.O. Box 983
Koloa, Kauai, HI 96756
800-325-5701, 808-742-7220

GREAT AMERICAN
MANAGEMENT CO.
P.O. Box 89678
Honolulu, HI 96830-8678
808-926-1144

HANALEI ALOHA
RENTAL MANAGEMENT, INC.
P.O. Box 1109
Hanalei, Kauai, HI 96714
808-826-7288

HANALEI HOLIDAYS
P.O. Box 3099
Princeville, Kauai, HI 96722
808-826-7204

HANALEI NORTH
SHORE PROPERTIES
P.O. Box 607
Hanalei, Kauai, HI 96714
800-367-8047, 808-826-9622

HAWAIIAN ISLAND
RESORTS, INC.
P.O. Box 212
Honolulu, HI 96810
800-367-7042

HAWAIIAN PACIFIC
RESORTS
1150 S. King Street
Honolulu, HI 96814
808-531-5235

HAWAIIANA RESORTS
1100 Ward Ave., Suite 1100
Honolulu, HI 96814
800-367-7040, 808-523-7785

ISLAND PACIFIC RESORTS
4334 Rice Street, #203C
Lihue, Kauai, HI 96766
808-245-3668

KAUAI AINA ENTERPRISES
P.O. Box 280
Hanalei, Kauai, HI 96714
808-826-6557

KAUAI VACATION
RENTALS & REAL ESTATE
P.O. Box 3194
Lihue, Kauai, HI 96766
800-367-5025, 808-245-8841

NA PALI PROPERTIES
P.O. Box 475
Hanalei, Kauai, HI 96714
808-826-7272

PRINCEVILLE
MANAGEMENT CORP.
P.O. Box 3040
Princeville, Kauai, HI 96722
800-367-7090, 808-826-3820

PROSSER REALTY
P.O. Box 367
Lihue, Kauai, HI 96766
1-800-367-8047, Ext. 117
808-245-4711

RHK ENTERPRISES
P.O. Box 3292
Lihue, Kauai, HI 96766
800-367-2912, 808-826-6855

R & R REALTY & RENTALS
R.R. 1, Box 70
Koloa, Kauai, HI 96756
800-367-8022, 808-742-7555

SUITE PARADISE
4480 Ahukini Rd., Ste. 2
Lihue, Kauai, HI 96766
808-245-6600

VILLAGE RESORTS, INC.
9090 Fort Street Mall
Suite 1540
Honolulu, HI 96813
800-367-7052, 808-531-5323

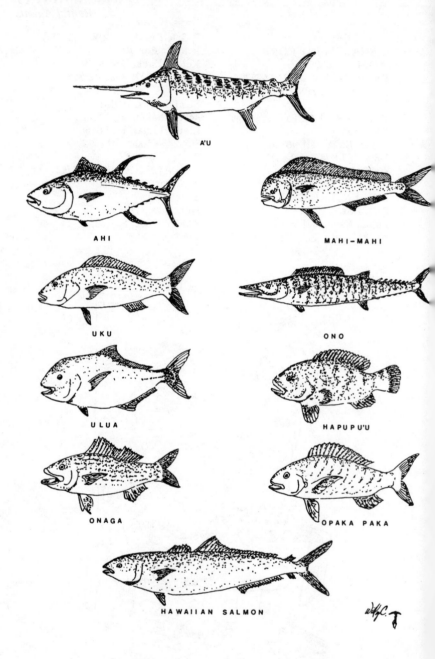

A'U

AHI

MAHI-MAHI

UKU

ONO

ULUA

HAPUPU'U

ONAGA

OPAKA PAKA

HAWAIIAN SALMON

WHERE TO EAT

INTRODUCTION

Because of the greater cultural diversity that is still found on Kauai, we have a wider variety of authentic ethnic foods to enjoy than on the other Hawaiian islands. The only exception is Honolulu itself. Food is as much a part of the way of life here as speech, song or dance. You may find yourself "talking story" with a grizzled, retired pineapple worker over cone sushis at a country store, invited to a neighborhood backyard luau, sharing a bag of malasadas with a stranger who becomes a friend, or staring at something odd on your plate that doesn't appear to be quite dead. Actually, it may not be! Samoans, for example, are fond of live sea urchins. While they are digging one open, another may be walking off the plate!

To really appreciate the food here, you have to leave behind some preconceptions that all of us have. There are only a few sophisticated restaurants on Kauai, with a maitre d' in tux, continental cuisine, superb service, and an extensive wine list. But you can find that in Honolulu or on the mainland. Here you should have a sense of adventure and savor the strange flavors.

One characteristic of Kauai is that not much care goes into the appearance of many of the eateries. You may find the best bentos (box lunches) in a place that looks like it's about to fall down, or taste the most fabulous kim chee served at a cheap chrome-and-plastic table, or enjoy delicious dim sum while trying to maintain your equanimity on a wobbly stool.

"Local" restaurants go one step further. They don't seem to care much about the appearance of the food, either. The top priorities are taste and amount, and they usually have a lot of both.

Of course, we have the usual fast-food outlets - McDonalds, Pizza Hut, Kentucky Fried Chicken, Wendy's, Burger King, and so on. When we discuss restaurants, little will be said about these unless they are in areas where you might stay with children and would want something fast and inexpensive.

75

We have our own forms of fast food, however, that you ought to try. **Barbecue sticks** are little pieces of chicken, beef or pork marinated in teriyaki sauce, then barbecued and served on a thin bamboo stick. They are delicious. A **bento** is the Japanese version of the box lunch, and is not only appealing to the eye but to the palate as well. **Cracked seeds**, pronounced "crack seed", are spiced preserved fruit seeds of Chinese origin. Children find them delicious and parents are content that they are nutritious as well. **Kulolo** is a Hawaiian pudding made with taro, coconut and raw sugar that can be found in local grocery stores. **Macadamia nuts** are another treat that are available roasted or in almost everything from cookies and candy to ice cream. **Poke** is a seafood salad – each one is different and delicious. These can be found in the deli department of the Big Save stores and are a popular take-out item. **Portuguese sausage** is something you should sample at least once. It is tangy in a distinctive way – more so than the sausage you are used to – but you can find varieties that are only mildly spicy. The **rice** here is "sticky" so you can handle it easily with chopsticks. Delicious sushi – rice in a seaweed wrapper – is available everywhere. **Taro chips** are thicker, crunchier and tastier than potato chips. And nothing is more uniquely Hawaiian than **shaved ice**. Notice in pronouncing this that the last "d" is left off so it comes out "shave ice." This is not the finely ground air-filled snowcone you have at home. A block of ice is actually shaved in front of you while you choose the flavor of your syrup. Strawberry usually wins out, but if you are not sure, ask for a "rainbow." Some are served with ice cream on the bottom, or azuki beans – sweet Japanese dessert beans. All come in a cone-shaped paper cup with a straw and spoon, and you will need both.

HAWAIIAN FRUIT

Fresh Hawaiian fruit is another gastronomic reward for visiting Hawaii – and Kauai in particular. Many will be unfamiliar to you. Here is an alphabetical list of some with a brief description:

Apple bananas, also known as Brazilian bananas, may be a new experience. They have a distinct personality, one that is totally different from the bland and blah bananas you had on the mainland. Try one and find out.

Breadfruit is a large, round, yellow-green fruit that is hard to find in the store, but you often see them while you are hiking. If you spot a breadfruit tree in someone's backyard, stop and ask for one if it looks ripe, usually in August and September. It is delicious steamed or baked with butter. Be sure to poke holes in it before cooking or it will explode.

When it comes to **coconuts**, forget all that you knew about the coconuts you bought in the stores at home. Here you should look for the green, or "spoon meat", cocos. This means they are not completely ripe, so the meat inside can be easily spooned out of the shell. For best results, chill, lop off the top, insert a straw and enjoy the delicious milk. Then comes the fun with the spoon.

Guavas are found along the roadsides and trails, but be sure you pick the right thing. They are green to yellow, thick-skinned and filled with seeds in a soft pinkish pulp. When picked at the right time, they have a penetratingly delicious sweet-sour taste which is not approximated by any manufactured drink, jelly or jam bearing the name "guava."

The *limes* grown here have a more tangy taste than those at home. Try them to flavor your drink or sprinkle the juice on almost anything to improve the flavor.

Lychee is a delicious grape-like fruit that has a hard but easily-peeled reddish shell. Its season is June and July, and proper technique involves biting through the tough skin, sucking out the juice, then opening the shell like a hard-boiled egg and popping the entire morsel inside into one's mouth. Be careful of the seed, though!

Lilikoi, or passion fruit, is also in season in the summer. The technique for eating this fruit is similar to that for lychees, and a delicious drink is prepared from it.

Mangos come in several varieties on Kauai. They are in season June and July. Some look as if they have been painted by an artist – red except for patches of green and yellow, with streaks of purple. The most common variety has the color of a peach when it is ready to eat. The best time to eat them is when they are still firm but not quite soft. Just peel it and slice the fruit away from the large pit. Some people are allergic to the skin of the mango and develop "mango mouth", so be sure to peel it well.

Mountain apples are a treat in the early summer. They are a pear-shaped, small, tart, juicy red fruit that come from the deep mountain valleys.

The *Methley plum* is a bright red plum both on the outside and on the inside. It is found in the Kokee area in May and June, when the locals flock there with buckets in hand to pick them.

Papaya – The most common variety is the sunrise papaya that has a yellowish-orange color and is best eaten when it is just slightly soft. It is delicious with a squeeze of lime.

Poha, or the cape gooseberry, has a lot of seeds so is most commonly cooked for jam, but it is edible and delicious raw.

Pineapple – Although the commercial hybrids available in the grocery store are tasty, there is nothing quite like those grown by the locals in their own backyard. You find these at small fruit stands. Test to see if it is ripe by feeling and sniffing it, and the leaves should snap off the top easily.

Soursop – This is a large, heart-shaped fruit with a thick, spiny skin. It can be eaten raw, but more often the juice is made into drinks and a puree into sherbets.

Starfruit, or carambola, is a yellow-green fruit with a thin, waxy skin. It has five prominent ribs which gives the cut fruit a star shape. It is available in the winter and adds a decorative and tasty touch to fruit salads.

Tamarind – This has a brittle brown pod and a sticky, slightly acid-tasting pulp around a black seed.

Let's get ethnic now and talk about some of the terms you should know in the various languages before you try the food.

HAWAIIAN FOOD TERMS

'alaea salt – a coarse sea salt mixed with ocherous red earth ('alaea).

haupia – a dessert pudding made from coconut cream, cornstarch and sugar.

huli huli chicken – barbecued chicken.

limu – any of several varieties of edible seaweed.

manapua – the Hawaiian version of Cantonese dim sum; a steamed bun filled with spicy bits of pork.

'okolehao – this was originally a liquor distilled from the ti root, but the term now applies to any liquor.

'opihi – a limpet that is found on rocks at low tide and a favorite of the Hawaiians, mixed with limu and salt and eaten raw.

poke – a seafood salad made of slices of raw fish or octopus mixed with kukui nut, limu and other ingredients. Each is different.

pupu – this word literally means a small gastropod (like a snail), which the Hawaiian's loved to munch on. In current usage, it applies to any appetizer.

In many restaurants, the menu will list only Hawaiian names for the fish, and because fish is the feature at most, the following is what you are getting:

'ahi – yellowfin tuna.

aku – the skipjack or bonita tuna.

'ama 'ama – mullet.

a'u – swordfish.

hapu'u pu'u – sea bass.

kaku – barracuda.

mahi mahi – this is the true dolphin – a fish, not to be confused with the porpoise, which is a mammal.

ono – wahoo – a long, slender tuna-like fish.

'opae – shrimp.

'opakapaka - pink snapper.

uku - a deep-sea gray snapper.

'ula'ula - red snapper.

ulua - the jackfish, or crevalle.

JAPANESE FOOD TERMS

daikon - a white radish.

beef sashimi - chilled raw beef.

dobin - a mixture of bits of shellfish, vegetables and a truffle-like mushroom.

ishiyaki - any food cooked in the old-fashioned way with hot stones.

isonotsuyu - the Japanese version of bouillabaisse.

miso soup - fermented soybean soup.

sake - rice wine.

sashimi - any type of raw fish sliced thinly, most commonly ahi.

shabu shabu - thin slices of beef with various vegetables cooked in hot chicken broth, then dipped in a sauce of sake, sesame oil and shoyu.

tempura - any food dipped in a light batter and then deep-fried.

teppanyaki - teppan means "metal plate" and yaki is "broiled" or "fried." Any food, usually beef, cooked on a teppan grill.

teriyaki - thinly sliced beef, chicken or pork marinated in a sauce that is predominantly shoyu but also contains ginger, garlic and sake. After marination, items are broiled.

tofu - a bland curd made from soybeans.

yakitori - pieces of chicken and vegetables marinated in various sauces, then skewered and broiled.

yosenabe - a mixture of seafood cooked in a clay pot.

CHINESE FOOD TERMS

There are three generally recognized styles of Chinese food, although gourmets will tell you of dozens. The most common on Kauai is Cantonese, from southern China. The usual ingredients are vegetables and seafood which are seasoned mildly and stir-fried. Mandarin style is from northern China. It is lightly seasoned and the emphasis is on meats, duck and breads. Peking duck is an example. Szechuan comes from central China and is characterized by the use of various peppers. Hot and sour soup is an example.

We will not go into Chinese food terms here because any one of a number of dialects may be on the menu or used by your waiter. Let's just mention one thing that is a favorite on Kauai and is Cantonese in origin – dimsum. The word literally means "delight of the heart", which is true. They are dumplings stuffed with pork, seafood and vegetables, then either deep-fried, baked or steamed.

KOREAN FOOD TERMS

karbi – barbecued ribs.

kim chee – spicy salad of pickled cabbage. Watch out for this – it looks benign, but is *hot.*

kun koki – meat barbecued with soy sauce and sesame oil.

PORTUGUESE FOOD TERMS

malasada – A small round doughnut – this is where all the holes went!

pao duce – sweet bread.

FILIPINO FOOD TERMS

adobo – simmered pork or chicken spiced with vinegar, garlic, salt, green pepper and bay leaves.

bagoong – a tangy fish sauce.

pochero – meat cooked with bananas and vegetables.

RESTAURANT INDEX

FOOD TYPE INDEX

Any attempt to classify the restaurants on Kauai by food type is bound to be frustrating. One, for example, lists three types of food on its sign, but the menu has *five!* Then, too, the types are subject to individual interpretation, e.g., "International" and "Continental" can mean something different to different people. One decision we made helps some – rather than separate out those featuring steaks or seafood as a "type", we elected to indicate those that serve reliably good steaks or seafood by indicating the appropriate word in parentheses.

AMERICAN

Al & Don's Restaurant.........87
Bali Hai Restaurant.............85
Beach House Restaurant (Seafood)98
Beamreach Restaurant..........85
The Boathouse Supper Club.....92
The Breakers Restaurant........98
Brennecke's Beach Broiler
    (Seafood).................98
The Bull Shed
    Waipouli (Steaks).........87
The Bull Shed
    Harbor Village (Steaks).....92
Buzz's Steak & Lobster.........88
Cafe Hanalei..................85
The Carriage House Restaurant..93
Charo's......................85
Chuck's Steak House (Steaks)...85
Cook's at the Beach...........93
Courtside Bar & Grill..........99
Duane's Ono-Char Burger.......88
The Flame Room...............88
Great Gourmet.................94
Hale Kai Dining Room.........88
Hale Kapa....................86
Hale Ohana...................99
Hanalei Dolphin Restaurant.....86

Hanalei Shell House (Seafood)...99
House of Seafood (Seafood).....95
Jacaranda Terrace..............90
Jolly Roger Restaurant.........90
J.J.'s Boiler Room (Steaks)......90
J.J.'s Broiler (Steaks)...........90
Jacaranda Terrace..............95
The Kahili Room...............90
Kalaheo Restaurant.............99
Kapaa Fish & Chowder House
    (Seafood).................90
Keoki's......................95
Keoki's Paradise...............99
Kiahuna Clubhouse Restaurant..100
Kokee Lodge.................100
Koloa Broiler.................100
Koloa Coffee & Bake Shop.....100
Koloa Ice House..............100
Kountry Kitchen Restaurant.....90
Kukui Family Kitchen..........96
Kukui Nut Tree Inn Restaurant...96
The Lagoon Dining Room.......90
Lanai Restaurant..............86
Nobles.......................86
Oar House Saloon.............97
Ono Family Restaurant........91

RESTAURANT REVIEWS

These are arranged alphabetically in each of the four major areas. We have made an effort to include all of those you might be interested in, including a few snack shops and local places. Those restaurants we especially liked are indicated by a ★.

After each description, a one-word comment is made about the price range. *"Inexpensive"* means that an average dinner is under $10, exclusive of tax, tips, drinks and dessert. *"Moderate"* is from $10 – $17, and *"Expensive"* is over $17.

Except as indicated, all restaurants take Visa and Mastercard. Many do not take American Express, Carte Blanche or Diners Club.

In the interest of conserving space, pizza places have been left out. There are a lot of them – at least one in each area – and some deliver. Check the phone book. Also, most major hotels have poolside snackbars for lunch service, which are not listed. Big Save and some other grocery stores have adjacent local-type restaurants and takeout places which are not listed, either.

Because chefs and management can change overnight, we would appreciate your comments to help us keep up-to-date.

If you are a stickler for good service, we should give you a general rule, one that is true more than not. Service is most attentive, efficient and friendly at the established family-run restaurants. In second place are the larger operations, which usually means hotels. Because of their size, they manage to keep a nucleus of well-trained personnel through thick and thin. The medium-sized and smaller restaurants are variable. You just have to take a chance – the service may be awful, or it may be awfully good.

Almost always (there are some exceptions) at the bottom of the list in quality of service are the one-person snack shops that are run without supervision. We have our druggies and drifters here, and this is one type of work they do to collect minimum wage for a few weeks before moving on.

One good place to test this "rule" is the Coconut Plantation Marketplace. Start with the surrounding hotels, then the larger restaurants. You will probably be pleased at most of them. The mid-sized restaurants *are* variable as the "rule" would indicate. Then the snack shops. At the bottom of even these is a Mexican food place there where insolence is carried to an art form. We have seen fully one-fourth of the potential patrons get up and leave even before their order arrives.

NORTH (HANALEI/PRINCEVILLE)

BALI HAI RESTAURANT
Hanalei Bay Resort, Princeville (826-6522). HOURS: Breakfast 7 to 11 a.m., lunch 11:30 a.m. to 4 p.m., dinner 5 to 10 p.m. daily. COMMENTS: Noted for its beautiful view at sunset, so go before then and ask for the upper tier. The decor is attractive, but the food and service are uneven. Reservations. *Expensive.*

BEAMREACH RESTAURANT
Princeville, 1-1/2 miles from main gate on the right hand side in the Pali Ke Kua condominium complex (826-9131). HOURS: Dinner 6 to 10 p.m. daily. COMMENTS: This restaurant has no view, but the service and food are excellent. It is famous for its steaks. Reservations. *Moderate to Expensive.*

BLACK POT LUAU HUT
Near the corner of Kuhio Highway and Aku Road, Hanalei (826-9871). HOURS: Open at 10:30 a.m. for lunch and dinner until 10 p.m. daily. COMMENTS: This is a good place to stop for lunch on a tour of the north shore. Menu contains Hawaiian, American and International food. *Moderate.*

CAFE HANALEI
Sheraton Princeville Hotel, Princeville (826-9644). HOURS: Open at 6:30 a.m. for breakfast, lunch and dinner daily. COMMENTS: Main dining room of the hotel. Meals are served on the terrace with a spectacular view of Hanalei Bay. Sunday brunch is a feature, as is the prime rib buffet every night but Friday. Good food and service. *Expensive.*

CASA DI AMICI
Adjacent to the Kong Lung Store, Kilauea (828-1388). HOURS: Opens at 11 a.m. for lunch and dinner daily. COMMENTS: The decor is in a garden motif and the Italian food is reliably good. Service is friendly and efficient. The only drawback is that their pasta is not made fresh daily, but flown in dried from Italy. Takeouts are available. Reservations. *Expensive.*

CHARO'S
Next to the Hanalei Colony Resort, Haena (826-6422). HOURS: Lunch 11:30 a.m. to 3 p.m., pupus and cocktails 3 to 5:30 p.m., dinner 5:30 to 10 p.m. daily. COMMENTS: A wonderful place to have a cocktail on the oceanfront lanai, but the food and service are unreliable. Reservations. *Expensive.*

CHUCK'S STEAK HOUSE
Princeville Center, Princeville (826-6211). HOURS: Lunch 11:30 a.m. to 2:30 p.m., dinner 6 to 10 p.m. daily. COMMENTS: Just like the Chuck's Steak Houses on the mainland. The steaks are good, they have a fine salad bar, but the service is impersonal at best. Reservations. *Moderate.*

THE FLATS GRILL & BAR
Princeville Center, Princeville (826-7255). HOURS: Lunch 11 a.m. to 5 p.m., dinner 5:30 to 9:30 p.m. daily. COMMENTS: Good American and Mexican food, as well as some Cajun cookery. Service is uneven. *Moderate.*

FOONG WONG CHINESE CUISINE
Second floor of the Ching Young Village, Hanalei (826-7434). HOURS: Opens at 11 a.m. for lunch and dinner every day except Sunday and Monday, when dinner only is served 5 to 9 p.m. COMMENTS: Folding chairs and formica decor. The features are won ton soup and roast duck. The service is excellent, but the quality of the food doesn't match up. Takeouts are available. *Moderate.*

HALE KAPA ★
Sheraton Princeville Hotel, Princeville (826-9644). HOURS: Dinner 6 to 10 p.m. daily. COMMENTS: Jacket only required. Beautifully designed and decorated with an early Hawaiian "country home" motif. Handmade Hawaiian quilts are hung on the wall which is said to give the room its name, but someone goofed – the term for quilt is "kapa kuiki." Excellent service, good food. Reservations. *Expensive.*

HANALEI DOLPHIN RESTAURANT
On the river near the highway, Hanalei (826-6113). HOURS: Dinner 6 to 10 p.m. daily. COMMENTS: Ideal location with river view. Serves mostly seafood and steaks. Attractive decor, fine service and good food. It would be nice if it were open for lunch, as many who are doing a north shore tour would appreciate a place like this to stop for lunch. This restaurant would deserve a star except for one serious drawback, their "no reservations" policy. We don't go on weekends or after 7 p.m. *Expensive.*

HANALEI SHELL HOUSE
Corner of Kuhio Highway and Aku Road, Hanalei (826-9301). HOURS: Breakfast 8 to 11 a.m., lunch and dinner from 11 a.m. to 10 p.m. daily. COMMENTS: A varied menu, but seafood is their specialty. Excellent clam chowder. Dining is outdoors – only eight tables. The food is great, but the service is somewhat variable and the automobile traffic at your elbow can be bothersome. *Moderate.*

LANAI RESTAURANT
Princeville Clubhouse, Princeville (826-6226). HOURS: Dinner 5 to 9:30 p.m. daily. COMMENTS: Nothing sensational, but pleasant ambience, good service, and fine food. Fresh fish, steaks and pasta are featured. Reservations. *Moderate.*

NOBLES
Sheraton Princeville Hotel, Princeville (826-9644). HOURS: Dinner 6 to 10 p.m. daily. COMMENTS: Jacket only required. Totally enclosed on a site which *would* have a fabulous view. Opulent decor and superb service. A four-course prix-fixe menu (changed nightly) of uneven quality; some evenings it's simply great, others its not. The only restaurant on Kauai that presently exceeds the "expensive" category – *Very Expensive.*

PAPAGAYO AZUL
Ching Young Shopping Village, Hanalei (826-9442). HOURS: Open at 11 a.m. for lunch and dinner daily. COMMENTS: A Mexican restaurant with the expected fare, plus its specialty – chicken cooked on a grill, Mexican style. NO CREDIT CARDS. *Inexpensive.*

TAHIT! NUI ★
East end of Hanalei on Kuhio Highway (826-6277). HOURS: Lunch 11:30 a.m. to 3 p.m., dinner 5:30 p.m. to 9:30 p.m. daily, Luaus Monday, Wednesday and Friday evenings. COMMENTS: This is a favorite of ours. The structure itself is over one hundred years old and looks it. The hostess, Louise Marston, is originally from Tahiti and organizes what she calls the "spontaneous entertainment." Her son, Christian, is a superb chef. The seafood is excellent and they also serve French continental cuisine. Usually live Hawaiian music every night but Sunday, when they feature country music. Warm and pleasant ambience. Reservations. *Moderate.*

THE VILLAGE SNACK & BAKE SHOP
Ching Young Shopping Village, Hanalei (826-6841). HOURS: Breakfast 6 to 11 a.m., lunch 11 a.m. to 5 p.m. daily. COMMENTS: A local favorite offering takeout bakery products including malasadas, taro chips and other local foods. Try their homemade pies. Not oriented toward the tourist trade. NO CREDIT CARDS. *Inexpensive.*

EAST (WAILUA/WAIPOULI/KAPAA)

AL & DON'S RESTAURANT
Kauai Sands Hotel, Wailua (822-4221). HOURS: Breakfast 7 to 10 a.m., dinner 7:30 to 9 p.m. daily. COMMENTS: A bit hard to find. Perhaps the best food value (but not the best food) on this side of the island, ocean view. *Moderate.*

AN NYONG RESTAURANT
Makai side of Kuhio Highway, heart of Kapaa. (822-9816) HOURS: Lunch and dinner Monday through Saturday 10:30 a.m. – 8:30 p.m. COMMENTS: Just opening as we go to press. Not reviewed, but Korean food reportedly excellent. *Inexpensive.*

ALOHA DINER
971-F Kuhio Highway, Kapaa (822-3851). HOURS: Lunch 10:30 a.m. to 3 p.m., dinner 5:30 to 9 p.m., closed Sundays. COMMENTS: This is one of the best places to go on Kauai for tasty, authentic Hawaiian food. That is all they serve. Takeouts are available. NO CREDIT CARDS. *Inexpensive.*

ATAMI RESTAURANT ★
4-901 Kuhio Highway (in the Waipouli Plaza), Kapaa (822-1642). HOURS: Lunch 11 a.m. to 2 p.m., dinner 5:30 to 9:30 p.m., closed Tuesdays. COMMENTS: No atmosphere, but it is clean and comfortable. Good service. The specialty is authentic Japanese food, perhaps the best on Kauai. Takeouts are available. *Moderate.*

THE BULL SHED, WAIPOULI
796 Kuhio Highway, Waipouli (822-3791). HOURS: Dinner 5:30 to 10 p.m. daily. COMMENTS: This restaurant, like its twin in Harbor Village Shopping Center, is a favorite with the steak crowd. It is on the ocean with a fabulous view, so request a window table when you arrive. The fish and all types of beef are good, and their canoe salad bar is famous. Perhaps the best thing on the menu is prime rib. One serious drawback: No reservations are taken, so go early on a weeknight or don't go at all. Be prepared for the consistently bad service – forewarned is forearmed. *Expensive.*

BUZZ'S STEAK & LOBSTER ★
At the back of the Coconut Plantation Marketplace, Wailua (822-7491). HOURS: Dinner 5 to 10 p.m. daily. COMMENTS: Same owners as restaurant of the same name in Waikiki. Tasteful Polynesian decor. The food is excellent and the service is surprisingly good for such a recent opening (June 1987). *Moderate to Expensive.*

CHOPSTIX CHINESE FOOD
4-356D Kuhio Highway (in the Kinipopo Shopping Village), Wailua (822-0560). HOURS: Open at 11 a.m. for lunch and dinner to 8 p.m. daily. COMMENTS: So-so Chinese food and service. *Moderate.*

DRAGON INN CHINESE RESTAURANT
4-901 Kuhio Highway (upstairs in the Waipouli Plaza), Kapaa (822-3788). HOURS: Lunch 11 a.m. to 2 p.m. Tuesday through Saturday, dinner 4:30 to 9:30 p.m. Tuesday through Sunday, closed Monday. COMMENTS: Good Chinese food and service, the best on this side of the island. Takeouts available. *Moderate.*

DUANE'S ONO-CHAR BURGER ★
Anahola (822-9181). HOURS: 10 a.m. to 6 p.m., closed Sundays. COMMENTS: Takeouts only, but there is a large poinciana tree outside with tables under it. Simply the best hamburger on the island. NO CREDIT CARDS. For what you get, *Inexpensive.*

FAST FREDDY'S DINER
4-1302 Kuhio Highway, Kapaa (822-0488). HOURS: Breakfast 7:30 a.m. to 1 p.m., dinner 5:30 to 8:30 p.m. daily. COMMENTS: This little place lacks atmosphere, but it is clean and comfortable and the food is good. NO CREDIT CARDS. *Inexpensive.*

THE FLAME ROOM
Coco Palms Resort, Wailua (822-4921). HOURS: Dinner 6 to 10 p.m. daily. COMMENTS: The decor is reminiscent of old Hawaii, with a nearby lagoon and torch-lit gardens. Prime rib is their specialty, but the seafood and other dishes are also good. All entrees include salad bar. Service is smooth. *Moderate.*

HALE KAI DINING ROOM
Kauai Beachboy Hotel, Wailua (822-3441). HOURS: Breakfast 6:30 to 10 a.m., dinner 7 to 10 p.m. daily. COMMENTS: International cuisine for the nightly buffet and a prime rib buffet each Saturday. Champagne brunch on Sunday. The tables are well-spaced for easy conversation, and in the evenings there is music to dine by. Reservations. *Moderate.*

T. HIGASHI STORE
On Kuhio Highway across from the old Kapaa Ballpark, Kapaa (822-5982). HOURS: Open at 6 a.m. for breakfast, lunch and dinner until 7 p.m. daily. COMMENTS: This tiny place specializes in teriyaki, which is undoubtedly the best on the island. Oriented toward locals. NO CREDIT CARDS. *Inexpensive.*

J.J.'S BOILER ROOM
At the entrance to Coconut Plantation Marketplace, Wailua (822-4411). HOURS: Dinner 5 to 9:30 p.m. daily. COMMENTS: This is a twin to J.J.'s Broiler in Lihue and has a similar menu. Food good, service fair. The Slavonic Steak is a specialty here, also. *Moderate.*

JOLLY ROGER RESTAURANT
At the back of the Coconut Plantation Marketplace, Wailua (822-3451). HOURS: Open from 6 a.m. for breakfast, lunch and dinner daily. COMMENTS: Although we have tended to omit fast-food restaurants, this one is something special. Good food, with entertainment nightly from 9 p.m. to 1:30 a.m. *Inexpensive.*

THE KAHILI ROOM
Kauai Resort Hotel, Wailua (245-3931). HOURS: Breakfast 6:30 to 10 a.m., lunch 11:30 a.m. to 2 p.m., dinner 6 to 8:30 p.m. daily. COMMENTS: Luaus are offered Sunday and Tuesday through Friday. Prime rib is featured on Mondays and Saturdays. Good food. *Moderate.*

KAPAA FISH & CHOWDER HOUSE
4-1639 Kuhio Highway, Kapaa (822-7488). HOURS: Dinner 5:30 to 10 p.m. daily. COMMENTS: The garden setting of the previous restaurant on this site has been preserved, as has the boat on the roof. The menu offers a wide selection, including prime rib and seafood, with a good salad bar. However, the quality of the food and service are not dependable. *Moderate to Expensive.*

KINTARO JAPANESE RESTAURANT
4-370 Kuhio Highway, Kapaa (822-3341). HOURS: Dinner 5:30 to 9:30 p.m. daily. COMMENTS: This restaurant admittedly lacks authenticity, which detracts from the dining experience. The ambience and food are exactly what an American tourist wants, but the food *is* tasty. Try their yakitori, yosenabe or shabu shabu. The sashimi is superb. Featured are teppan tables, which were first introduced in Japan a dozen years ago for the tourists *there.* *Expensive.*

KOUNTRY KITCHEN RESTAURANT ★
1485 Kuhio Highway, Kapaa (822-3511). HOURS: Open at 6 a.m. for breakfast, lunch and dinner until 9 p.m. daily. COMMENTS: This restaurant is something special. It looks ordinary, but is clean and comfortable, service is friendly, and the quality of the food is excellent. Breakfasts are the best around. *Inexpensive.*

THE LAGOON DINING ROOM
Coco Palms Resort, Wailua (822-4921). HOURS: Open at 6:30 a.m. for breakfast, lunch and dinner until 9 p.m. daily. COMMENTS: A buffet for breakfast and lunch in addition to regular menu service. Food is fair, service good. They also have a champagne brunch each Sunday (10 a.m. to 2 p.m.). *Moderate to Expensive.*

NORBERTO'S EL CAFE ★
4-1373 Kuhio Highway, Kapaa (822-3362). HOURS: Dinner 5:30 to 9:30 p.m. daily. COMMENTS: This may look hokey on the outside, but inside the food preparation is presided over by Norberto himself, and the result is the best Mexican food on Kauai. Service is friendly, and the margaritas are delicious. Takeout food is available. *Moderate.*

OLYMPIC CAFE
1387 Kuhio Highway, Kapaa (822-5731). HOURS: Breakfast and lunch 7 a.m. to 1 p.m., dinner 5 to 9 p.m. daily. COMMENTS: This small restaurant serves both Japanese and American food. Although it caters more to the local crowd, you will enjoy it. NO CREDIT CARDS. *Inexpensive.*

ONO FAMILY RESTAURANT
4-1292 Kuhio Highway, Kapaa (822-1710). HOURS: Breakfast 7 to 9 a.m., except Sunday, 8 a.m. to 2 p.m., dinner 5 to 9 p.m. daily. COMMENTS: Homestyle cooking is the feature here, in clean and attractive surroundings. Three things we especially enjoyed were the paniolo ribs, the macadamia nut cream pie, and the Portuguese bean soup – something you have to taste to believe. Service is friendly, but not fast. *Moderate.*

RIB 'N' TAIL
In the Kapaa Shopping Center, Kapaa (822-9632). HOURS: Dinner 5 to 9:30 p.m. daily. COMMENTS: This place is a runner-up to the nearby Bull Shed in popularity, but the food is equivalent and THEY ACCEPT RESERVATIONS, so for us it comes out ahead. Famous for its steaks and seafood. Service is good. Live entertainment Wednesday through Sunday which may be Hawaiian, country or contemporary. *Moderate.*

SEA SHELL RESTAURANT
Across from Coco Palms Resort, Wailua (822-3632). HOURS: Dinner 5:30 to 10 p.m. daily. COMMENTS: Indifferent salad bar (extra), good steaks, prime rib and island fish. But they feature blackened fish, New Orleans style! We lived in New Orleans, and the main reason for this highly-spiced style is to disguise fish that is not quite fresh. Ridiculous on Kauai! A touristy place and the service is slow. *Expensive.*

SHARON'S SAIMIN BOWL ★
4-1296 Kuhio Highway, Kapaa (822-5140). HOURS: Lunch 11 a.m. to 2 p.m., dinner 6 to 10 p.m., closed Sundays. COMMENTS: Sharon offers twenty-one varieties of delicious saimin, and it is a close tug-of-war between hers and Hamura's. We suggest you try both several times and decide for yourself. NO CREDIT CARDS. *Inexpensive.*

THE SIZZLER
4361 Kuhio Highway (in the Wailua Shopping Plaza), Wailua (822-7404). HOURS: Open at 6 a.m. for breakfast, lunch and dinner until 10 p.m. daily. COMMENTS: Good standard American fare. Excellent salad bar. No reservations. NO CREDIT CARDS. *Moderate.*

TROPICAL TACO
Kapaa Shopping Center, Kapaa (822-3622). HOURS: Open at 11 a.m. for lunch and dinner until 9:30 p.m. daily. COMMENTS: The Mexican food is good, the service fair. *Inexpensive.*

THE VOYAGE ROOM
Sheraton Coconut Beach Hotel, Wailua (822-3455). HOURS: Breakfast 6:30 to 11 a.m., lunch 11 am. to 2 p.m., dinner 6 to 9:30 p.m. daily. COMMENTS: Roomy with spaced tables. The decor is "ancient seafarers of Hawaii." Lunch and dinner are buffet in addition to a la carte. The service is so-so, and the food is too. It is less crowded in the evenings, but reservations are recommended. *Expensive.*

WAILUA MARINA RESTAURANT
In Wailua River State Park, Wailua (822-1128). HOURS: Breakfast 8:30 to 11 a.m., lunch 11 a.m. to 2 p.m., snacks 2 to 5 p.m., dinner 5 to 9 p.m. daily. COMMENTS: The cooking is plain homestyle, but your table has a view of the river from the lanai. A large selection on the menu and service is pleasant. Best during the evening when the crowds taking the boats up the Wailua River have gone. *Inexpensive.*

WAIPOULI DELI & RESTAURANT
Waipouli Town Center, Waipouli (822-9311). HOURS: Open at 7 a.m. for breakfast, lunch and dinner until 9 p.m. daily. COMMENTS: Caters to locals more than tourists, but tasty stuff. NO CREDIT CARDS. *Inexpensive.*

ZIPPY'S RESTAURANT
4-919 Kuhio Highway, Kapaa (822-9866). HOURS: Open twenty-four hours. COMMENTS: We included this fast-food restaurant because it is always open for the "hungries" at odd hours. NO CREDIT CARDS. *Inexpensive.*

CENTRAL (HANAMAULU/LIHUE/NAWILIWILI/PUHI)

BARBECUE INN ★
2982 Kress Street, Lihue (245-2921). HOURS: Breakfast 7 to 10:30 a.m., lunch 10:30 a.m. to 1:30 p.m., dinner 4:30 to 8:30 p.m., closed Sundays. COMMENTS: Basically American food, with a touch of Japanese, Chinese and Filipino. Some thirty to forty items on the menu, and all meals come with soup, salad and dessert. This restaurant, which has been a tradition for nearly fifty years in Lihue, gained its fame by providing ample amounts of good food at low prices. It still does. Service is friendly and efficient. NO CREDIT CARDS. *Inexpensive.*

THE BOATHOUSE SUPPER CLUB
In the Westin Kauai Resort, Nawiliwili. (245-5050). HOURS: 6:30 – 9:45 p.m. nightly except Monday. COMMENTS: Dinner and show. Six entrees to choose from, with quality unreliable but improving. Service good. The show itself is tops. Price for one cocktail, dinner, show ("broadway-style" polynesian), tax and tip presently $49.

THE BULL SHED, HARBOR VILLAGE
Harbor Village Shopping Center, Nawiliwili (245-4551). HOURS: Lunch 11 a.m. to 2 p.m., dinner 5:30 to 10 p.m. daily. COMMENTS: This, like its twin in Waipouli, is a favorite with steak lovers. Unlike its twin, it has no view. Featured are midwestern beef, prime rib and seafood. Attractive decor. Reservations are taken for four or more. Food is good, service is acceptable. *Expensive.*

THE CARRIAGE HOUSE RESTAURANT
In Kilohana, Puhi (245-9593). HOURS: Dinner 5 to 9 p.m. daily. COMMENTS: An attempt at a home barbecue atmosphere with self-service and dining at picnic tables. But paper plates, paper napkins, and plastic cups at these prices? One or the other has to change. "Daddy Cool" on the piano is the best part of the evening. Several varieties of fish are offered, as well as steaks. The salad bar is ample, but that's all you can say about it. *Moderate.*

CASA ITALIANA
2989 Haleko Road, Lihue (245-9586). HOURS: Dinner 5:30 to 10 p.m. daily. COMMENTS: Anthony and Rosario Iaskolk make their pasta daily, and the veal dishes are tasty, too. Two criticisms: 1) The downstairs part is noisy (upstairs less so, but warm in the summer) because of hard surfaces on the floors, walls, and ceiling, which almost prevents conversation when crowded; 2) The waiters and busboys do not wait for a pause, but invariably interrupt whatever conversation you do manage to get started. These two things could be changed. Reservations. *Moderate to Expensive.*

CLUB JETTY RESTAURANT & CABARET ★
On the jetty, Nawiliwili (245-4970). HOURS: Dinner 4:30 to 9:30 p.m., closed Sundays. COMMENTS: This has been a tradition on Kauai for forty years. American and Cantonese/Chinese food are featured, but almost anything is obtainable. Twice a week the inter-island steamer leaves from close by, so when you request a window table, verify the time of departure so you can watch it leave. Emma "Mama" Ouye presides over the preparation of your meals and the service. Both are excellent. The place undergoes a metamorphosis about 9:30 p.m. Wednesday through Saturday evenings. A combo sets up, locals drift in, and it becomes a bouncing nightspot. *Inexpensive to Moderate.*

COOK'S AT THE BEACH
At the Westin Kauai Resort, Nawiliwili (245-5050). HOURS: The only three meal restaurant at the Westin, open from 6:30 a.m. – 11 p.m. daily. COMMENTS: Eclectic menu of good quality. Service is acceptable and still improving. Informal indoor-outdoor setting near the fountain pool. *Moderate.*

DENMAR'S RESTAURANT & BAKERY
In the Harbor Village Shopping Center, Nawiliwili (245-3917). HOURS: Breakfast 7 a.m. to 1 p.m., lunch 11 a.m. to 4 p.m., happy hour 3 to 6 p.m., and dinner 6 to 9 p.m. Sunday through Wednesday, 6 to 10 p.m. Thursday through Saturday. COMMENTS: From the name of this restaurant, it is hard to figure out exactly what it offers. Pancakes for breakfast are their specialty, and they are delicious. Then the place turns into a Mexican restaurant at lunchtime. This fare is fair. Service is not overly efficient. *Inexpensive.*

EGGBERT'S
4483 Rice Street, Lihue (245-6325). HOURS: Breakfast 7 to 11 a.m., lunch 11 a.m. to 3 p.m. daily; dinner 5:30 to 9:30 p.m. Wednesday through Saturday only. COMMENTS: This was originally named The Egg and I, and its breakfast array of omelets tells you why. Typical of the unusual entrees on the lunch and dinner menu is the "loco moco", a large scoop of rice with a hamburger patty and egg on top, and the whole thing drowned in gravy. *Inexpensive.*

GAYLORD'S ★

In Kilohana, Puhi (245-9593). HOURS: Lunch 11 a.m. to 4 p.m., dinner 5 to 10 p.m. daily. Sunday brunch. COMMENTS: This restaurant offers fine dining in a courtyard atmosphere. An extensive wine list is available. The service is uneven, but they are working on it. Lunch – *Moderate.* Dinner – *Expensive.*

GREAT GOURMET

Kukui Grove Shopping Center, Lihue (245-7115). HOURS: Lunch 10 a.m. to 4 p.m., Sundays to 3 p.m. COMMENTS: The best delicatessen on the island, but the service can be erratic – even exasperating when the counter help allows every phonecall to interrupt your purchase. Breads are baked on the premises, and unique items such as turkey torte and artichoke lasagna are on the menu. You may buy wine, imported cheese and other items to take with you. *Expensive.*

HALO HALO SHAVE ICE ★

2956 Kress Street (next to Hamura's), Lihue (245-5094). HOURS: "When the girl is there who knows how to do it." COMMENTS: Actually, it's part of Hamura's and under the same roof. Serves the best shave ice on the island, prepared Filipino style with fresh fruit, ice cream, or azuki beans at the bottom. You can also purchase manju and fresh manapua here at times. They do take credit cards, but then give them right back. In other words, cash only. *Inexpensive.*

⚡ HAMURA SAIMIN STAND ★

2956 Kress Street, Lihue (245-3271). HOURS: Open at 10 a.m. for breakfast, lunch and dinner until 2 a.m. Monday through Thursday, until 4 a.m. Friday and Saturday, and 4 p.m. until midnight on Sundays. COMMENTS: To say that the building is unpretentious is to understate the case. However once you enter, settle yourself on a stool and read the sign "Please Do Not Put Gum Under the Counter", you'll become aware of the aroma of perhaps the best saimin anywhere. Twenty varieties to chose from, all prepared before you by Aiko Hamura herself. Also delicious are the barbecued beef and chicken sticks. Sometimes fresh malasadas and other goodies are available. The lilikoi pie is exceptionally light and delicious – take one home. A real find, this place. NO CREDIT CARDS. *Inexpensive.*

HANAMAULU RESTAURANT TEA HOUSE ★

On Kuhio Highway in Hanamaulu (245-2511). HOURS: Lunch 9 a.m. to 1 p.m., dinner 4:30 to 9:30 p.m., closed Mondays. COMMENTS: This restaurant, operated by the Miyakes, serves delicious Japanese and Chinese food in private tea rooms overlooking a Japanese garden. Service is marvelous. Attached is Ara's Sushi Bar, where Aramaki Koichi makes the excellent sushi also served in the restaurant. Reservations. *Moderate.*

HO'S GARDEN RESTAURANT

3016 Umi Street, Lihue (245-5255). HOURS: Lunch 10:30 a.m. to 2 p.m. Monday through Friday, dinner 4:30 to 9 p.m. Monday through Friday, 5 to 9 p.m. Sunday, closed Saturdays. COMMENTS: A garden this place is not, small it is. But once inside, you'll find surprisingly delicious Cantonese food with a local touch. NO CREDIT CARDS. *Inexpensive.*

THE INN ON THE CLIFFS

In the Westin Kauai Resort, Nawiliwili (245-5050). Separate restaurant with ocean view, reached by carriage or over lagoon by canoe or launch. Will be featuring pasta and seafood for lunch and dinner when open in early 1988. Not reviewed.

JACARANDA TERRACE

In the Kauai Hilton & Beach Villas, three miles north of Lihue (245-1955). HOURS: Open at 6 a.m. for breakfast, lunch and dinner until 11 p.m. daily. COMMENTS: Garden view, two tiers with attractive decor, offering fixed menu and a la carte at breakfast and lunch, menu only at dinner. Good food, pleasant service. Less crowded in the evenings. Reservations. *Moderate.*

J.J.'S BROILER ★

3971 Haleko Road, Lihue (245-3841). HOURS: Dinner 5:30 to 9:30 p.m. daily. COMMENTS: Jim Jasper took over an old plantation foreman's building twenty years ago and set up a great restaurant here. Simple decor but good service and food. A selection of mainland beef, lobster and seafood, as well as a fine salad bar. Slavonic steak is the specialty of the house. Reservations. *Moderate.*

JONI HANA/LOCAL GRINDS ★

Kukui Grove Shopping Center, Lihue (245-5213). HOURS: Open 9:30 a.m. to 5 p.m. daily, except Fridays when they are open until 9 p.m. COMMENTS: These small twin takeout restaurants are a delight if you happen to be near them during lunch hour. The Joni Hana part offers the best selection of bentos, or Japanese box lunches, available anywhere, along with sushi, saimin and oriental candy. On the Local Grinds side are foods designed for the local crowd. These are well-prepared, tasty, and filling. NO CREDIT CARDS. *Inexpensive.*

JUDY'S OKAZU & SAIMIN ★

Lihue Shopping Center (corner of Rice and Kuhio Highway), Lihue (245-2612). HOURS: 7 a.m. to 3 p.m., closed Sundays. COMMENTS: Don't let the word "okazu" fool you, it just means "all kine food." Judy has retired, but Sue's warm personality has taken over. Takeouts available. NO CREDIT CARDS. *Inexpensive.*

KAUAI CHOP SUEY

In the Harbor Village Shopping Center, Nawiliwili (245-8790). HOURS: Lunch 10 a.m. to 2 p.m. Tuesday through Saturday, dinner 4:30 to 9 p.m. Tuesday through Sunday, closed Mondays. COMMENTS: Service is scanty – one waitress! Some say that this place has the best Chinese food on Kauai, but after several samplings we'd say that the food is only adequate. The *amount* is abundant – that's really why its famous. Like most Chinese restaurants it is noisy, and if you arrive before the crowd, they'll play a recording of their busiest hour from the night before as loudly as you wish. We're kidding about that. NO CREDIT CARDS. No alcoholic beverages. *Moderate.*

KEOKI'S

3474 Rice Street, Nawiliwili (245-3260). HOURS: 9 a.m. to 5 p.m. daily. COMMENTS: During the construction of the Westin Kauai Resort, this restaurant has had to cater to workmen, but is once again becoming a great snack shop now that the Westin is open. Good charburgers and plate lunches. Handy if you're spending the day at Kalapaki Beach. Cash only. *Inexpensive.*

RESTAURANT KIIBO ★

2991 Umi Street, Lihue (245-2650). HOURS: Lunch 11 a.m. to 1:30 p.m., dinner 5:30 to 9 p.m. closed Sundays. COMMENTS: Here you can pretend you are in Japan. The menu has photographs just as the small restaurants like this do there and it features a similar authentic menu. The food is great and the prices are reasonable. The bubble may burst when you notice the waitress is Filipino. Oh well One of our favorites. *Moderate.*

KUKUI FAMILY KITCHEN

Kukui Grove Shopping Center, Lihue (245-3581). HOURS: Open at 7:30 a.m. for breakfast, lunch and dinner until 9:30 p.m. daily. COMMENTS: This is a small cafeteria specializing in local delicacies with sandwiches, shortribs and other offer ings. NO CREDIT CARDS. *Inexpensive.*

KUKUI NUT TREE INN RESTAURANT ★

Kukui Grove Shopping Center, Lihue (245-7005). HOURS: Open at 7 a.m. (Sun days at 7:30 a.m.) for breakfast, lunch and dinner until 8 p.m. (except Sundays when they close at 3 p.m. and do not serve dinner). COMMENTS: The decor, with lattice work over each booth, provides a summer garden atmosphere. A wide rang of American and local foods is offered. A good family restaurant and the service is friendly and courteous. We recommend reservations for lunch, when it can be ver busy. *Moderate.*

LIHUE CAFE & CHOP SUI

2978 Umi Street, Lihue (245-6471). HOURS: Dinner 4:30 to 9 p.m. Monday through Friday. COMMENTS: This is another of those unpretentious restaurants in fact, it looks a bit more like a nightclub than a restaurant. The food is adequate to good, but the atmosphere leaves something to be desired. *Inexpensive.*

MA'S FAMILY, INC. ★

4277 Halenani (behind B.J.'s furniture off Rice Street), Lihue (245-3142). HOURS Open at 5 a.m. for breakfast and lunch to 1:30 p.m. ("oah whatevah") Monday through Friday, weekends breakfast only 5 to 10 a.m. No dinners served. COM MENTS: From the outside, this restaurant resembles one of the rundown roadside restaurants you find on the mainland. But once you are inside and talk to Ma or her sister and enjoy their warm welcome, and especially if you try Ma's pancakes of waffles, you will change your first impression. Some of the specialties for lunch in clude laulau, pepe kaula and lomi lomi. Service is fast and friendly. Try breakfa early in the morning – the locals you meet are fascinating. *Inexpensive.*

THE MASTERS

In the Westin Kauai Resort, Nawiliwili (245-5050). Featuring Continental cuisine the golf and racquet club, this will be the only restaurant at the Westin Kauai to r quire a jacket for men when it opens in 1988. Dinner only.

MIDORI ★

In the Kauai Hilton & Beach Villas, three miles north of Lihue (245-1955). HOUR Dinner only 6 to 10 p.m. daily. COMMENTS: Japanese name and decor, but co tinental cuisine and seafood are served. Fine food and service. *Expensive.*

MOKIHANA CAFE ★
4261 Rice Street, Lihue (245-8999). HOURS: Lunch 11 a.m. to 2 p.m., dinner 5 to 10 p.m. Monday through Saturday, closed Sundays. COMMENTS: Mixed menu – sandwiches, steaks, seafood and local. Fine food and service. Guitarist on weekends. The manager, Jay Mollicone, and the chef, Mike Salomone, are formerly from the Kauai Hilton & Beach Villas. Recently opened and really trying to please. *Moderate.*

OAR HOUSE SALOON
Nawiliwili (245-4941). HOURS: Open at 10 a.m. for lunch and dinner until 2 a.m. daily. COMMENTS: Essentially a saloon *cum* pool hall, but offers grilled and other sandwiches. The atmosphere of this place makes you feel that you should strap on your guns before you enter. *Inexpensive.*

THE PLANTER'S
On Highway 56 in the center of Hanamaulu (245-1606). HOURS: Open from 11 a.m. for lunch and dinner until 10 p.m. daily, with a happy hour from 3 to 5 p.m. COMMENTS: Food and service are good. The specialty is kiawe charcoal-broiled steaks. *Moderate.*

PRINCE BILL'S
In the Westin Kauai Resort, Nawiliwili (245-5050). HOURS: Buffet and a la carte breakfast Monday through Saturday 7 a.m. – 11 a.m. Brunch on Sunday 9 a.m. – 2 p.m. No lunch served. Dinner nightly 6 p.m. – 10 p.m. COMMENTS: A modified prix fixe dinner menu featuring an ample selection, primarily broiled items. The food and service are both superb under the management of Jay Bohling. Spectacular view from top of the ocean tower. *Expensive.*

RAINBOW COFFEES ★
Kukui Grove Shopping Center, Lihue (245-3703). HOURS: 9:30 a.m. to 6 p.m. daily. COMMENTS: Not a restaurant, but such a pleasant place for coffee and croissants or pastries after browsing in the bookstore or Stone's Gallery that we thought we'd list it. *Moderate.*

ROSITA'S MEXICAN RESTAURANT
Kukui Grove Shopping Center, Lihue (245-8561). HOURS: Open at 11 a.m. for lunch and dinner to 10 p.m. daily. The cantina, or bar part, remains open until midnight. COMMENTS: This restaurant is in a pseudo-Mexican stucco style with Tijuana-type stained glass and wrought iron, but manages to be rather pleasant nonetheless. The food is good but not great. The service is the same. *Moderate.*

THE TEMPURA GARDEN
In the Westin Kauai Resort, Nawiliwili (245-5050). HOURS: Lunch Monday through Saturday 11:30 a.m. – 2 p.m. Dinner nightly from 6 – 10 p.m. COMMENTS: Formal Japanese setting and dining. Kaiseki style cuisine prepared by chefs from Kyoto. Service is excellent. Separate sushi bar. Highly recommended, but for the sophisticated palate only. *Expensive.*

THE TERRACE RESTAURANT
In the Westin Kauai Resort, Nawiliwili (245-5050). To open late in 1988 with breakfast, lunch and light fare in the golf and racquet club.

TIP TOP MOTEL CAFE & BAKERY
3173 Akahi Street, Lihue (245-2333). HOURS: Open at 6:45 a.m. for breakfast, lunch and dinner until 8 p.m. daily. COMMENTS: spartan, but two reasons we put this on our list besides the friendly service: the macadamia nut pancakes (until noon) and the macadamia nut cookies to take with you. NO CREDIT CARDS. *Inexpensive.*

TONY'S DELI
2696-A Kress Street (next to Hamura's), Lihue (245-3244). HOURS: Lunch (take-outs only) 9:30 a.m. to 12:30 p.m., closed Sundays. COMMENTS: Located in a building that looks like its about to fall down. However, Tony produces take-out lunches that are exceptionally tasty. Popular with locals. DOES NOT DEAL IN PLASTIC. *Inexpensive.*

SOUTH & WEST (POIPU/KALAHEO/HANAPEPE/WAIMEA/KOKEE)

THE AQUARIUM RESTAURANT
2301 Nalo Road, Poipu (may be hard to find – head east along Hoone Road, past Brennecke's Beach, turn left on Nalo Road at a sign directing you mauka, and you will come to the restaurant) (742-9505). HOURS: Dinner 4 to 10 p.m., closed Tuesday. COMMENTS: Leonard Zalopany and his family specialize in pasta dishes. The pasta is freshly prepared daily. Fish and steak are also on the menu. This restaurant does have a nice family atmosphere, but their food is distinguished more for quantity than quality. *Moderate.*

BEACH HOUSE RESTAURANT
5022 Lawai Beach Road, Poipu (742-7575). HOURS: Dinner 5 to 10 p.m. daily. COMMENTS: This establishment strives for elegance (or something) in replacing the funky old restaurant destroyed by Hurricane Iwa. The famous personal touch apparently blew away, too. The tables are now arranged in a larger building to provide more window tables for the fabulous view, but they are also crushed closer together. Reservations are recommended, but you are almost always asked to wait in the lounge. You may be left there, so we advise that you stand and wait. The specialties are fresh fish, shellfish and steaks, which are all excellent. The service is rushed and inattentive, which detracts from the fine food. We still have early cocktails and pupus in the lounge and watch the sunset from the lawn. *Expensive.*

THE BREAKERS RESTAURANT
In the Sheraton Kauai Hotel, Poipu (742-1661). HOURS: Dinner 5:30 to 10 p.m. daily. COMMENTS: Not much atmosphere. Kiawe-broiled steaks are featured. The food and service are fair to good. *Moderate.*

BRENNECKE'S BEACH BROILER ★
Opposite Poipu Beach Park, Poipu (742-7588). HOURS: Lunch and dinner 11:30 a.m. to midnight daily. Late happy hour from 10 to 11:30 p.m. COMMENTS: This second-floor restaurant offers an ocean view and sparkly atmosphere, catering to a younger crowd. The specialty is kiawe-broiled fresh fish of the day, which is the best on the island, bar none. Bob and Christine French ensure that both the food and service are of top quality. Reservations. *Moderate.*

COURTSIDE BAR & GRILL
By the Kiahuna Tennis Courts, Poipu (742-9497). HOURS: Open at 7 a.m. for breakfast and lunch to 2 p.m. daily. COMMENTS: Pleasant surroundings. "Design-your-own" omelets are featured for breakfast and sandwiches for lunch. Cleanliness and the mosquitoes could both stand a little attention. NO CREDIT CARDS. *Moderate.*

GREEN GARDEN
On Highway 50, Hanapepe (335-5422). HOURS: Breakfast and lunch 7 a.m. to 1 p.m. daily, dinner 5 to 8:30 p.m. (closed for dinner on Tuesdays only). COMMENTS: The restaurant opened in 1948 and is still run by Gwen Hamabata in the style her parents began. It has been enlarged several times, and the rambling architecture itself is attractive. The plants everywhere, with orchids on every table, give you the feeling you truly are in a green garden. We recommend that you call first because it is often closed for local functions; and it is crowded at lunch time – tourist buses stop here. The food is good, not gourmet quality, but hearty and plentiful. For dessert try their macadamia nut or lilikoi pie – *ono. Inexpensive.*

HALE OHANA
Poipu Beach Hotel, Poipu (742-1681). HOURS: Breakfast 7 to 10 a.m. Monday through Saturdays, 7 a.m. to noon on Sunday, dinner 6 to 9 p.m. daily. COMMENTS: Offers nothing unusual. A standard hotel dining room with good food and service with a view of the pool. *Moderate.*

HOUSE OF SEAFOOD
1941 Poipu Road, Poipu (in the heart of the Poipu Kai Condominium Complex), Poipu (742-6433). HOURS: Lunch 11:30 a.m. to 3 p.m., dinner 6 to 10 p.m. daily. COMMENTS: The menu is varied, and the pastry is from their own bakeshop. The view from the window tables over the tennis courts out to the ocean is pleasant. But the food is only fair and the service inattentive. This is an ideal location for a good family restaurant. Someone should put one here. *Expensive.*

KALAHEO RESTAURANT
Near the stoplight on Highway 50 , Kalaheo (332-9755). HOURS: Open at 7 a.m. for breakfast, lunch and dinner until 9 p.m. daily. COMMENTS: Homestyle American and oriental food is offered. The best value is hamburger with fries. *Inexpensive.*

KEOKI'S PARADISE
Kiahuna Shopping Village, Poipu (742-7534). HOURS: Seafood and taco bar from 4:30 p.m. and dinner 5:30 to 10 p.m. daily. COMMENTS: The fisherman's chowder is excellent, as is their hula pie. The rest of the menu is fair to good, which cannot be said of the service. The place is ideally located so is popular and usually crowded – reservations are a must. But be prepared – the fake decorations and tourist crush may do just that to your mood. At least they have turned off the tape recording of frogs croaking! *Expensive.*

KIAHUNA CLUBHOUSE RESTAURANT ★

Poipu (up Kiahuna Plantation Drive past Keoki's Paradise, left turn to the golf course clubhouse) (742-6055). HOURS: Breakfast 7 to 11:30 a.m., lunch 11:30 a.m. to 3:30 p.m., dinner 5:30 to 9 p.m. daily. COMMENTS: The food and the service are superb. There is usually a chef's special – be sure to ask. You are never crowded or rushed and the ambience is sparse but pleasant. *Moderate.*

KOKEE LODGE

Kokee State Park, Kokee (335-6061). HOURS: Open at 8:30 a.m. for breakfast and lunch until 5:30 p.m. daily, dinner Fridays and Saturdays only until 10 p.m. COMMENTS: You will pass this on the way to the Kalalau Valley Lookout and might want to stop for lunch. Good food and service. *Moderate.*

KOLOA BROILER

On Koloa Road, Koloa (742-9122). HOURS: Open at 11 a.m. for lunch and dinner until 10:30 p.m. daily. COMMENTS: As you walk in, you will see a sample display on ice of the steak, fish, chicken and kabob that you can choose from and cook yourself. Salad, baked beans and rice are on a side table. The ambience is that of a tired warehouse. But while you are broiling your own selection, camaraderie develops with other patrons, advice is exchanged, and you will enjoy the apron on the wall with "Known Worldwide for our Famous Chefs!" Bring the kids – the burgers are a buy. Reservations advised at peak hours. *Inexpensive.*

KOLOA COFFEE & BAKE SHOP

On Koloa Road, Koloa (no phone). HOURS: 6:30 a.m. to 10 p.m. daily. COMMENTS: This small establishment prepares its own exquisite baked goodies. It is included here because it offers a continental breakfast if you are staying in the Poipu area and are underway early for a tour around the island. Conversely, you can pick up some of their specialties the night before and enjoy a continental breakfast on your own lanai. It also offers those famous Lappert's ice cream cones to drip off your elbow as you stroll around Koloa. *Moderate.*

KOLOA ICE HOUSE

On Koloa Road, eastern end of Koloa (742-6063). HOURS: Open at 10:30 a.m. for lunch and dinner until 9 p.m. daily. COMMENTS: They offer a variety of snacks such as "veggie" sandwiches, burritos, delicious soups, shave ice and Lappert's ice cream. Order the hula pie – its delicious. There is limited seating space, but a small picnic garden across the way provides more. The service was variable in the past, but has been good for nearly a year now. *Inexpensive.*

MANGOS

On Koloa Road, Koloa (742-7377). HOURS: Lunch 11 a.m. to 3 p.m., dinner 5:30 to 9:30 p.m. daily. COMMENTS: The first restaurant on Kauai to change its name and character so far in 1988 is Mangos – which was formerly the Koloa Fish and Chowder House. The decor, service and quality of the food have all been improved substantially under the new owners Allan and Charlotte Beall. The Szechuan dishes may lack authenticity, but the rest of the menu is excellent. *Moderate.*

NANIWA
Sheraton Kauai Hotel, Poipu (742-1661). HOURS: Dinner 5:30 to 10 p.m. daily. COMMENTS: This restaurant features good, but not great, Japanese food while looking out over a carp-filled lagoon. However, the prices will shock you for what you get. *Expensive.*

THE OUTRIGGER ROOM
Sheraton Kauai Hotel, Poipu (742-1661). HOURS: Breakfast 7 to 10 a.m., lunch 11:30 a.m. to 2 p.m., dinner 6:30 to 9:30 p.m. daily. COMMENTS: The main dining room of the hotel. The food and service are good, and the Sunday brunch is recommended. *Expensive.*

PLANTATION GARDENS RESTAURANT ★
Kiahuna Plantation, Poipu (742-1695). HOURS: Dinner 5:30 to 10 p.m. daily. COMMENTS: The finest overall dining experience on the south shore *if* you are seated when and where you request. Request a window or lanai table, and if you get one, the view of the Moir gardens is delightful. Seafood is featured. Their prime rib and steaks are also good. Ask about the specialties of the evening. The service has been excellent for nearly a year now, but reservations are still a problem. Even if you have them you are often asked to wait, and your request for a window or lanai table is often ignored. Cocktails and pupus are available on the outside lanai if you want to avoid these two problems. We do. *Expensive.*

THE TAMARIND ★
Waiohai Resort Hotel, Poipu (742-9511). HOURS: Dinner 6 to 10 p.m. daily. COMMENTS: This is one of the few places on Kauai that request a jacket for men, although a long-sleeved shirt with a collar will pass. No tie. They feature a continental cuisine and their appetizers are justifiably famous. The wine list is extensive, and after your meal you are offered an excellent selection of pastries. The service is perfect; however, there is no view. One constant complaint is that it is air-conditioned for the comfort of waiters in jackets, not ladies in sleeveless dresses. Reservations. *Expensive.*

THE WAIOHAI TERRACE
Waiohai Resort Hotel, Poipu (742-9511). HOURS: Open at 6:30 a.m. for breakfast, lunch and dinner until 10 p.m. daily. Sunday champagne brunch 10 a.m. to 2 p.m. COMMENTS: The main dining room of the hotel. Menus are mostly a la carte. The food is generally good, but the service tends to be indifferent. Something *has* to be done about the flies in the summer. The feature of The Waiohai Terrace is the Sunday champagne brunch. Although the line for this begins to form about 9 a.m., they do take reservations for parties of ten or more. If your group comes to a half-dozen or so, you could make reservations and pick up four companions in the line. Otherwise, come about 1:30 p.m. for the shortest wait. Plans are in the works to offer a daily brunch. *Expensive.*

WRANGLER'S RESTAURANT
9852 Kaumualii Highway, Waimea (338-1218). HOURS: Open at 10:30 a.m. for lunch and dinner until 9 p.m. daily. COMMENTS: Perhaps the best aged beef on the island. They also have good hamburgers and some fairly good Mexican dishes. *Moderate.*

LUAUS

If luaus are your thing, the best on Kauai is at the *Tahiti Nui* in Hanalei (826-6277). These are Monday, Wednesday and Friday nights, and reservations are required. They are warm, local affairs presided over by "Auntie" Louise Marston. Cocktails start at 6:45 p.m., with buffet dinner and show at 8:30 p.m. The cost is $20 per person including tax, but exclusive of drinks.

Others listed alphabetically are:

Kauai Resort Hotel, Wailua (245-3931) – Luaus are in the Garden Court every night except Monday and Saturday. The imu ceremony is at 6 p.m., cocktails 6:15 to 7:15 p.m., dinner at 7:15 p.m., and a Polynesian show at 8 p.m. The cost, including drinks, is $34 per person, plus tax.

Sheraton Kauai Hotel, Poipu (742-1661) – Every Sunday and Wednesday evening at 6:30 p.m. a buffet dinner is offered with a wide choice of Hawaiian, American and oriental food. This is followed by a Polynesian show at 8 p.m. The cost, exclusive of drinks is $34 per person plus tax.

Smith's Tropical Paradise, Wailua (822-4654) – Luaus Tuesday, Wednesday and Thursday nights. The gates open at 5 p.m. for a stroll around the gardens. The imu ceremony is at 6 p.m., followed by open bar from 6:10 p.m. and a buffet at 6:45 p.m. featuring Hawaiian and other food. An international show, partly Hawaiian, begins at 8 p.m. nearby. The cost for everything is $36 per person plus tax.

Sheraton Coconut Beach Hotel, Wailua (822-3455, ext. 651) – A luau every night but Monday in The Kahili Room. Shell lei greeting at 7 p.m., open bar 7 to 8 p.m., buffet dinner starts at 8 p.m., and the show at 8:30 p.m. The total cost is $36 per person, tax included.

The Westin Kauai Resort, Nawiliwili (245-5050) "Broadway-style" polynesian shows with dinner in the Boathouse Supper Club.

NIGHT LIFE

Night life is scant on Kauai, but there is some! The features of this island are the beauty and the quiet. Alphabetically, the night spots are:

Club Jetty, Nawiliwili (245-4970) – Music nightly from 9:30 p.m.

Coco Palms Resort, Wailua (822-4921) – At dusk every night, torch-lighting ceremony followed by Grace Guslander's recitation of local history. It's recorded now – she retired. In the Lagoon Bar, Hawaiian music from 5 to 7 p.m. and 9:30 p.m. to 12:30 a.m. Polynesian shows are Sunday, Tuesday, Thursday and Saturday in the interval.

The Flats Grill & Bar, Princeville (826-7255) – A hula show Thursday and Sunday evenings at 8 p.m.

Jolly Roger Restaurant, Coconut Plantation Marketplace, Wailua (822-3451) – A guitarist or other entertainment from 9:30 p.m. to 1:30 a.m.

Kauai Beach Boy Hotel, Coconut Plantation Marketplace, Wailua (822-3441) – The Boogie Palace is open nightly from 9 p.m. with live bands.

Kauai Hilton & Beach Villas, three miles north of Lihue (245-1955) – Live music and dancing nightly in Gilligan's.

Kauai Resort Hotel, Wailua (245-3931) – This hotel sometimes has the finest entertainment from Honolulu for one or two nights. Watch the newspaper or call to see who may be in town.

Park Place, Harbor Village Shopping Village, Nawiliwili (245-5775) – Music video system from 8 p.m. to 4 a.m. Tuesday through Sunday. This is the hottest spot in town for the locals.

The Rib 'n' Tail, Kapaa (822-9632) – Live entertainment Wednesday through Sunday nights.

The Poipu Beach Hotel, Poipu (742-1681) – Live music in the Poipu Beach Club Wednesday through Sunday from 9:30 p.m. on.

Seaview Lounge (upstairs in Kapaa Trade Center Building), Kapaa (822-7273) – Hawaiian music on Friday nights.

Sheraton Coconut Beach Hotel, Wailua (822-3455) – In the Paddle Room, Kaholokula plays Hawaiian tunes Monday, Thursday and Friday nights. Cook's Landing usually has a singer and guitarist or a small combo.

Sheraton Kauai Hotel, Poipu (742-1661) – Live music and dancing nightly in the Drum Lounge.

Sheraton Princeville Hotel, Princeville (826-9644) – Ukiyos, a nightclub disco.

Tahiti Nui, Hanalei (826-6277) – Pickup entertainment Tuesday and Thursday, and a combo on weekends.

Westin Kauai Resort, Nawiliwili (245-5050) – The Verandah Disco is open nightly.

WHAT TO SEE

INTRODUCTION

We thought long and hard about how best to lay out an exploratory tour of Kauai. Some visitors just want to browse around the area where they are staying when they have a spare hour or so. Most are here for a week or two and spend a couple of days adventuring. And there are a few who would like to explore every inch of the island, which would take forever.

What we decided to do was include most of the points of interest so that you can read about them ahead of time with a pencil in hand. Those who live here are reassured that some of their most special places are not mentioned. The idea is to mark those that you want to see in the time available, "connect the dots", and you have your own personalized tour! No times can be given for any portions of the tours, but rough estimates can be made from the distances involved, then adding how long your interest might hold you at each spot.

Because the highway mile markers start in Lihue, this is the best place to begin. If you are staying at one end of the island, it is easy to check the places you want to see in reverse as far as Lihue, and then those along the opposite shore in the order described. The overall length of the north shore tour is almost the same as the south, so we have divided our description of the tour along the shore into these two parts, with Waimea Canyon and Kokee as the third part.

No long hikes that would disrupt the tours will be described – only a few taking half an hour or less. Longer hikes and overnight camping are covered in "What to Do." But bring along appropriate shoes and clothing even for these shorter hikes. Mosquito repellant is a good idea for some places, and bathing suits, mask, snorkel and fins, beach towels and whatever else in case you want to go for a swim. Some of the gorgeous beaches may be irresistible.

Small sectional maps are included, but a good map of Kauai is also advised; better yet, a trusty co-pilot beside you to read maps and pertinent parts of this guide book as you drive. Check the weather before starting out. Some of the roads require a four-wheel drive when muddy.

There is one important thing to do ahead of time. Most of the interesting places on Kauai are on land owned by sugar plantations or access to them is through such property. Of the four plantations on Kauai, two are the most important in this

107

regard, and permission to go on their property must be obtained. This is a relatively recent requirement due to the rapid increase in tourists, many of whom don't understand cane operations. This brought with it a sharp rise in the number of accidents and lawsuits, whether the visitors were driving, bicycling or walking on cane roads. In the past, local residents were allowed admission under a laissez-faire policy almost to the point where they regarded cane lands as public property. Now the plantations are increasingly concerned about liability and have tightened up on tourists and locals alike. Guided tours of the mills stopped three years ago, and in 1985 locked gates began appearing on the major access cane roads.

Throughout the tour descriptions to follow, the key words "cane road" will be at the start of the directions to each site where such permission is required. In most cases, clearance from your rental car agency is also necessary to drive on these unimproved roads.

The **Lihue Plantation Company** controls the cane land from "Halfway Bridge" over the Huleia River between Koloa and Lihue, all the way north to Kealia. Write their main office at 1970 Kele Street, Lihue, Kauai, HI 96766, or telephone 808-245-7325. If your stay is to be short, obtain an application in advance by mail and apply the same way. The committee that passes upon the applications meets only once a week. If you wait until arriving on Kauai, their headquarters is in a two-story white building behind the First Hawaiian Bank on Rice Street in Lihue.

The **McBryde Sugar Company** controls most of the cane land west of the Huleia River up to that of the Olokele Sugar Company, which starts at the Hanapepe River. Write the McBryde Sugar Company Ltd., P.O. Box 8, Eleele, Kauai, HI 96705, or telephone 808-335-5111. If you are already here and want to find their headquarters, head west out of Lihue on Highway 50 and pass through Kalaheo. Just out of Kalaheo, Route 540 (a paved road) turns to the left. The other end of this loop can be picked up in Eleele. Once on Route 540, head toward the high smoke stack. Their headquarters is in Numila, the Hawaiian adaptation of "new mill." When you are close to the stack, the headquarters building can be found easily.

Read the rules and restrictions of both companies, and be careful to observe them. The harsh reality is that if we don't, and if some of us can't resist calling in "mainland-type" lawyers for every little thing, most of the beauty of Kauai will be closed to everyone soon – and to posterity forever.

Each company will provide an identification card and a copy of your signed release of liability. You should have both with you whenever you are on their property. Each also issues a decal for your car. As a tourist, you should not affix this to a rental car, but keep it easily visible in the lower right-hand corner of the front windshield and destroy it when you leave the island.

NORTH SHORE TOUR

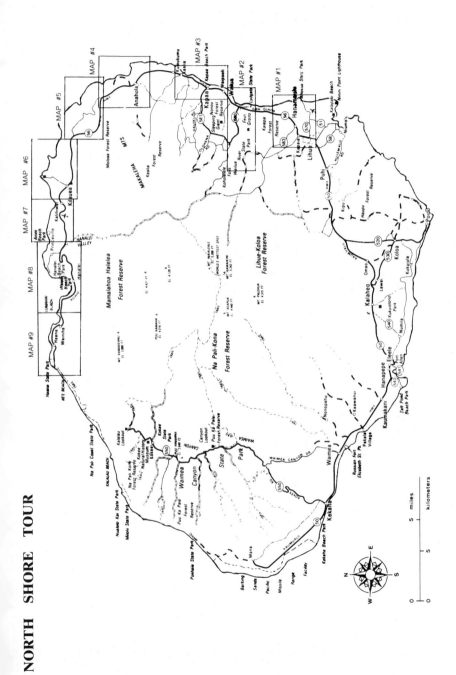

109

NORTH SHORE TOUR
LIHUE TO HANAMAULU
MAP #1

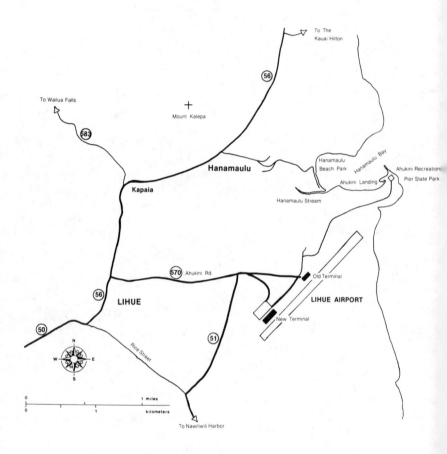

To The Kauai Hilton

To Wailua Falls

56

+ Mount Kalepa

583

Hanamaulu

Hanamaulu Beach Park

Hanamaulu Bay

Ahukini Recreation Pier State Park

Ahukini Landing

Kapaia

Hanamaulu Stream

570 Ahukini Rd.

Old Terminal

LIHUE AIRPORT

56 LIHUE

New Terminal

50

Rice Street

N
W E
S

51

0   1 miles
0   1   kilometers

To Nawiliwili Harbor

NORTH SHORE TOUR

LIHUE TO HANAMAULU - MAP #1

Before leaving Lihue, Ahukini Road, the road that you took from the airport, leads to one place of interest. Pass the airport and continue makai (towards the ocean). From time to time the road crosses portions of the narrow-gauge track that was used to transport bags of sugar to **Ahukini Landing** until the bulk loading facility was built at Nawiliwili. Tracks like this were also used for the small trains that carried cut cane to the mills until trucks began to be used early in this century. The track was taken up and laid down by hand to each area as it was harvested.

Park at the end of the road. You are in **Ahukini Recreation Pier State Park**. Although the rocky shoreline could not be called a beach, this is a good spot to remember for snorkeling and scuba diving during Kona winds. At those times, the normally calm south shore spots can be rough or even closed out altogether. Walk out on the dock to your left. This was a major port for the sugar industry until Nawiliwili Harbor took over in 1924, and it closed officially in 1951. Time seems to stand still here. If you see some locals fishing, stop and "talk story" with them. Enjoy the fabulous view of Hanamaulu Bay and on down the coast to the "Bali Hai" peaks. These are the peaks that, through cinematographic wizardry, were transformed into the island of Bali Hai for the movie "South Pacific." That's what there is of interest at Ahukini – a moment of history, a beautiful view and some local lore.

We're going to pass a lot of *sugar cane* on these tours, so this may be a good point to tell you about the growing, harvesting and processing of sugar on Kauai. First, selected cane is cut by hand into eighteen-inch lengths, each of which has several buds. This is planted by a machine that digs furrows, drops in the segments, adds fertilizer, and covers the furrows. Sometimes old roots are just allowed to grow after the cane is harvested, a process which is called "ratooning", but this produces a smaller crop than planting "seed" cane and it is not economical to do this more than once or twice.

Irrigation is accomplished either by ditches and furrows from reservoirs or drip systems using black plastic tubing. Approximately a ton of water is required for every pound of refined sugar, so irrigation has to supplement natural rainfall most places on the island. Weeds are sprayed by airplane or tractor early in the growing cycle, and then by hand. After a few months, the cane stalks are tall enough to block out the sun and no more herbiciding is necessary.

The cane matures in about two years. Large areas are then burned to remove the dry leaves. The stalks are then cut close to the ground by V-cutters, cranes load it into huge cane trucks, and the cane is taken to the mill. There it is washed, chopped, and rolled two or three times to squeeze out the juice, which is mixed with calcium carbonate and heated to clarify it. Most of the water is removed from the juice in evaporators, which forms a syrup. The syrup is then boiled in vacuum pans to thicken it, and then centrifuged to separate molasses from golden raw sugar crystals.

The raw sugar is sent to the mainland for refining, and the molasses is used for cattle feed and other products. The residual cane fiber, or bagasse, is burned by the mills to generate approximately one-fourth of the electricity used on Kauai.

The sugar planters of Hawaii collectively own the California and Hawaiian Sugar Company refinery on San Francisco Bay, which produces C & H Sugar for the western states. A small refinery in Aiea on Oahu produces refined sugar for consumption in Hawaii. The sugar industry faces a bleak future beyond 1991, when federal price supports are scheduled to end.

Back on Kuhio Highway, or Highway 56, just north of Lihue are two or three vintage buildings. This is the visible part of the small town of **Kapaia**, which means "the bowers" – probably because it is enclosed by verdant bluffs on either side of the Hanamaulu Stream. The few remaining homes in Kapaia are in the valley to your right, connected by a suspension foot bridge to the hundred-year-old Immaculate Conception Church.

Route 583, Maalo Road just beyond Kapaia, leads left to **Wailua** (two waters) **Falls**. Turn here, and at about 3-1/2 miles there are small pullouts where you can pause and view the valley. The large parking lot at the end of the road marks the main lookout over Wailua Falls on the south fork of the Wailua River. If the falls are full, there may be a rainbow arched over them. In ancient times, Hawaiian chiefs would dive from the top of the falls into the pool below to demonstrate their courage. A trail goes to the top of the eighty-foot falls where there are some pools and caves, but the footing along the stream is slippery. In the last dozen years, nine visitors have fallen into the stream and were carried over the falls. Seven were killed and two are paralyzed. Heed the warning sign and don't go up this trail. About 100 yards downstream are three or four paths leading down a steep and slippery slope to a pool at the bottom of the falls. Getting down is not a problem – getting back up is. You have to cross the river to reach the pool, so don't go if the paths are muddy or the falls are full.

Once again on Highway 56, enter Hanamaulu and turn right on Hanamaulu Road. Another right on Hehi Road takes you to **Hanamaulu** (tired from walking) **Bay**. On the way is an overpass that was used for the old narrow-gauge railroad that once ran all the way from Koloa to Kealia. By the time of your visit, the new Ahukini cutoff road may also pass overhead.

Hanamaulu Beach Park is about six acres in area with tables, restrooms, a pavilion, barbecue facilities and showers. Camping is allowed with a County permit. The surf is gentle and swimming is safe, even for children, any time of the year. The waves are usually too small for any type of surfing, however. Snorkeling is poor due to the limited visibility. Because this park is close to large population centers, local toughs in the past would occasionally rough up overnight campers here. But Hurricane Iwa in 1982 had a miraculous effect. Tourism almost died for two years after that and the island realized how heavily it depended on tourists. Communities rallied together and straightened out the young punks. There hasn't been a single such incident that we are aware of in the last five years anywhere on Kauai.

As you return mauka to Hanamaulu proper and Highway 56, you see **Mount Kalepa** just behind. This name means "the flag" literally, but because Hawaiians hoisted a piece of kapa (or tapa) to indicate they had poi or other articles for sale, by extension it means "trader." This part of the shore on Kauai is the nearest to Oahu, and in ancient times flags were raised on the mountain to indicate a willingness to trade with canoes coming from other islands. More recently, lookouts were stationed there to warn of an invasion from Oahu when Kamehameha threatened Kauai. The slopes of the entire range were once covered with sandalwood. The sand dunes to the right as you head north out of Hanamaulu are an old Hawaiian burial ground; bones and artifacts are still turned up here from time to time.

HANAMAULU TO WAILUA - MAP #2

The road to the right just before the Wailua County Golf Course takes you to **Nukolii Beach**, a sandy beach that runs for about two miles. It is the first exposed beach on the eastern coast as we go north from Lihue, so safety precautions start here.

Because of the tragic consequences following the publication of another guide that described beaches only as the author, who is a part-time visitor, found them on pleasant summer days, no description of activities at beaches is given in this guide except for the south shore beaches, which are usually safe. Our purpose in this edition is merely to appeal to the explorer in all of us, lead you to each beach, and make a simple precautionary statement on safety. John Clark, who has written exemplary guides to the beaches of other islands that balances the recreational activities against the potential dangers, is currently working on a guide for Kauai that will appear in 1988. Those who wish to enter the water at any but south shore beaches are urged either to await his guide or exercise appropriate caution.

The surf at Nukolii is usually rough during the winter, but a reef offers some protection at spots. All along, the shore is steep and a shore break with backwash is present most of the time, but especially strong at high tide. A southerly current of one to two knots along shore sweeps out to sea just north of Hanamaulu Bay.

The Kauai County Correctional Center (jail) is directly across Highway 56 from the Wailua Golf Course clubhouse.

At the 5 mile marker, a sign indicates the Lydgate Area, named for the Reverend J.M. Lydgate who was the founder of the Lihue Union Church over 100 years ago. Turn right on Leho Drive, then right again to reach **Lydgate State Park** makai of the Kauai Resort Hotel. The park is forty acres in area and has restrooms, a pavilion and showers, but no camping is allowed. As at Hanamaulu Beach Park, some overnight campers were bothered by local toughs here before 1982, so the State simply closed it to camping and left it closed. Behind the breakwater, the protected beach is ideal for beginning snorkelers. There is a sandy bottom with many small fish near the rocks. The rest of the beach - a continuation of Nukolii Beach - is wide and pleasant, but swimming outside the protected area is not advised for the reasons mentioned.

NORTH SHORE TOUR
HANAMAULU TO WAILUA
MAP #2

To: U. of Hawaii Agricultural
    Experimental Station
    Kuilau Ridge Trail
    Keahua Arboretum

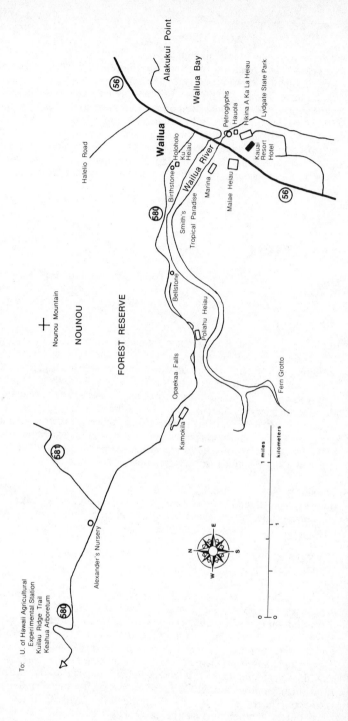

Alexander's Nursery

580
581

Nounou Mountain

NOUNOU

FOREST RESERVE

Opaekaa Falls

Kamokila

Poliahu Heiau

Bellstone

580

Smith's
Tropical Paradise

Wailua River

Fern Grotto

Halelio Road

Birthstone
Holoholo
Ku
Heiau

Wailua

56

Alakukui Point

Wailua Bay

Petroglyphs
Hauola
Hikina A Ka La Heiau
Lydgate State Park

Marina

Malae Heiau

Kauai
Resort
Hotel

56

1 miles

kilometers

N
E
W
S

Stroll around here. Just behind the north end of the beach are many large black rocks. Some have been moved to line the road, but those still in place mark one end of the *Hikina a Ka La* (rising of the sun) *Heiau*, an ancient Hawaiian temple. It went due north from here 395 feet, and this orientation means it was lined up with the north star. It was unique in being only fifty-six feet in width for most of its length. The size of the boulders as well as other evidence indicates that it was built in the Marquesan period around 800 A.D. This heiau was given its name because it was built on the first spot in the Wailua area that the rays of the rising sun touch each day.

At the northern end of the heiau are boulders set in a rough square. This is all that is left of *Hauola* (dew of life), one of the two ancient places of refuge on Kauai. If Hawaiians had broken a tabu or were part of an army that had been defeated in war, they tried to gain entry to a place of refuge such as this. Once they had gone through the rites prescribed by the kahunas (priests) there, they were then free to return to their homes. A flat stone once used to sharpen adzes is on the site, but would have been used with sand and water at the shoreline nearby.

From the bronze Hauola plaque, walk about sixty feet towards the mouth of the Wailua River. At the shore to your left is a separated group of large black rocks with about a dozen petroglyphs inscribed on the surface. The only spiroglyph ever found in the Hawaiian Islands is on the side of one. The dilapidated bridge was once part of the old narrow-gauge railroad that ran to Kealia, and remnants of the old highway bridge are beside it.

Back on Highway 56, look mauka of the highway to find a large overgrown mound above a parallel cane road. Here are the key words "cane road" for the first time. You will be going on Lihue Plantation land here, and permission is required. Park near the gate. A trail on the left leads up to the massive *Malae* (clear or calm) *Heiau*. This was once 300 x 300 feet with walls six feet high and ten feet thick. We will see this from another heiau farther up the hill, and sacred rites were often performed conjointly at both sites.

Smith's Tropical Paradise is below the Malae Heiau on the west bank of the Wailua River. This consists of thirty acres of gardens and simulated Polynesian village, Japanese island, and Filipino village. This is so cloyingly commercial that it has never appealed to us, despite the interesting plants and birds there. The hours are 8:30 a.m. to 4:30 p.m. daily, and the charge is $3.00 for a walking tour or $5.00 for a narrated tram ride.

The wide *Wailua River* is in front of you here. It is often called the only navigable river in the Hawaiian Islands, but that depends on the size of your boat. We have navigated up seven rivers on Kauai alone in our Zodiac boat. Motorboat tours leave from the marina every half hour from 9:00 a.m. to 4:00 p.m. for the 1-1/2 hour trip to the *Fern Grotto* and back. This is a narrated ride that includes the singing of Ke Kali Nei Au, the "Hawaiian Wedding Song", at the Grotto. Two firms operate these tours – Waialeale Boats and Smith's Motorboat Service. Waialeale Boats tends to be less crowded, but the price for each is the same – $8.00. The trip itself is beautiful, so perhaps everyone should go once. All boats are somewhat less crowded in the late afternoons.

Now take Route 580, or Kuamoo Road, mauka (towards the mountains) from Highway 56 just past the river. You are on the ancient path up which high chiefs were borne in their canoes from the beach to their homes by the lagoon. This path and the surrounding area were once kapu to commoners – on penalty of death. Deborah Kapule, widow of Kaumualii, the last high chief of Kauai, lived near the lagoon from 1830 until her death in 1855.

The palms on the grounds of the Coco Palms Resort and farther east along Highway 56 are not a "royal grove" as you may be told. They were planted by William Lindemann in 1896 for copra (dried coconut meat) for its coconut oil. The venture was not a commercial success.

The Hawaiians constructed seven sacred heiaus from Hikina a Ka La at the mouth of the Wailua River to the top of *Mt. Waialeale* (rippling or flowing water). The altar on Mt. Waialeale is still there today beside a large pond whose waters ripple in the wind and flow to nourish the island – hence the name.

About .1 mile up Route 580 is a structure designated *Holoholo Ku* (run run stand fast) *Heiau*. Because this doesn't look anything like a heiau, we visited the site with Dr. William Kikuchi, the preeminent archeologist on Kauai. He informed us that the sign was put there in error by a State official when Route 580 was built. The structure is actually the pigpen that belonged to Deborah Kapule. A heiau by that name did exist in ancient times on top of the hill just behind the site, but its remnants were replaced by the cemetery now there. The low opening in the wall was for two purposes – drainage and to keep the larger sows in. Apparently the piglets passed freely out of the pen to forage, but always returned to their mothers inside the pen. When they became too large to pass through to forage on their own, it was time to have a feast.

The largest stone adjacent to the cliff just inland from the pigpen is the *birth stone*, or *Pohaku Hoohanau*. This is a marker stone only to indicate the sacred site of royal births on Kauai. Births did *not* take place with the woman's back against this stone. The square, double-walled rock foundation had a grass shack on it. This shelter next to the birth stone is where both labor and delivery took place. Afterward, the umbilical cord and placenta were wedged into cracks in the *Pohaku Piko* (navel stone), the cliff behind the birth stone, with pieces of wood and small rocks. The slab of sandstone in front of the doorway to the birth shelter has dog bones under it, an ancient ritual performed to make the birthsite kapu.

A short way farther up Route 580 is a turnout on your right from which you can view Opaekaa Valley. About one mile from the start of 580, watch for a dirt road angling sharply back to your left. Take this and follow it (over bumps and all) to the end where two huge boulders stand. Between them, a path starts that winds down the bank of the river to *the bellstone*. You can tell which it is at the end of the path because it shows ample evidence of having been hammered upon for centuries. When struck sharply, a resonant note rings out over the entire valley. The announcement of royal births was made this way. A path along the river bank on which the kahunas walked to perform this rite once connected the birth site and bellstone directly. Traces of the path are still visible today.

About .1 mile farther up Route 580 is a paved one-way loop to the left. Take this to enjoy a panoramic view of the **Wailua Valley**. The **Poliahu Heiau** to the right was named for the snow goddess of the Island of Hawaii. Walk around it to the north-west corner where there is a bronze plaque. There you might find offerings – a flower or a leaf under a rock – left by a devout Hawaiian. If you rummage in the dirt along the east wall and at one spot near the south wall, you will find chips of volcanic stone left over from making stone adzes and other implements. The rocks for these were selected and brought up from the streambed nearby. The heiau is overgrown inside now, but under the growth are several terraces, idol sites, and a vertical "god stone" five feet high. It measures 242 feet by 165 feet, approximately one acre in area, and is the largest heiau on Kauai. Ceremonies were held here conjointly with the Malae Heiau you saw before. This heiau was discovered when Route 580 was built, as was another one 3/4 mile farther up 580 on the bank of a small stream.

About 1.3 miles from the start of Route 580 is a parking area for **Opaekaa** (rolling shrimp) **Falls**. Some shrimp are still in the pool, hiding under rocks during the day and emerging at night. The best view is from the path along the highway.

If you cross the highway, you can look down on **Kamokila** (the stronghold), a restored Hawaiian village. To see Kamokila, follow the signs at the first road to your left as you leave the parking area. The hostesses are part-Hawaiian and have an extensive knowledge of Hawaiiana. For a $5.00 admission fee, you will see poi pounding, breadfruit trees, a petroglyph, and many other interesting things. The hours are 9:00 a.m. to 4:00 p.m. Monday through Saturday, closed Sundays. It seems to us that a wharf along the riverfront would allow much easier access by boat so that this operation could do better financially.

About two miles beyond Opaekaa Falls, **Alexander's Nursery** is set in the tall trees on your right just past the Route 581 turnoff. The entry with its small sign is hard to see, but is worth watching for if you are interested in tropical flora.

At a sharp bend to the left on Route 580, shortly after the 4 mile marker, is the **University of Hawaii Agricultural Experiment Station**. From the road you can see the different crops under study, but visitors are not encouraged.

Notice the many homes along Route 580. This area is a desirable place to live because it is cool in the summer. The temperatures are about five degrees below those at sea level and the trade winds are unobstructed.

At 6.6 miles from the start of Route 580 is the trailhead of the **Kuilau Ridge Trail**. This hike takes about two hours, so you may not have time on this tour. It goes by waterfalls, through hau trees, wild orchids, and ti plants (that were once used to make hula skirts), to two spectacular viewpoints.

Continue on now potholed Route 580 until you splash through **Keahua** (the mound) **Stream**. Just beyond on the right is a parking area. The trail to your left goes to the **Keahua Arboretum**. Although this area was devastated by Hurricane Iwa, there are still about a dozen numbered posts designating interesting plant life. These numbers correspond to an explanatory pamphlet obtainable from the District Forester, and several other plants and trees are labeled. The pool in the stream is perfectly located to splash in after you after your stroll. Route 580 continues to the Power Line Trail, which is on the old Waimea to Wailua trail.

Return to Highway 56, turn left and drive along *Wailua Bay*, and reflect that this bay was the last place on Kauai where Hawaiians gathered for hukilaus. The Coco Palms Resort on your left grew out of a small hostelry that Grace Buscher began to manage in the late 1940's. She later married the owner, Lyle Guslander. It was the major tourist hotel on Kauai for many years. *Wailua Beach* is gorgeous and on some days it is safe. However, when there is heavy surf the steep shore causes a strong backwash. *Alakukui Beach*, the small strip of sand to the north is somewhat protected by Alakukui Point. The remains of a heiau can also be seen on this point.

The *Coconut Plantation Marketplace* in Wailua was conceived and constructed primarily for tourists. Inside are over seventy shops including restaurants, fast-food outlets, and a twin cinema. A free Polynesian show is presented here Thursdays, Fridays and Saturdays at 4:00 p.m.

WAILUA TO KEALIA – MAP #3

It is hard for visitors to tell where Waipouli leaves off and Kapaa begins. One "Kapaa" sign at the entrance to Waipouli doesn't help things, nor do the Waipouli Plaza and Waipouli Complex farther on that are actually in Kapaa. The town of *Waipouli* (dark water) is small, consisting of the group of buildings just south of the first small stream you cross after leaving Wailua. The Waipouli Town Center *is* in Waipouli. Some day Waipouli probably will be swallowed up by Kapaa, so the distinction will no longer matter.

Kapaa (the solid, or closed up) is a much larger town by comparison. It originally started near Kapaa Stream, then filled in the space between Waikaea Canal on the south and Moikeha Canal on the north. Now it laps over both canals approximately a mile north to Kawaihau Road and half a mile south to Hoi Road. A beautiful waterfall, *Hoopii Falls*, is a short hike from the end of the narrow road that angles back to the right 2.5 miles from the start of Kawaihau Road.

Kapaa Beach Park has a long beach with a fifteen-acre park, a pavilion, pool, picnic tables, restrooms and showers. The same precautions mentioned before apply to this beach at high tide, although at low tide the reef offers protection so that kids can usually play in the shallow water. The best place to swim when it is calm is north of the Waikaea Canal in front of the Pono Kai condominiums.

Kapaa is a curious combination of a sleepy 19th century plantation town and large modern hotels and condominium complexes. The entire Wailua-Waipouli-Kapaa area seems to be laid out for tourists, and, of course, most of it was. But a large number of local residents live inland so it is the major shopping place for them on this side of the island.

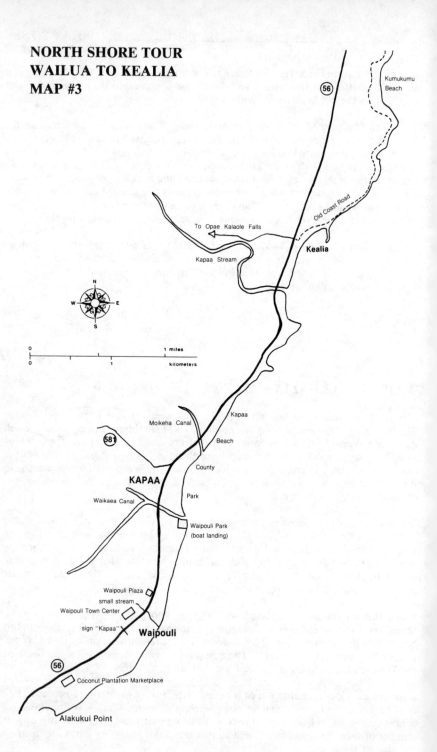

NORTH SHORE TOUR
WAILUA TO KEALIA
MAP #3

Kumukumu
Beach

56

Old Coast Road

To Opae Kalaole Falls

Kealia

Kapaa Stream

N
W   E
S

0   1 miles
0   1
kilometers

Kapaa

Moikeha Canal

581   Beach

County

KAPAA

Waikaea Canal   Park

Waipouli Park
(boat landing)

Waipouli Plaza
small stream
Waipouli Town Center

sign "Kapaa"   **Waipouli**

56

Coconut Plantation Marketplace

Alakukui Point

Nounou (throwing) *Mountain*, also called "*Sleeping Giant*", is seen best from Kapaa. The name Nounou comes from a Hawaiian legend. A giant named Puni lay down to rest there and some rocks thrown to awaken him landed in his mouth, choking him to death. He lies there today, and will forever. Two trails lead up to his chin. The east trailhead is found by turning inland on Halelio Road just east of the Coco Palms Resort. A sign indicating the trailhead is at 1.2 miles. The west trail starts from a higher elevation so is not as steep and is shorter. This trailhead is found by going inland on Route 580 to Route 581 (Kamalu Road), and at 1.2 miles along 581 the trailhead is also marked. Each trail takes at least an hour, so will not be described here.

Just before Kealia is a turnout on the right from which there is a dramatic view of the coastline.

Near the 10 mile marker along Highway 56 is *Kealia* (salt encrustation) *Beach*. This long beach is not a park so there are no facilities. The beach is always beautiful, but can be dangerous due to a surface current along the coast, rough surf, a shore break and backwash. A point provides some protection farther north up the beach. The little plantation town of *Kealia* is long gone, leaving only one or two buildings.

The first road inland after crossing Kapaa Stream goes past Spalding Monument to the *Waipahee Slippery Slide*, a portion of a natural lava tube down which Hawaiians used to slide to the pool below. Unfortunately, the slippery slide is now private property, closed and fenced. Entry to it is forbidden because of liability problems. However, the beautiful *Opae Kalaole Falls* can be reached by a short hike along a ditch between the two Kenaha Reservoirs, which are about seven miles up this road.

The old coast road parallels Kealia Beach, and although in poor repair requiring some tricky cross-country four-wheel drive trekking followed by a hike, it will take you to bays on either side of *Anapalau Point*, and to *Lae Lipoa Bay*, south of Lae Lipoa Point, for fabulous snorkeling.

KEALIA TO PAPAA BAY – MAP #4

Kumukumu (tree stumps) *Beach* used to be called "*Donkey Beach*" by hippies in the 60's because of the mules (not donkeys) that grazed there then. It is difficult to reach now because the access cane roads have been barred by gates that are closed most of the time. However, if you park near (but not in front of) any gate past the 11 mile marker, it is only a quarter-mile walk along a cane road to the beach. Swimming is usually dangerous for the same reasons given for Kealia Beach. Nudity, although illegal, still seems more or less tolerated here.

Between Kumukumu Beach and *Anahola Bay* are several small beaches and rocky coves with interesting coral reefs, accessible only with a four-wheel drive. Take Anahola Road at 13.4 miles, follow the double-yellow lines to the right at the first "y", and then bear left at the second "y" – a dirt road. Go past the beach, up the dirt road at the end of the parking area, and then south on the bluffs past the automated beacon and radio tower on Kahala Point. The road connects here with Kukuihale Road, which is an alternate way to get to this spot, but goes through

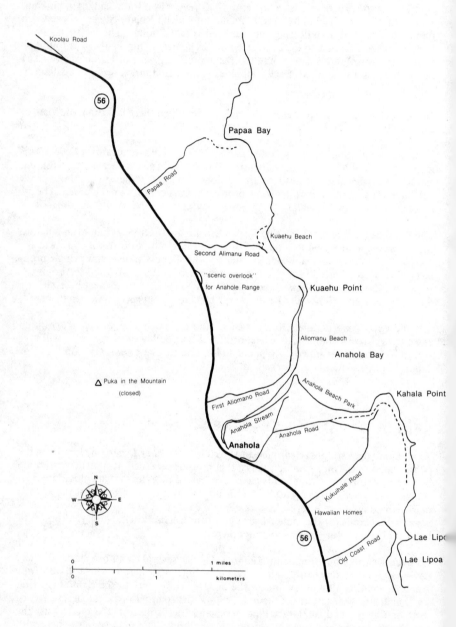

Koolau Road

56

Papaa Bay

Papaa Road

Kuaehu Beach

Second Alimanu Road

"scenic overlook"
for Anahole Range

Kuaehu Point

Aliomanu Beach

Anahola Bay

△ Puka in the Mountain
(closed)

Anahola Beach Park

Kahala Point

First Aliomano Road

Anahola Stream

Anahola Road

Anahola

N
W   E
S

Kukuihale Road

Hawaiian Homes

56

Lae Lipo

Old Coast Road

Lae Lipoa

0   1 miles
0   1
kilometers

Hawaiian Homes Land from Highway 56 and the Hawaiians there like their privacy. The first beach south of Kahala Point is *Lae o Kailio Beach*, just south of the point by that name. The cane road then continues along the bluffs to *Opana Beach* north of Opana Point. The coast is mostly rocky south of Opana Point, but at Lae Lipoa Point and about a mile farther south on both sides of Anapalau Point, the coral is profuse and the snorkeling is fabulous on a calm day, as we mentioned before.

Return along the bluffs to the parking lot at *Anahola* (no known meaning) *Beach Park*. Here there are picnic tables, restrooms and showers. However, it may be best to avoid this park for the time being. Militant Hawaiians have been brought over from Waimanalo on Oahu to camp here in an effort to claim the beach. This is why camping for the rest of us is not now permitted by the County. The beach stretches more than a mile around the bay to the northwest, past the mouth of Anahola Stream and Aliomanu Beach. The sand dunes inland around the bay were an ancient burial site. All of the south shore of Anahola Bay is fully exposed to the northeast trade winds, so it is rough at high tide. The reef protects the beach at low tide, but then it is too shallow for swimming.

Back on Highway 56, a hole through the *Kalalea* (prominent) *Mountain Ridge* once could be seen from the Anahola area at a viewpoint one mile past the first Aliomanu Road. A landslide in 1982 closed the hole completely. It was featured in "South Pacific" as the coastwatcher's hideout.

The first Aliomanu Road off Highway 56 at the 14 mile marker leads to the right just after you cross Anahola Stream. About .7 miles down a beautiful drive is *Aliomanu* (canoe groove) *Beach*, where you can park under the ironwoods. The beach itself is not safe most of the time for the same reasons as at Kealia, but the lagoon can be if the rivermouth is blocked off by sand, as it sometimes is in summer. During the winter the stream runs high and you may be carried out to sea. Past Kuaehu Point, Aliomanu Road ends because of tsunami damage, but a quarter-mile hike will take you to the other, more secluded part of Aliomanu Beach.

Because this tsunami damage to about a half-mile of the seaward portion of the Aliomanu Road loop has not been repaired, what we call the second Aliomanu Road starts just past the 15 mile marker. Take this, and at .6 mile go left on Kukuna Road. Just .2 mile farther on is room for two cars to park. *Kukuna Beach* is a short walk down the bluff, and stretches over half a mile north and south from the parking spot. The same precautions apply except where there is protection from the reef.

The small but delightful beach at *Papaa* (secure enclosure) *Bay* can be reached with a four-wheel drive from Papaa Road. Go half a mile to two gates, pass by them and continue another quarter-mile on a terribly bumpy cane road to a place where there is room for only one car to park. Don't try this road it if is muddy. The shore is rocky there, but a beautiful sand beach is a short walk to your left, and the bay is more sheltered than Anahola Bay. A heiau, housesites, an oven, and taro terraces can be found on the east bank of the Papaa Stream just inland of the highway.

123

NORTH SHORE TOUR
PAPAA BAY KILAUEA BAY
MAP #5

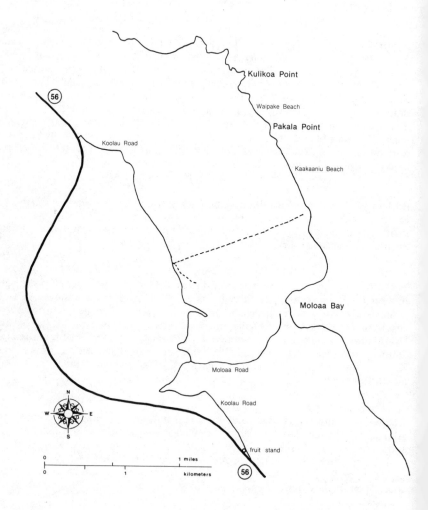

Kulikoa Point

Waipake Beach

Pakala Point

Koolau Road

Kaakaaniu Beach

Moloaa Bay

Moloaa Road

Koolau Road

fruit stand

N
W   E
S

0   1 miles
0   1   kilometers

PAPAA BAY TO KILAUEA BAY - MAP #5

The turnoff from Highway 56 to **Moloaa** (matted roots) **Bay** is Koolau Road, which leads off at an angle by the Sunrise Fruit Stand about 16.6 miles from Lihue. This is actually the old coast road. Go 1.2 miles and turn right on Moloaa Road, which leads directly to the beach. Park off the road and look for the beach access sign. This is a spectacular beach and bay. When the surf is rough, the currents in the bay are tricky and add to the hazard of the shore break. But you can always go exploring or shell hunting. The name Moloaa comes from the paper mulberry trees that still grow here and were once used to make kapa. Trails lead north and south from Moloaa Bay along the coast. A rugged hike (in spots) of about five miles north along the shore takes you to Kilauea Bay.

Kaakaaniu (rolling coconut) **Beach**, formerly called "**Larsen's**" because David Larsen, a manager of Kilauea Plantation in the 1920's, had a cottage here, is a mile-long beach with a coral-fringed lagoon that is hard to get to but well worth the effort. Instead of turning right from Koolau Road onto Moloaa Road, continue 1.1 miles farther on to a sharply angled dirt road on the right marked by a beach access sign. Take this, then an immediate left at a second beach access sign. Follow this road .8 miles to the end. There you will see a "cattle guard" opening in the fence with a path beyond, and it is only a six or seven minute walk to the beach from there. Observe the conditions carefully from the top of the bluff. Tide changes, and even a moderate surf, cause a strong current to flow out the reef openings. Snorkeling and swimming are hazardous because of this, and people are carried out to sea here almost every year. If you do go in the water, stay well away from the openings and watch your location at all times.

Kaakaaniu Beach ends at Pakala Point, but it is possible to walk around this rocky point to **Waipake Beach** between Pakala Point and Kulikoa Point. The name Waipake means "weak water", because the Waipake Stream dribbles out and disappears before reaching the shore. This is one of the most secluded beaches on Kauai, but the same precautions apply as at Kaakaaniu Beach.

WAIAKALUA BEACH TO KAUAPEA BEACH - MAP #6

Two isolated beaches along here are a real challenge to reach. Take the paved Waiakalua Road, and a half-mile from the start take the cane road to the right. Follow this to its end at the coast near Keilua Point. A short walk to the right leads to **Waiakalua** (water hole) **Beach**. A quarter-mile inland from Kakiu Point just to the east is the **Kapinao Heiau**, which overlooks a waterfall and is well-preserved. The second beach, called **Waiakalua Iki**, is near Pohaku Malumalu at the mouth of a small stream. It can only be reached by a hike along the coast because the cane road previously allowing access is now blocked by a gate. Safety precautions apply at both beaches because of hazards.

The beach at **Kilauea Bay** is reached by taking the turnoff to Kilauea at 23.3 miles (Kolo Road), and then left on Lighthouse Road. Pass through the town of Kilauea, ignore the first road to the right, and take the next old cane road to the right at an angle. The trip down this road, about a mile, is bumpy, rough, and may be overgrown. Don't try it if it has rained recently. At the bottom of the road is the

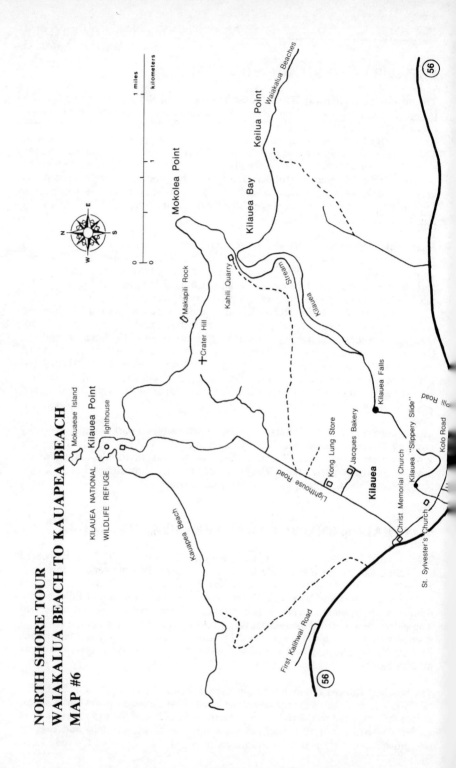

NORTH SHORE TOUR
WAIAKALUA BEACH TO KAUAPEA BEACH
MAP #6

defunct Kahili Gravel Quarry, where the gravel for the main street of Kilauea came from. Take off your shoes (or whatever, if the water is high) and wade across Kilauea Stream to the beach. It will probably be all yours. The surf is usually rough and dangerous, but children can play in the lagoon if the rivermouth is closed. If it isn't and the river current is not strong, they may be able to safely swim well back from the mouth.

The paved right angle turnoff from Kilauea Road just beyond the one that took you to Kilauea Bay leads to *Crater Hill*. Go to the dead end, turn left, and then go on up the hill. Take any cane road that leads to the tower on the crest. Crater Hill is the 138-acre site that residents of Kauai are trying to have added to the sea bird sanctuary at Kilauea Point. Most of the crater ridge has slipped into the sea, but from the portion remaining where you are standing, there is a spectacular view of the coastline and sea birds soaring. Take care not to disturb the birds nesting here.

Return to Lighthouse Road and continue north to the *Kilauea Point National Wildlife Refuge*. This is a half-hour self-guided stroll for a recently imposed $2 admission charge. Binoculars and informative literature can be obtained at the small shop staffed by volunteers. The lighthouse itself, with its Fresnel lens, was constructed in 1913, and its beam once reached ninety miles to sea. The lens is the largest of its type ever made. The lighthouse has not been in service since 1976 when a smaller high-intensity beacon was installed in front of it. The area is open from 10:00 a.m. to 4:00 p.m. Monday through Friday, closed Saturday and Sunday. If the gate is closed, it is still worth stopping near it for the view. At Kilauea Point, you are at the northernmost point of the Hawaiian Islands.

The town of *Kilauea* has an interesting history. The sugar plantation dating from the 1870's closed in 1970, but the workers refused to let their community become a ghost town as other plantation camps have. They purchased lots, built homes and created an attractive town. One industry they succeeded in bringing here is a 300-acre prawn farm about a mile north, mauka of Highway 56.

St. Sylvester's Catholic Church on Kolo Road east of Lighthouse Road has a unique octagonal shape and was made of lava rock cleared from the nearby fields. The murals of the stations of the cross are by Jean Charlot. The quaint *Christ Memorial Church*, near the intersection of Lighthouse Road and Kolo Road, was built in the 1940's of the same lava fieldstone and has a beautiful altar carved by Mrs. William Hyde Rice and stained glass windows imported from England.

The *Kong Lung Store* on the corner of Keneke Street and Lighthouse Road was first operated by the Lung family in 1896 as a plantation store. Kwai Chew Lung bought it from Kilauea Plantation in 1955 and sold it to the present owners in 1979. He lived behind the store until his death in July, 1987. Browse around inside – we think it is the best gift store on Kauai. The two glass lanterns once graced the old Halekulani Hotel in Waikiki; the sconces with the mirror between them are from the original Princeville Plantation manager's home.

While in Kilauea, visit *Jacques Bakery* one block off Lighthouse Road on Oka Street. The quonset hut was once the powerhouse for the sugar plantation. Jacques Atlan is a friendly type, and swears he can tell which travel guide you have read by what you order. Let's confuse him. One of us likes his croissants and the other his onion bread.

NORTH SHORE TOUR
KAUAPEA BEACH TO ANINI BEACH
MAP #7

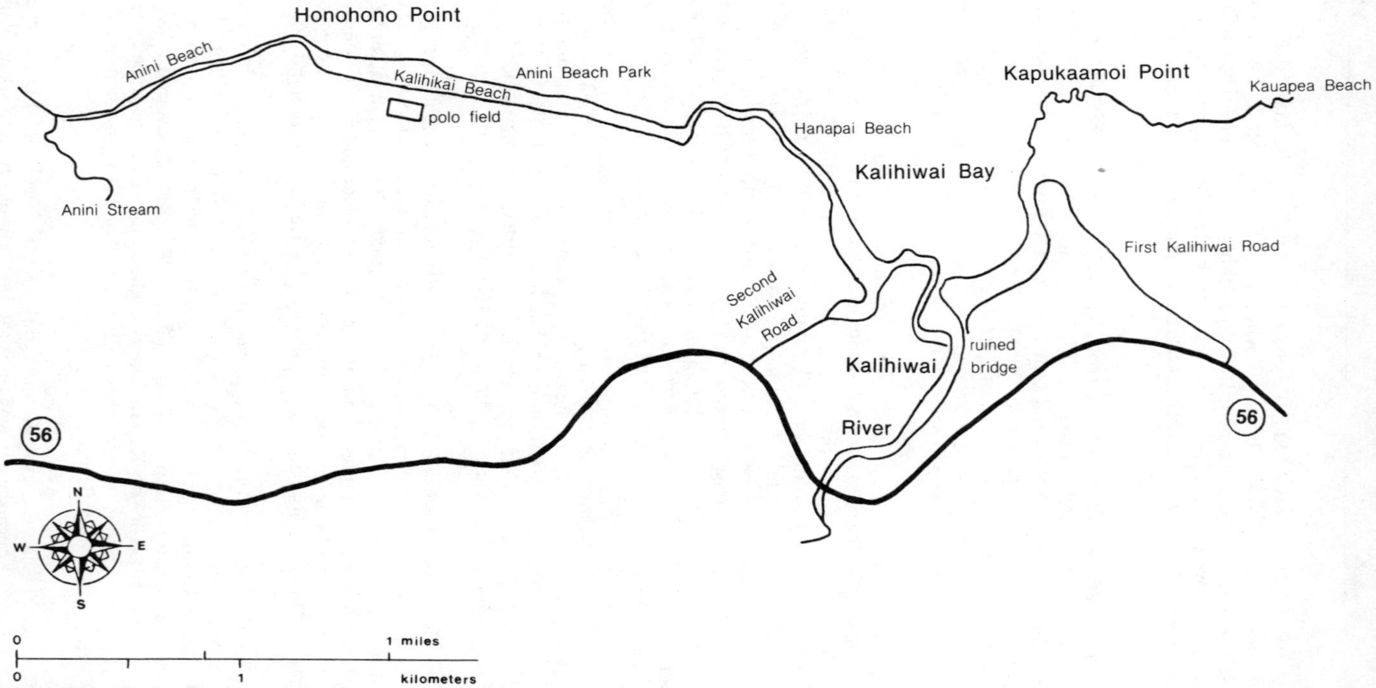

Kauapea Beach

Kapukaamoi Point

First Kalihiwai Road

56

Kalihiwai Bay

ruined bridge

Hanapai Beach

Kalihiwai River

Second Kalihiwai Road

Honohono Point

Anini Beach Park

Kalihikai Beach

polo field

Anini Beach

Anini Stream

N E S W

56

0   1   1 miles

0   kilometers

The Kilauea Slippery Slide may be viewed from a distance, but not used. This is a cement tube that was constructed for the movie "South Pacific" using the natural lava tube of Waipahee as a model. Continue southeast on Kolo Road and park just before the bridge. Walk down the west bank of Kilauea Stream to see the falls and slide. The owner had to close the area because of liability problems. If you are adventurous, a half-mile hike farther down Kilauea Stream takes you to the larger *Kilauea Falls*.

Return to Highway 56, and .3 mile north of Kolo Road is the turnoff to *Kauapea* (the fair rain) *Beach*, also called "*Secret Beach*" by those who can't pronounce the correct name. Turn right and wiggle towards the water. The road seems to end nowhere, near a goat enclosure, but a "beach trail" sign is there to guide you. It is less than a ten minute walk down to the beach. The trail will be slippery if it is muddy. This beach is beautiful, secluded, and something to see at times in the winter. We have watched twenty to thirty foot waves crashing ashore that made the ground tremble. Even during the summer there are strong along-shore currents to the west, and sharks are often sighted here. For all these reasons, swimming is never advisable. A short walk left over a lava point takes you to another part of Kauapea Beach. It is possible to hike from here all the way to Kalihiwai Bay. It isn't just the ocean that you have to watch out for at Kauapea Beach. Its *third* name is *Nude Beach* and you may run into nude campers and sunbathers, so if nudity disturbs you, don't go. Fortunately, the last time we were there, one was at least wearing a guitar. The time before, two were only wearing beards, and they weren't nearly long enough!

KAUAPEA BEACH TO ANINI BEACH – MAP #7

Kalihiwai (the edge with a stream) *Bay* is one of those places you dream about. From Highway 56, take the first or easternmost Kalihiwai Road to your right and drive slowly. About one-quarter mile along, look back over your right shoulder to a green glade with a waterfall. When you round the bend, pause to see the beautiful arc of the beach with the rugged coastline beyond it.

At the far end of the beach, park under the ironwoods – but not in the sand or you may be there longer than you had intended. Walk out on the sandbar and dabble your feet in the lagoon. This is not a park, so there are no facilities. The tsunami of April 1, 1946 destroyed all the homes here, as did the March 3, 1957 tsunami caused by the Alaska earthquake. The latter took out the bridge, which has not been repaired, which is why there are now two Kalihiwai Roads. During the summer Kalihiwai is a delightful place, but during the winter it is usually dangerous because of the high surf and cross-currents in the bay. Swimmers are sometimes carried out to sea off the rivermouth by a combination of river currents and ocean surface currents moving to the left.

Once more on Highway 56, watch for the paved turnout at the 24 mile marker. Park there, walk out on the bridge along the narrow walkway on the mauka side, but be careful of the traffic. Look up the valley to see the *Kalihiwai Falls*. You can reach the falls by renting a kayak and starting from the mouth of the Kalihiwai River, or along the dirt road by hiking or with a four-wheel drive. For now, from your vantage point on the bridge, smell the fragrance of the flowers, dream a little, and in a quiet moment listen to the falls. A small waterfall is just beside the highway on the mauka side a short distance up the hill from the parking lot.

Back again in your car, the second Kalihiwai Road leads to Kalihikai Beach. Don't take a right at the "y" or you will go down to Kalihiwai Bay on the other side of the ruined bridge you have just seen. Bear to the left instead and pause at the point by the ocean. The stretch of sand there and to your right is *Hanapai* (raised bay) *Beach*. An offshore reef offers some protection, but most of the hazards mentioned for Kalihiwai Beach are present here also. Continue on down the road. The mile-long beach along the straight section of road is *Kalihikai* (the seaward edge) *Beach*, and around Honono Point is the shorter *Anini* (dwarfed or stunted) *Beach*. Locals still torch-fish here at night, and it is something to see. At Kalihikai is the two-acre *Anini Beach Park* with pavilion, restrooms, showers, tables and barbecue facilities. Camping requires a County permit.

Because of the offshore reef, Kalihikai Beach is perhaps the least hazardous beach on the north shore. The sailboarding is fabulous at the park. Board sailing, or sailboarding, is, by the way, just poking around on one of these boards in calm water, which any of us can do after a couple of lessons and about a hundred falls into the water. Windsurfing requires skills several levels above this. With a modified board and sail, windsurfers jump the waves going out, sometimes doing a complete turn in the air, and then ride them back in faster than the wind. At the park, there are usually two or three trucks with sailboard equipment to rent and someone to give you lessons. The polo field past the park is in use all summer, with matches on Sunday afternoons.

You may see at least one sign, "Wanini Beach", while you are here. This is the old spelling. The "w" has been dropped and in its place is a glottal stop to give the more proper: "'Anini."

ANINI BEACH TO LUMAHAI BEACH – MAP #8

Once more on Highway 56, the next point of interest is *Princeville*. This is the site of a coffee plantation started in 1853 by R.C. Wyllie. When King Kamehameha IV and Queen Emma visited him in 1860, they brought their two-year-old son Prince Albert, Ka Haku o Hawaii, with them. Wyllie was so taken with the young prince that he renamed his plantation after him – Princeville. The coffee enterprise failed, as did several others at Princeville.

Development of Princeville as a resort started in 1969, and it is now the largest planned development on Kauai – over 11,000 acres in size. Except for the weather and spectacular mountain vistas, you might think you are at any affluent resort on the mainland, not Kauai. It has excellent golf courses and most of the condos are comfortable – many even luxurious. A beautiful view of Hanalei (crescent bay) and on down the coast can be seen from the Hanalei Bay Resort. Notice that the word "bay" in the name of this resort is redundant. The Po'oku Stables are back across Highway 56, with horseback riding daily and rodeos on some Sundays. The Hanalei Athletic Club is also here, along with several restaurants and the opulent Sheraton

Princeville Hotel that appears to cascade down the bluff. Two small beaches can be reached by trail. The best, **Kaweonui Beach**, is a small strip of sand at the end of the path that starts from the road near The Cliffs condominiums, and the other, **Kenomene Beach**, mostly rocky, is reached from a path starting at the parking lot of the Pali Ke Kua. The surf is usually too rough and the currents too strong for swimming at either one, however.

Returning to Highway 56, the mile markers start again at Princeville. The 28 mile marker in the series we have been following stands right beside one marked "0" as Highway 56 turns into Route 560. The next stop is the **Hanalei Valley Lookout**. This view is perhaps the most famous of all on Kauai. Most of the taro grown for the Hawaiian Islands comes from this valley. The one-way bridge you see before you was originally built in 1912, then substantially reinforced after sustaining severe damage in the 1957 tsunami, retaining its quaint style. Linger a while at the lookout and let your thoughts wander back in time. This beautiful valley has changed very little over hundreds of years.

Many yachts anchor in the bay in the summertime, but not during the winter because of the surf that is sometimes thirty feet high. The small beach in front of the Sheraton Princeville is **Puu Poa** (thumping point) **Beach**, and public access is provided. At open spots in the coral, you can dip your body and listen to the surf "thump" on the outer reef, but there really isn't any swimming. Kayaks can be rented at the Sheraton's Beach Activities Center to explore the river.

From here on, you will be passing through the most beautiful part of Kauai. In fact, it reminds many of Tahiti. Going down the hill, pause for a moment at the slightly widened spot in the road for a spectacular view of the bay and the coast beyond. Note the waterfalls cascading down the far bluffs. At the bottom of the hill to your right are buffalo roaming the range behind the eight-foot fence in the distance. The fence is that high because buffalo can jump seven feet! Bill Mowry's Hanalei Garden Farm comprises the 155 acres between the bluff and river to the shore. He hopes to market his buffalo steaks, which are tastier and lower in fat than beef. The few weeping willows on the banks of the Hanalei River were brought as cuttings around the Horn in a crusty sea captain's shaving mug – taken from St. Helena when Napoleon was exiled there.

The lower 917 acres of Hanalei Valley mauka of Route 560 is the **Hanalei National Wildlife Refuge**, under the jurisdiction of the U.S. Fish and Wildlife Service. Hanalei Valley Road, which leads inland through the valley along the old "China Ditch", is a County road within the Refuge. Thus, you are allowed to drive on the road but not to get out of your car and walk around. About a half-mile inland on the right, the **Haraguchi Rice Mill** has recently been restored as a museum. This is the one place along the road where you can stop and get out of your car. There is another at the very end of the road. From there, a trail leads through a bamboo forest and two stream crossings to a picnic spot. This trail is just beyond the Refuge, so be careful to stay on the path.

The one-way bridges in "Hano Hano" Hanalei set the pace of life here. Etiquette requires that all cars on one side wait until the bridge clears completely from the other side before crossing. Hanalei still shows evidences of the counter-culture influence of the sixties, but is slowly recovering.

131

NORTH SHORE TOUR
ANINI BEACH TO LUMAHAI BEACH
MAP #8

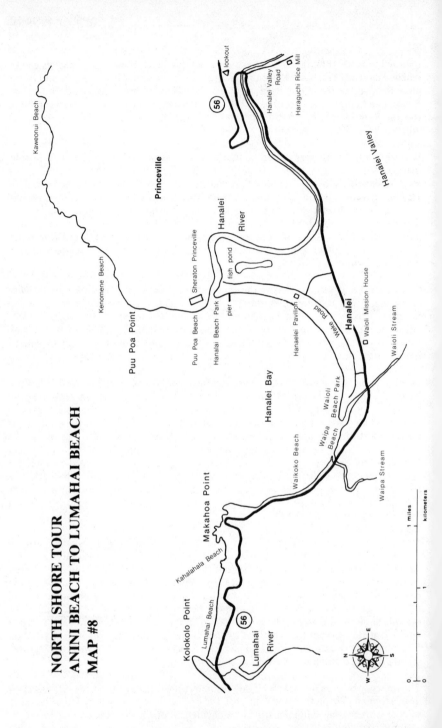

Kaweonui Beach

Kenomene Beach

Princeville

Puu Poa Point

Sheraton Princeville

Puu Poa Beach

Hanalai Beach Park

fish pond

pier

Hanalei
River

Hanalei Beach Park

Hanaelei Pavilion

Waioli Mission House

Hanalei

Wake Road

Waioli Stream

Hanalei Valley Road

Haraguchi Rice Mill

lookout

Hanalei Valley

Hanalei Bay

Waikoko Beach

Waioli
Beach Park

Waipa
Beach

Waipa Stream

Makahoa Point

Kahalahala Beach

Kolokolo Point

Lumahai Beach

Lumahai
River

N
E
W
S

0   1 miles

0   1   kilometers

On the left near the 2 mile marker (in the new system) is the small **Hanalei Museum**, which is housed in a building dating from 1860. It has interesting Hawaiian artifacts and old photographs. In Hanalei, turn right on Aku Road (all the roads parallel to this in Hanalei are named for fish) and then another right on Weke Road to go past the Hanalei Pavilion to **Hanalei Beach Park** and **Hanalei Pier**. This was the site where much of "South Pacific" was filmed, and you can see why. The only safe swimming in Hanalei Bay is by the pier. A contract lifeguard is often here, and it is a nice spot for a picnic under the ironwoods. Tables are provided and restrooms are nearby. The pier was constructed in 1912 and still has narrow-gauge tracks on it that were once used for loading bags of rice grown in the valley. The mouth of the Hanalei River is the departure point for most of the Na Pali Zodiac tours.

The part of Hanalei Beach Park at the mouth of the Hanalei River is also called **"Black Pot Beach."** For over fifty years, starting early in this century, it was a gathering place for locals. Hukilaus took place here then, a grass shack was put up, and each member of the "club" hung his bottle from the eaves. Just outside the door was a three-foot wide wok in which whatever fishermen and others brought was cooked under the careful eye of "Uncle Henry" Tai Hook. Every night locals would eat, drink, and talk story. It was this fire-blackened wok that gave the beach its nickname, although it rusted out and has been gone now for almost thirty years.

Return on Weke Road and pause a moment near the **Hanalei Pavilion** to see the 1896 Albert Wilcox home set back on the spacious lawn, and contemplate the pace and style of life here then. Behind the home is an old Hawaiian fish pond. The surf-break offshore between here and the pavilion is called **"Pinetrees"** by surfers because of the ironwood trees there. As everyone knows, ironwoods are *not* pinetrees. Near the end of Weke Road at Waioli (water of happiness) Stream is **Waioli Beach Park**. All three parks have restrooms and showers, and camping requires a County permit.

Return to Route 560 from the end of Weke Road. We have bypassed most of the town of Hanalei by taking Weke Road, so must turn back on Route 560 to see two or three places of interest there.

The **Native Hawaiian Trading and Cultural Center** in the century-old Ching Young Store in Hanalei has a small museum. If there are craft demonstrations or entertainment, it may be worth dropping in.

The **Waioli Mission House** is a "must" stop. It was built of coral limestone blocks in 1837, and the Reverend William Alexander "laid up" the chimney himself. The house was restored in 1921 by the three granddaughters of the first Wilcox family missionaries assigned here, Abner and Lucy, and is fascinating to visit. Something of the mindset of the early missionaries is indicated by the large bedwarmer they brought with them to the tropics. The Mission House is open for tours on Tuesdays, Thursdays, and Saturdays from 9 a.m. to 3 p.m. Volunteers conduct the tours, which are free but donations are accepted.

The **Waioli Mission Hall** and the unrestored bell tower behind it both date from 1841. The hall was the original church, and when it was first built had a thatched roof (as you can see from its lines) and a pebble floor. The green and white **Waioli Huiia Church** was founded in 1834, although the present structure only dates from

1912. Services are conducted in a combination of Hawaiian and English at 10:00 a.m. on Sundays, and the choir is famous for its hymns sung in Hawaiian. If you have gone to a luau at the Tahiti Nui, you will see two or three of the entertainers in the choir. Attend if you can, and buy a tape of the choir in the Mission Hall afterward if you wish. It was recorded under the supervision of Graham Nash of Crosby, Stills and Nash, who has a home on Kauai.

Between Hanalei and the road's end there are no gas stations, so be sure to check your gas gauge before going on from here.

Between Waioli Stream and Waipa Stream is **Waipa** (touched water) **Beach**. From there to the end of Hanalei Bay is **Waikoko** (blood water) **Beach**. A reef shelters the latter, so it would be a second site in Hanalei for safe swimming except that it is too · shallow. It is fun for kids to splash in, however.

The first beach past Makahoa Point is **Kahalahala** (the great sin) **Beach**, which goes from the point to the tongue of black rock projecting into the ocean. Just beyond that protrusion is half-mile long **Lumahai Beach**. The name Lumahai means "to tumble and break in the surf" and is appropriate. This may not be the *most* beautiful beach on Kauai, but with Kahalahala is certainly one of them. The latter (*not* Lumahai) was made famous as "Nurses' Beach" in the movie "South Pacific." If you happen to see "South Pacific" again, note how the camera pans back and forth as Mitzi Gaynor washes that man out of her hair. At each angle, the black rock, white sand and blue sea make a dramatic backdrop. This is probably why the shorter Kahalahala was chosen rather than Lumahai.

There are almost always several cars parked near here. The best place to park is at a sharp curve by one of the low stone walls. Be sure to park off the road with your car headed in the direction of the traffic or you may get a ticket. As you get out, look up on the bluffs for the rare white lehua blossom which is found nowhere else in Hawaii. The steep trails down are through pandanus trees, and because of the frequent rains, the trails are usually muddy so hang on and watch your step. Don't swim at either beach or walk out on the rocks unless it is one of those rare summer days when it is absolutely calm and flat. The surf is usually high, rogue waves are frequent, and the shorebreak causes a strong backwash. A westward current is almost always present and sometimes reaches a speed of three or four knots. This combination takes swimmers from the shallows, then along shore and out to sea off Kolokolo Point. More tourists have drowned at Lumahai and Kahalahala than on any other beaches on Kauai. Yesterday, as we write this, one was swept out and his body has not yet been found.

You can stroll along the beach to the western end of Lumahai Beach where the **Lumahai River** enters the ocean. Look for the "sunrise" shells which abound here, or park under the ironwood trees near the 6 mile marker and emergency telephone. Here you can at least dabble your feet in the river. During the summer a sand bar sometimes closes the mouth of the river and children can swim in the lagoon. Don't ever try this if the rivermouth is open, however. Unofficial camping is tolerated under the trees, but there are no facilities.

At the 5 mile marker, a Hawaii Visitor's Bureau sign on the top of **Lumahai Hill** marks a spot where there is room for just one or two cars to pull off the road. This is the best place to take a picture of Lumahai and Kahalahala Beaches.

LUMAHAI BEACH TO KEE BEACH – MAP #9

Just before crossing the *Wainiha* (unfriendly water) *River* is a town about 100 yards long, *Wainiha*, and the Wainiha General Store. Stop for a moment to "talk story" with the Olanolans who own the store or the locals on the bench outside.

The river and lagoon behind *Wainiha Beach* are what gave this place its name – both are "unfriendly." Don't swim in either one at any time. The ocean is dangerous, also, for reasons similar to those at Lumahai.

Past the store are two bridges with white railings in a beautiful pastoral setting. These are the "temporary" bridges built to replace the ones destroyed by the tsunami of 1957. The first road beyond them is *Powerhouse Road*. This goes inland two miles through a lush and beautiful valley, past waterfalls, heiaus, perfectly preserved taro terraces, ancient housesites and the gorgeous estate of Jerry Lynn, to a dead end at the powerhouse where the Powerhouse Trail starts. Another trail takes off from there to the west and goes along (but under) the Wainiha Pali. At about 2-1/2 miles, it crosses Maunahina Stream which comes from the Alakai Swamp. From there you can see the beautiful *Puuwainui* (big heart) *Falls* of the Wainiha River.

Once more on Route 560, continue to *Kepuhi Point*. The view of the coastline is dramatic from here. Look for the blowhole. The beach just to the right is *Wainiha Kuau* (end of unfriendly water) *Beach*. To the left of the point is *Kaonohi* (bright spear) *Beach*, then *Kanaha* (the shattered) *Beach*. All of these are beautiful but dangerous except on calm days when the reef offers sufficient protection. The latter two somewhat difficult to reach because the beachfront property is private. You can walk on one of the "beach access" paths or west around Kepuhi Point from Wainiha Kuau Beach.

At the 8 mile marker is *Camp Naue* belonging to the YMCA, the site of many local functions such as luaus and hula contests. If one is taking place, stop and join the fun. A large Hawaiian settlement was once on this site.

At 8.5 miles, (1/4 mile before the Dry Cave) is a "narrow bridge" sign and a dirt road to the right marked by a tree with a red stripe. This leads into the ironwoods to a parking area for *Makua* (parents) *Beach*. Surfers call this beach "*Tunnels*" because of the wave forms caused by the wide break in the reef. Snorkeling inside the reef is good at almost any time, but it is absolutely fabulous on calm days in the summer when it is possible to venture outside the reef.

Back on Route 560, just past Makua Beach on the left, are a cluster of homes on the mauka side of the highway. In them live the descendants of the last Hawaiians to live in Kalalau Valley. From here on, you are in Haena, and *Haena Beach* extends from Haena Point until it disappears west of Haena Beach Park. Cross Manoa Stream (it's a dip in the road – you sometimes splash through the stream itself), enter *Haena Beach Park*, and stop at *Maniniholo* (swimming Manini fish) *Dry Cave*. It was almost twice as large before the 1957 tsunami half-filled it with sand. This cave goes into the mountain about 300 yards, gradually narrowing, to emerge as a small hole on the side of the mountain. As you face the cave entrance on the outside, look up to your left and you will see carefully constructed stone terraces from an unknown period.

135

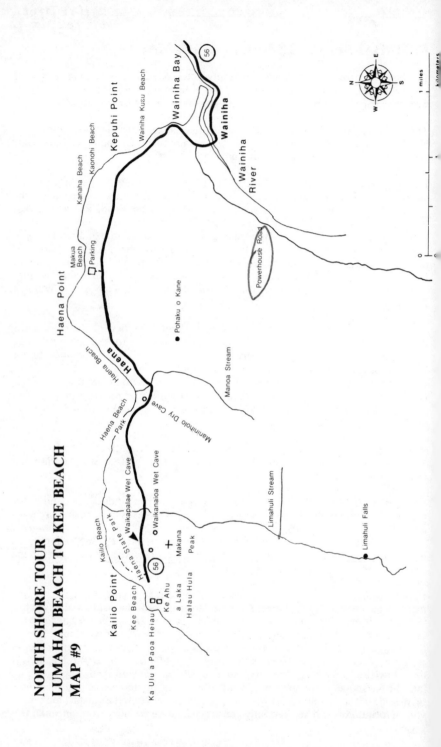

NORTH SHORE TOUR
LUMAHAI BEACH TO KEE BEACH
MAP #9

Haena Point

Kepuhi Point

Wainiha Bay

56

Wainiha

Wainiha River

Wainiha Kuau Beach

Kaonohi Beach

Kanaha Beach

Makua Beach

Parking

Pohaku o Kane

Powerhouse Road

Haena

Haena Beach

Manoa Stream

Maniniholo Dry Cave

Haena Beach Park

Limahuli Stream

Waikapalae Wet Cave

Waikanaioa Wet Cave

Kailio Beach

Kailio Point

Haena State Park

Kee Beach

Makana Peak

Limahuli Falls

Ka Ulu a Paoa Heiau

Ke Ahu a Laka Halau Hula

56

Haena Beach Park is a five-acre County park with all facilities. Camping, of course, requires a County permit. Swimming is sometimes safe in the summer at the west end behind the reef. Try to visualize this entire area destroyed by the tsunamis of 1946 and 1957. Not a building was left standing either time from Kepuhi Point to here. A group of twenty-one people gathered in a church about a mile down the road in 1957 and were swept away with it. At the top of the bluff just to the west is a large rock called **Pohaku o Kane**. The Hawaiians have a legend about Kane and this stone that is similar to our legend of Sisyphus.

Just before you ford the next stream, Limahuli Stream, a cement road goes up **Limahuli Valley** to the garden formerly owned by Juliet Rice Wichman, one of the last descendants of the Rice family. This garden is world-famous. The beautiful **Limahuli Falls** is at the apex of the valley, which can be reached with some difficulty on an overgrown trail. The 1,000 acre garden is now part of the Pacific Tropical Botanical Garden. If you join that Garden, you may also visit this one from 8 a.m. to 5 p.m. Park outside the chain, walk in, and show your card to the gardener. There is no charge. The swimming hole in Limahuli Stream on both sides of the highway is a favorite with locals. They call it "cold pond" for a good reason – it is.

Haena State Park, not to be confused with the County park we have just left, starts at the sign near the Wet Caves. The infamous "**Taylor Camp**" was just east of here, where Elizabeth Taylor's brother, Howard, started a hippie settlement in the 1960's. Trash piled up amid marijuana fumes, pollution killed the fish in the ocean, and trees and other natural features were desecrated. Finally, in the 1970's, the area was condemned, torched, and added to the State Park.

The **Waikapalee** (water of the lace fern) **Wet Cave** is reached by a short trail to the left of **Waikanaloa** (water of Kanaloa, a god) **Wet Cave**. The latter has been explored about 100 yards in by scuba divers. The peak above is **Makana** (gift or reward) **Peak**. This was climbed by selected youths on festive occasions in ancient times. They carried spears of dried hau and papala wood strapped to their backs, set them afire and hurled them seaward. When the wind was right, updrafts carried them far to sea, showering sparks all along the way. This ceremony was last recreated in 1923.

JANORA BAYOT

Kailio (the dog) **Beach** is the last discrete beach in the State park before **Kee Lagoon**. Kailio Beach is reached by dirt road and is somewhat protected by a reef. Inland from the sand dunes of Kailio Beach are remnants of irrigation systems built about 800 A.D. **Kee** (avoidance, as too far) **Beach** is at the end of the road on the west end of Haena State Park. On a calm day, snorkeling is marvelous in the lagoon and through the passage on the left outside the reef. This opening was named Puka Ulua by Hawaiians for the fish that can still be caught there. Be sure to observe the conditions before you enter the lagoon at Kee. If the surf is coming over the reef, this causes a strong current going out the opening. Swimmers are frequently carried out to sea and drown here.

The trailhead to Kalalau Valley is just off the Kee parking area. At a spot a half-mile up this trail, one has a spectacular view back of Kee Beach, and just beyond, of Na Pali Coast. Note that "na" means (plural) the, and "pali" means cliff or cliffs, so you don't say *the* Na Pali *Cliffs*. The hike to **Hanakapiai** is a fabulous experience, but once there you would want to hike up to the falls. All told, the hike would take four or five hours, so let's return another day.

The former Allerton house is nestled against the slope behind Kee Beach. Follow the path along the shore in front of it, turn inland at the west end of the wall, and hike uphill. You have arrived at one of the most sacred spots in all of the Hawaiian Islands. The first structure there is **Ka Ulu a Paoa Heiau**. The name means "the inspiration of Paoa." Paoa was a hula master and friend of Lohiau. Let's pause here to tell you a legend.

This is the story of **Pele**, the fire goddess, and her youngest sister **Hiiaka**. There are various versions of this legend in different chants, but this is the one we like best. Pele wanted to live where there was fire, so left home to search the world over for it. When she came to the hula halau here, she was drawn toward the sound of nose flutes and drums. A hula ceremony was taking place, and there she saw **Lohiau**, the young and handsome chief of Kauai. She decided to have him for a husband, enchanted him, and he agreed.

But Pele told Lohiau she could not be his wife until she found a suitable place for them to live. She dug twice for fire nearby, creating the wet caves, and then departed to search on the other islands. She finally found fire at Halemaumau on the island of Hawaii, and decided that would be her home. She released Hiiaka, whom she had carried as an egg under her arm, and sent her back for Lohiau. Hiiaka's journey was long due to many adversities, "dragons" and demons. By the time she arrived at Haena, Lohiau had hung himself in lonely despair. Hiiaka saw his spirit hovering over the peaks, captured it in a small blue flower that still grows there, and carried it up to his body which had been buried above the wet caves. She worked the spirit back into his body for seven days and nights, until on the eighth day Lohiau returned to life.

The two then set forth for the island of Hawaii and Pele. Their journey was long because of many difficulties encountered along the way. They fell in love during their arduous trip, but stoically kept this from each other. When they arrived at Halemaumau, Hiiaka was so overcome with relief at having returned safely that her love burst forth, she threw her arms around Lohiau, and kissed him. Pele saw this, was angered, and destroyed Lohiau on the spot with molten lava. Being divine, Hiiaka escaped death and returned to Haena where she mourned for Lohiau. Two brothers of Pele restored Lohiau's life once again and carried him back to Kauai. He wandered along the shore in search of Hiiaka, came to the hula halau here at Kee, and at a singing contest sang of his loneliness for his lost love. Hiiaka was nearby, heard him, and echoed his song. The two embraced, declared their love for each other, and lived happily ever after at Haena.

An incidental note. The famous song *"**Ke Kali Nei Au**"*, which you may have heard at the Fern Grotto and elsewhere, was written by Charles E. King in 1926 with this legend in mind. It is *not* a wedding song. Instead, the Hawaiian lyrics tell of two lonely lovers pining for each other. The woman hears the voice of her lover in song, responds, and in the beautiful duet the two pledge that their love will never end.

According to the legend, Hiiaka and Lohiau lived together at the foot of the bluff near the east end of Kee Beach. If you go a few yards up the start of the Kalalau Trail and take the faint trail to your left, you will come to a high rectangular stone wall. This supports a level site where it is said their house once stood. Whether this is true or not, the wall is old enough, according to archaeologists.

Back to our hike and Ka Ulu a Paoa Heiau. Approach this sacred spot with the reverence it deserves. The first fifty feet of the terrace up the slope is paved with flat stones, and the locations for wooden idols can be seen. This is the heiau proper. On the eastern end is a refuse pit where sacrificial offerings were thrown after their use. Above this is an incline with stone-lined terraces. You can just make out a narrow stone terrace above this with more sites for idols. The upper terrace is **Ke Ahu a Laka Halau Hula**, the location of a dancing pavilion and halau, or long hall, which was built over the entire seventy foot length and twenty-eight foot width of the terrace. The shrine to **Laka**, Goddess of the Hula, is the indentation in the cliff behind it.

For centuries, the best dancers from all the Hawaiian Islands were trained at this halau. It is now maintained out of reverence for the past by volunteer members of the finest hula halau on Kauai, the Kahiko Halapa'i Hula Alapa'i, under Kumu Hula Roselle Bailey. This group often performs here in devotion to Laka. The spot is sacred to all Hawaiians, and you may find floral offerings to Laka placed by them on her altar.

Return now to Kee Lagoon. If it is nearing sunset, wait to view it from here - it will be spectacular.

It is also the sunset of our north shore tour, but we still have the south shore tour and the magnificent Kokee area to see!

139

SOUTH SHORE TOUR

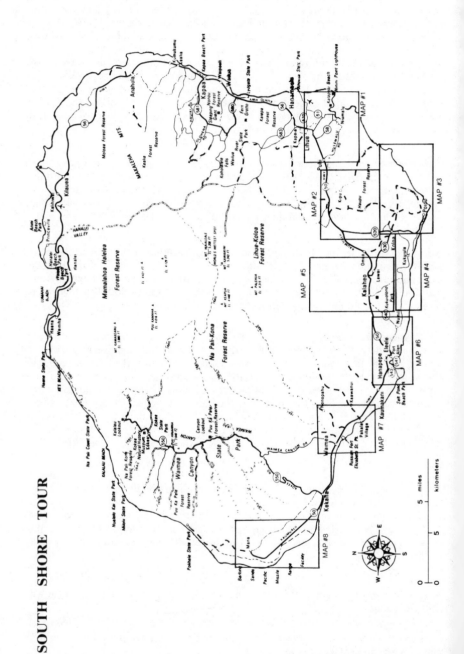

SOUTH SHORE TOUR

LIHUE TO PUHI – MAP #1

Before starting on the south shore tour, let's first look around **Lihue** for half an hour or so. You can get a feeling for Lihue from the County building in the center of town. Built in 1913, set back on a large lawn and surrounded by stately palms, it is from another era. Kauai (including Niihau) is a county of the State of Hawaii, and its mayoral government moves at a slower and simpler pace than its equivalent on the mainland. As you look around Lihue, you will be struck by the fact that there are no tall buildings in town, nor for that matter anywhere on Kauai, with the exception of the Westin Kauai Resort. When that hotel was originally constructed (as the Kauai Surf), its eleven-story tower sparked the controversy that eventually resulted in a law that no building on Kauai can be higher than the tallest coconut tree – four stories.

The two main streets of Lihue are the intersecting roads of Rice Street and Kuhio Highway (56). Drive down **Haleko Road** or "Old Mill Road." The aroma of molasses may fill the air if the Lihue Mill is operating. Four buildings, constructed with foot-thick concrete walls in 1910 for German plantation foremen, are along Haleko Road. Restaurants presently occupy these four buildings. A marble horse trough in front of them was brought around the Horn a few years before then, and was in use until automobiles replaced horses.

The **Kauai Regional Library**, a part of the State library system, at the corner of Hardy and Umi Street is a great source of information for visitors. With any valid identification card that has your picture, you can obtain a library card, check out books, and return them at any branch library near where you are staying. Browse through their Hawaiiana collection and ask questions of Donna Marie Garcia in the Reference Section. Library hours are: Monday and Tuesday, 8:00 a.m. to 8:00 p.m.; Wednesday, Thursday and Friday, 8:00 a.m. to 4:30 p.m.; Saturday, 8:00 a.m. to Noon; closed Sundays. Telephone 245-3617.

Another interesting place in Lihue for visitors is **The Kauai Museum**. The original Wilcox Building was constructed in 1924 as the first public library on Kauai and was converted to a museum in 1969. The Rice Building was added at that time. The Kauai Museum is a local history/art museum for the islands of Kauai and Niihau. It preserves, exhibits and interprets artifacts relevant to the various ethnic groups represented in the community, and houses a permanent exhibit telling the "Story of Kauai" through it's geology, flora, fauna, pre-contact Hawaiian lifestyle, and missionary and plantation influences. The book and gift shop has a wide selection of books on Kauai and Hawaii, as well as Hawaiian crafts for sale. If you do not see something you want, ask "Ba" Riznick, who keeps some of the less-demanded items in back and is most helpful in other ways. Walk through the courtyard into the Rice Building and watch the video about Kauai. The museum is at 4428 Rice Street. The hours are Monday through Friday, 9:00 a.m. to 4:30 p.m., and Saturday from 9:00 a.m. to 1:00 p.m. Telephone 245-6931.

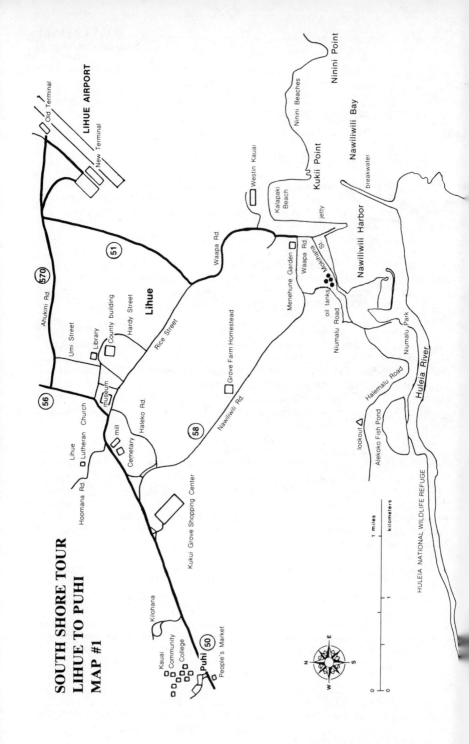

SOUTH SHORE TOUR
LIHUE TO PUHI
MAP #1

LIHUE AIRPORT

Old Terminal

New Terminal

Ninini Point

Ninini Beaches

Nawiliwili Bay

Kukii Point

Westin Kauai

breakwater

Kalapaki Beach

jetty

570

51

Ahukini Rd

Waapa Rd

Menehune Garden

Waapa Rd

Nawiliwili Harbor

Lihue

Umi Street

Library

County building

Hardy Street

Rice Street

Grove Farm Homestead

oil tanks

Mokihana St.

Niumalu Road

56

museum

Lutheran Church

Lihue

Haleko Rd.

Nawiliwili Rd

58

Niumalu Park

Hoomana Rd

Cemetary

mill

Halemalu Road

lookout

Alekoko Fish Pond

Huleia River

Kukui Grove Shopping Center

HULEIA NATIONAL WILDLIFE REFUGE

Kilohana

1 miles

kilometers

Kauai Community College

Puhi

50

People's Market

N E W S

0   1

0   1

142

Drive down Rice Street toward **Nawiliwili Harbor** (Rice Street becomes Waapa Road). The harbor was named for the wiliwili trees that were once abundant here. Their scarlet seeds were used by Hawaiians for necklaces. Note the fine **Kalapaki** (double-yolked egg) **Beach**, named because of the double contour of the bay. The surf is gentle and your children can swim safely or learn to ride body boards. You might want to try sailboarding there yourself. Snorkeling is not particularly rewarding, but it is a good place to practice. Walk through the grounds of the new Westin Kauai Resort and past the golf course along the bluff to the small and secluded **Ninini Beaches** – "first beach" and "second beach" – inside Ninini Point. These are small but secluded and protected by the point except during Kona winds. Swimming is safe and snorkeling is good. An offshore break is popular with board surfers.

Continue driving down Waapa Road. Look for the oil tank on the right that has a patch on it as the result of a Japanese submarine shelling in World War II. Turn left on Niumalu Road and stop at **Niumalu** (shade of coconut trees) **Park**. The park has three acres with tables, showers and restrooms. Camping is allowed with a County permit. Swimming is in the water of the Huleia River, which has a muddy bottom but children enjoy it. Kayaks may be rented here for a trip up the river, and sailboarding is also popular here. From the park you have a view of the small boat harbor and **Huleia Stream**. This name means "pushed through" because it was here that Kamapuaa, the pig god, raped Pele. This entire area was the site of a large settlement that was important to the Hawaiians. Canoes could pull up on the riverbank and remain protected here, but no trace of the settlement is seen today.

Return to Hulemalu Road and turn left. To see the **Alekoko Fish Pond**, take the dirt road angling off to the left. This property belongs to the Kanoa family, but they are gracious about allowing admission. Park near the gate and walk to the left past the gate and on a path at the end of the road. This fish pond, which allowed river and tidal influx to enter with smaller fish, but kept the larger fish in, was constructed over a thousand years ago by cutting off a loop of the Huleia River with a dike 900 yards long. The engineering is remarkable. Along the river surface of the first 600 yards from the west end, where the river current would erode the dike, it is faced with a double layer of dressed stone two to three feet thick and nine feet high from the river bottom. This stone facing becomes a single layer and then disappears toward the seaward end of the wall where the current would no longer erode it. One sluice gate is visible, built by a Japanese family in 1940 in an effort to restore the pond to use, but the original ones have collapsed and the fish pond is not in working condition at the present time.

Beyond this point up the Huleia River is the **Huleia National Wildlife Refuge**, the principal home of the endangered Koloa Duck. The only way to see this area is on one of the canoe or kayak tours that go up the river. Continue up Hulemalu Road to the lookout for a panoramic view of the fish pond.

Return to Nawiliwili the way you came, but turn left on Nawiliwili Road, Highway 58. Immediately on your right is a small sign "**Menehune Garden.**" This should reopen sometime in 1988 and you are in for a real treat. For a small admission you will be guided through a lush tropical garden by the owner, Melvin Kailikea, and see the largest banyan tree on Kauai. Mrs. Kailikea regales you with tales of old Kauai, and may do an impromptu hula. Their warm enthusiasm is what makes the tour a delight.

About half-way up Nawiliwili Road on the right is the entrance to the **Grove Farm Homestead Museum**. Tours are by reservation only, so for now just mark its location in your mind. This was formerly the eighty-acre plantation home of George N. Wilcox and of his sisters until 1978. Grove Farm was named for a grove of Kukui trees that once was here and also gave its name to the Kukui Grove Shopping Center. The Wilcox home, adjoining buildings and grounds have been preserved as a depiction of old sugar plantation life. The plantation office, washhouse, teahouse and guest cottage are just as they were then – actual papers and books used at the time are on Wilcox's desk.

Tours are conducted by docents who are knowledgeable about the history of Kauai and the Grove Farm. Your tour will be more rewarding if you first read the book *Grove Farm Plantation*, obtainable in paperback at most bookstores on Kauai. The book may also be purchased at the Homestead for later reading. Because the tours are often booked up well in advance, it is best to write ahead for reservations to Grove Farm Homestead, P.O. Box 1631, Lihue, Kauai, HI 96766, or telephone Pat Palama at 808-245-3202.

Just past Grove Farm on your left at the end of a double row of palms is a stately home built in 1913. This is the residence of the present manager of Grove Farm. Just glance as you go by – it is private property. The company no longer operates a sugar plantation. It is now involved in land development, quarrying and other interests.

Near the intersection of Nawiliwili Road and Highway 50, close to the mill, is a cemetery with headstones bearing the names of those who helped contribute to the history of Kauai.

About .1 mile to the right of the intersection along Highway 50, look for Hoomana Road ascending mauka from the highway. A Hawaii Visitors Bureau sign *"Lihue Lutheran Church"* marks the turnoff. Go up this road to what was known in the last century as "German Hill." Starting in the 1860's, a large number of German immigrants were brought in to work on the sugar plantations. They constructed a neat and orderly community here and the parishioners built their own church in 1883 which still stands. Their most skilled carpenter had only worked on wooden ships before, so the floor of the church slopes away from the center like a ship's deck. Prior to World War I, over a thousand Germans lived nearby.

Now return to Highway 50 and continue to the west. On the left is the **Kukui Grove Shopping Center**, the largest on Kauai. Beyond this is Mt. Haupu (named after a demigod) dominating the **Haupu Range**, and the adjacent **Queen Victoria's Profile** holding her admonishing finger in the air. The Hawaiians thought the face resembled the goddess Hina, and the slender peak a male phallus. They were quite happy with this male-female interpretation until the missionaries came and prevailed upon them to change it to a more "Victorian" meaning. The fragrant mokihana berry that grows only on Kauai is still found on the slopes. The berries are intertwined with maile leaves to make the traditional lei of Kauai.

Less than a mile out of Lihue on the mauka side is **Kilohana**. This was the home of Gaylord and Ethel Wilcox in the 1930's when sugar was king and he was the manager of the Grove Farm Plantation. The name was taken from the crater four miles west of Lihue which is seen clearly from here. The word Kilohana was used by Hawaiians for the outer layer of tapa on their bed coverings, which was the finest, so by extension means "superb" or "excellent." The Wilcox home has been beautifully restored. You can walk around and visit the array of fine shops, restaurants and gardens, or ride around the grounds in an old-fashioned carriage pulled by Clydesdale horses. Kilohana opens daily at 9:30 a.m., the museum and shops remain open until 7:30 p.m., and the restaurants until 9 or 10:00 p.m. There is no admission charge. Telephone 245-5608.

Next you come to the small community of **Puhi** (puff or blow). This was formerly a plantation town, and the plantation store building (containing an old-fashioned grocery store) is still there. The store was built in 1918 and the post office added later, extending the false front. Rarely today do you find a grocery store that has a counter where you *ask* for the items you want. The nearby **People's Market** is an excellent place to purchase fresh fruit and leis.

Kauai Community College, a two-year college and part of the University of Hawaii system, occupies the area north of the highway. This is also the site of the future Performing Arts Center of Kauai.

PUHI TO KOLOA – MAP #2

If you are in old clothes and shoes and ready for a little adventure, turn left from Highway 50 just west of Puhi at the sign "Kipu" (hold back). Go on Kipu road, ignore the left turnoff on Halemalu Road, and continue along the winding road until you come to the "one lane bridge" sign. Look for a small dirt road to the left just beyond that. Go approximately a half mile on this, listening for the sound of a waterfall. At a place where the road widens slightly, you can hear **Kipu Falls** on your right. Either park there, allowing enough room for a car to go by, or continue ahead for a hundred yards or so where there is enough room to turn around and return to park. Apply mosquito repellant because at times the mosquitos are very hungry here. If there has been a recent rain, be careful on the first part of the trail – it is steep and can be slippery. Go down the trail and you will see the beautiful waterfall plunging into a pool more than 100 feet in diameter. There is a rope to swing on, and you can climb out of the pool using roots as hand-holds or walk out downstream. Note the smooth holes in the rocks where the Hawaiians sharpened their adzes.

The surrounding area of **Kipu** is where William Hyde Rice, son of William Harrison Rice, started a cattle ranch in 1867 that is still operated by the Rice family today. The row of Norfolk pines once led to his home. The bronze plaque there was erected by his Japanese workers in 1925. He was exceptionally fluent in Hawaiian, wrote the famous *Hawaiian Legends*, and was loved by all who knew him.

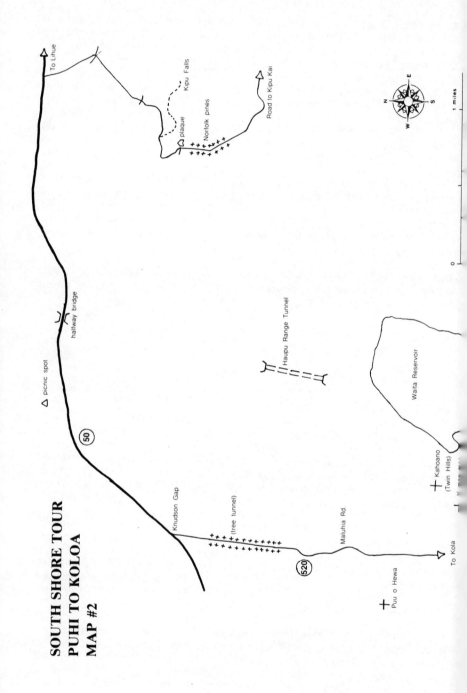

SOUTH SHORE TOUR
PUHI TO KOLOA
MAP #2

To Lihue

Kipu Falls

plaque

Norfolk pines

Road to Kipu Kai

picnic spot

halfway bridge

50

Haupu Range Tunnel

Waita Reservoir

Knudson Gap

(tree tunnel)

Kahoano
(Twin Hills)

Maluhia Rd.

520

Puu o Hewa

To Kola

1 miles

0

The road over the one-lane bridge continues and turns into a jeep road that leads up and over the Haupu Range. This is on private land blocked by gates, and permission to pass is granted only rarely. It is the only means of land access to a heavenly valley, called *Kipu Kai*, nestled between two arms of the Range. A cattle ranch owned by a branch of the Waterhouse family is now there. Kipu Kai has a sacred spring, petroglyphs, remnants of old Hawaiian housesites, and a small heiau. *Kipu Kai Beach* is a broad white sand beach where the swimming and snorkeling are absolutely fabulous. A visit by boat or kayak can be arranged – see the "What to Do" section. In this way you can swim, snorkel, and stroll on the beach up to the "debris and vegetation" line.

This is a good place to explain the Shoreline Law in Hawaii. The State owns all beaches up to the "debris and vegetation" line where private property begins. This is the highest place where the waves and tide deposit debris, and also the lowest where natural vegetation grows. Many routes from the nearest roads have been condemned through private property by the State to allow public access to beaches, and are marked "beach access." Unfortunately, this was not possible at Kipu Kai.

Back on Highway 50, you are now heading toward *Knudsen Gap*. This was named for an old family on Kauai that still owns all the land around here. It is the pass to the southern and western sides of the island between the Haupu Range and the *Kahili Ridge* which ascends to the peak of Kawaikini. Notice the total lack of billboards or other clutter that could obstruct this gorgeous panorama. To your right, the twin peaks of *Kawaikini* and *Waialeale* soar to the sky. These peaks, 5,243 feet and 5,148 feet high respectively, are usually shrouded in clouds except during Kona winds, when they stand out dramatically.

Before passing through Knudsen Gap, best indicated now by the junction of Route 580 with Highway 50, you go over the *Huleia Bridge*, halfway from Lihue to Koloa. This is why it is called "*Halfway Bridge*" by local residents. A road by the bridge leads down past a gravel quarry to a delightful picnic spot by a waterfall. However, you must have permission from Grove Farm to go there.

Turn left down Route 580, *Maluhia* (peaceful) *Road*, into the "*Tree Tunnel.*" The road is lined with a variety of eucalyptus trees called "swamp mahogany" that Walter Duncan McBryde donated in 1911. The dirt road into Koloa was often muddy here, and the roots of these trees added stability to it. The tree tunnel was considerably longer before the belt road was built in 1939. You can still see remnants of twin rows of trees mauka of Highway 50.

About two miles down Maluhia Road, there is a conical hill on the right known as *Puu o Hewa*. This name has an interesting origin. Literally, it means "hill of wrong." On one of the earliest maps of the area hung on the wall of the Koloa Plantation office, an erroneous name had been given this hill. An unknown Hawaiian crossed this out and wrote "hewa", or "wrong", above it. No one bothered to find out what the name really was. The hill has been called Puu o Hewa ever since and the correct Hawaiian name has long been lost. If you look carefully you can see an x-shaped scar on the hill. This was made by the Hawaiians while enjoying one of their favorite sports, hee holua, or sledding. They laid pili grass on the two paths to sled on. Only one such sled is still preserved in the Bishop Museum in Honolulu. The two paths on the hill crossed, and the danger of collision just added to the thrill.

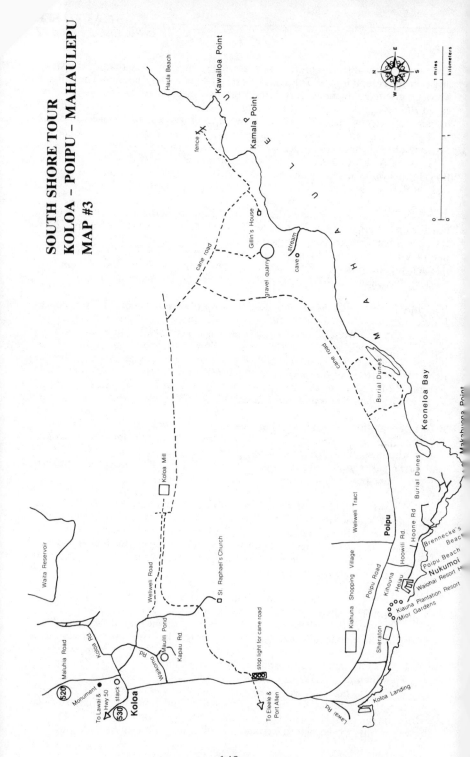

SOUTH SHORE TOUR
KOLOA – POIPU – MAHAULEPU
MAP #3

Waita Reservoir

Haula Beach

Kawailoa Point

Kamala Point

fence

Gillin's House

cane road

gravel quarry

Stream

cave

Burial Dunes

cane road

Keoneloa Bay

Makahuena Point

Maluhia Road

Koloa Rd

Koloa Mill

Weliweli Road

St. Raphael's Church

Maulili Pond

Kapau Rd.

Waikomo Rd

stop light for cane road

To Lawai & Hwy 50

Monument

stack

520

530

Koloa

To Eleele & Port Allen

Kiahuna Shopping Village

Weliweli Tract

Poipu Road

Kiahuna Heiau

Poipu Rd.

Poipu

Hoowili Rd

Hoone Rd

Burial Dunes

Brennecke's Beach

Poipu Beach

Nukumoi

Waiohai Resort H

Sheraton

Kiauna Plantation Resort

Mior Gardens

Lawai Rd.

Koloa Landing

The twin hills on the left beyond Puu o Hewa have both real names and Hawaiian nicknames. But you'll have to guess what the nicknames are. We'll give you a hint: Note that the lady appears to be growing hair on her chest.

KOLOA-POIPU-MAHAULEPU - MAP #3

You next arrive in **Koloa**. Please don't call it "Old Koloa Town." That name was whipped up recently for the tourist trade. Park on the grass just before coming to Koloa Road to see the monument depicting the different races of sugar workers, a brief inscribed history, and various types of sugar cane that have been important to this area. Nearby is the truncated stack of the sugar mill built in 1841. The foundation is also still there, and behind it on the banks of the Waikomo Stream are the remains of the dam used to power the mill.

As pointed out in the "History" chapter, this was actually the third mill in Koloa and the fifth or sixth on Kauai. The location of both the first and second Koloa mills can be found by taking Weliweli Road to Waikomo Road. Turn right on this, and just before the bridge over Waikomo Stream, turn left on Kapau Road. A dirt turnoff is immediately on your right. **Maulili Pond** at the end is the spot. It is enjoyed today by local kids as a swimming hole. The present mill at Paa about a mile east of Koloa was built in 1921. On the way back into town, look carefully at some of the small, older houses – they still bear their camp number in addition to modern street addresses.

Koloa developed in the mid 1800's as a plantation town around its mill. Kauai's first doctor, Thomas Lafon, and first public school, started by Daniel Dole, were here. It was the major population center of the island from about 1835 to 1879. The official port of entry then for Kauai was the small Koloa Landing nearby, and the island's only customs officer was stationed there.

Prior to the development of Koloa, the area was populated by some four thousand Hawiians. They did not cluster together in villages unless forced to by the topography, but instead built grass shacks, many with rock foundations, near their taro patches. In any area from Koloa to the ocean that has not been cleared for sugar cane, rock housesites can still be seen. The rock walls enclosed pig pens, marked boundaries, or were used for the extensive irrigation system from Waikomo Stream. Taro terraces lined with stones can also be found. Some of these structures are easier to see on the Kiahuna Golf Course, where they were preserved, and the black rocks stand out dramatically against the green grass.

The decline of Koloa Plantation, and the town itself, started when union agitation caused labor problems after the Second World War. This resulted in mechanization of the sugar plantation and the loss of a large part of the labor force. Sugar workers in Hawaii today are the highest paid in the world, and the industry faces demise largely because of this. The decline of Koloa was slowed in the early 1970's when tourism on the Poipu shore increased. All of the buildings in Koloa were carefully restored in a three-year program that ended in 1986.

Koloa is now over three acres in size with approximately thirty shops and restaurants. Its name comes from "ko", the word for cane, and "loa", which is Hawaiian for both long and tall. Sometimes translated as "long cane", a more appropriate translation in this context is "tall cane." Under the branches of a large monkeypod tree is the building that was Kauai's first hotel. Its five rooms now house a series of shops. Around the corner, the old plantation hospital is now The Garden Island Medical Clinic.

The New England-style Koloa Church was built in 1859. Its spire was visible from far at sea, and whalers and other mariners set their course by it to arrive at Koloa Landing. Behind the green Y.B.A. social hall, across the street from the Big Save market, is the Koloa Hongwanji which was built in 1910 by artisans from Japan. The Koloa Jodo Mission to the east of the Big Save market also dates from 1910. The larger temple next to it was completed in 1985. Both temples were built by master craftsmen from Japan who came here for that purpose. Note that kneeling mats are used. Look inside if one is open. The altar of the smaller Jodo Mission is especially stunning.

Saint Rafael's Church, the first Catholic church on Kauai built in 1854, can be seen by taking Weliweli Road out of Koloa. The turnoff to the right from that road is marked. There are three old structures there: the church, the rectory, and a small school. The newer church is the only building that is presently used. The cemetery nearby has many interesting names and dates.

The **Waita Reservoir** northeast of Koloa is the largest in Hawaii. At 424 acres, it is also the largest *lake* in the Hawaiian Islands! The reservoir was completed in 1906 on the site of an old marsh, and was an engineering feat in its time. Its official name is Koloa Reservoir, but the Japanese and Hawaiian laborers called it "Waita." "Wai" is the Hawaiian word for fresh water, and "ta" was added as a Japanese suffix meaning rice paddy. Local residents fish here and dig clams from the bottom.

Behind Waita Reservoir, just to the north, a half-mile long tunnel goes through Haupu Range. How this came to be is an interesting story. In 1948 Grove Farm, located in the Lihue area, merged with the Koloa Plantation – primarily for its mill. Grove Farm had none, and until then had used the Lihue Plantation mill. Once the mill was acquired, the problem presented itself of transporting cane from Grove Farm lands, around the north end of Haupu Range to the Koloa mill. After calculating carefully, it was determined that blasting a tunnel through the range would pay for itself within three or four years. Using surplus Army equipment found in a cave on Oahu made it even more economical. The tunnel is just large enough for one cane truck, and on harvesting days they roar through it at thirty or forty miles per hour. There is absolutely no room for a car with tourists in it, so the tunnel is declared a "restricted area" by The McBryde Sugar Company, which has leased this part of the Grove Farm land since 1974.

Going south towards Poipu from Koloa, less than a mile out of town, is a large cane road with its own traffic lights. Note this because it will be the start of an exploration trip later. Poipu Road continues to the left of the corner that has the "Welcome to Poipu" sign, past the **Kiahuna Shopping Village**. This is a wonderful place to shop. Across Poipu Road is a sign "Kiahuna Plantation." Turn down there to visit the *Moir Gardens*. When Hector and Alexandra Moir lived there in the 1930's, they started an unusual garden of cacti and succulents on the six-acre grounds and called it "Pau a Laka" (skirt of the goddess Laka), an ancient Hawaiian name for all of this area. Their residence was converted into the Plantation Gardens Restaurant in 1968.

After a stroll through the Moir Gardens, walk down the path to the grounds of the Sheraton Kauai Hotel and the Kiahuna complex. Note the absolutely gorgeous, crescent-shaped *Kiahuna Beach* which is shared by guests of the Sheraton Kauai. Public access is provided. It is always this beautiful here and always safe because of protective offshore reefs. Swimming and snorkeling are great. Body surfing and body boarding are fair during the summer, and some of the best board surfing sites on the island are off shore. See "What to Do" for more details. All equipment can be rented at various resort beach activities centers, and lessons are available. Catamaran rides leave from the beach. The adjacent *Poipu Hotel Beach* and *Waiohai Resort Beach* are similar.

In front of the Waiohai Resort is the restored *Kihouna Heiau*. If you are taking the south tour before the north one, this will be your first heiau, and you are certain to be disappointed. Try to visualize it as it was. It was built under the direction of the district chief Kina in the late 16th Century. Captain Cook described the walls as four to six feet high in a rectangle 100 feet by 130 feet. It had oracle towers, an altar, and several idols. The site was respected and preserved when both the old Waiohai Resort and the new one were built.

Back on Poipu Road continuing east, turn makai on Hoowili Road to reach *Poipu Beach Park*. This is a pleasant four-acre park with showers, restrooms, and covered pavilions for picnicking. There is a play area and a small sheltered wading beach for children. The beach itself is safe and one of the two on Kauai with a full-time lifeguard. Swimming and snorkeling are similar to the beaches mentioned above, as are other beach activities.

Just to the east is *Brennecke's Beach*. Dr. Marvin Brennecke owned the beach until the State appropriated it in 1976 for public use. His home next to it was destroyed by Hurricane Iwa in 1982 and he now lives in Waimea. This was the best body surfing beach on Kauai, and one of the best in Hawaii, before Iwa struck. It is still the best on Kauai for body boarding. The loss of sand and large rocks on the bottom brought in by the hurricane make body surfing a bit risky now. Sand, though, is slowly coming in. Locals now body surf at high tide. In two or three years this may again be as good as before for body surfing.

Inland from Brennecke's Beach are an old fish pond, taro terraces, walls and house sites, all completely overgrown and invisible from the road. Few are aware they are there.

Return to Poipu Road and turn east (right). Continue when it turns into a cane road. *Keoneloa Bay* on the right is the future site of a 506 bed luxury Hyatt Regency resort to be completed by Mel Ventura in 1990. Public beach access will be provided. For now, two or three cane roads lead down to the beach and access on these is allowed without special permission. The name "Keoniloa" appearing on maps has no translation. Whenever this occurs, it is usually due to a mistake in spelling somewhere along the line. Keoneloa means "the long sand", so this is almost certainly the correct name. It is sometimes still called **Shipwreck Beach** because the keel and ribs of a wooden vessel were there for many years prior to Hurricane Iwa, which washed the keel out to sea. It was on this beach that the ancient Kauaians first found iron in similar wreckage from Spanish galleons. Iwa also improved **Keoneloa Beach**, and it is now an attractive swimming, body boarding and board surfing site. Snorkeling is fair near the rocks, but breaking waves make this tricky. Storms south of the equator can cause a high surf here. Sometimes there are "wraparound" waves from the north and northeast, and trade winds cause a westward current. Otherwise, the beach is safe. There are no facilities at this beach.

You may hear about petroglyphs on the sandstone ledge along the shore of Keoneloa Bay. These have been seen on just three recorded occasions, the last of which was after a series of severe storms in 1914. An investigator came over at that time from the Bishop Museum and photographed them. A slab of sandstone with glyphs was removed and taken to the Bishop Museum where it is on exhibit. The ledge was then covered by sand again and the petroglyphs have not been seen since. Some people tell us they have seen the glyphs from time to time, but their descriptions do not match the photographs.

To explore **Mahaulepu** (and falling together) **Beach**, continue on the cane road two miles until it deadends on another east-west cane road with utility poles along it. Turn right, pass the first road on the right which leads to a gravel quarry, and you

will arrive at Mahaulepu. Remember, this is all private property and you need permission from McBryde Sugar Company to come here. Park at the end of this road to the right. Look for windsurfers. When the wind is right a dozen will be dancing on the waves like butterflies.

The name for this area, Mahaulepu, which implies warriors falling together in battle, comes from an interesting episode in history. When Kamehameha attempted his first invasion of Kauai in 1796, most of his war canoes were sunk or turned back by the stormy channel. However, a few made the crossing and landed here. Exhausted, the warriors collapsed beside their canoes and slept. Just before dawn, Kauai defenders fell upon them and slaughtered all but a handful. These survivors succeeded in launching one canoe and, afraid to face Kamehameha on Oahu, sailed all the way to the Island of Hawaii. This oral tale is confirmed by an identical one in Kawaihae, Hawaii, where the canoe landed.

Stroll east along Mahaulepu Beach (to your right facing the ocean) and you will pass an isolated house. This belongs to the Gillin Family. Elbert Gillin was the civil engineer who supervised the Haupu Range Tunnel project. His wife, Adena, still lives there with her daughter. It is marvelous for small children because of the protective reef and shallow water. Keep going until you come to a small stream. On the far side of the stream is a faint trail. This goes inland for approximately 200 yards to the entrance of a cave. We're not going to tell you about the surprise inside – just go all the way in and its there. You won't need a flashlight – just duck when you have to. The surprise is less than 100 feet in.

Back on Mahaulepu Beach, stroll in the other direction, past your car, and you will come to sandy **Kamala** (crude shelter) **Point**. This spot is ideal for sunbathing. There is not much left of the Waiopili Heiau inland from here to be worth the hike. Walk along the shore around Kamala Point or drive around behind it. Either way, you will come to **Kawailoa** (the long water) **Bay** another part of Mahaulepu, where "Islands in the Stream" was filmed. This spot used to be a secret and even locals rarely came here. However, in the past few years it has been "discovered." If you are lucky enough to be alone or nearly so, it is a fascinating place. The waters are clear and there are underwater caves off to the left to explore. The beach is almost always safe and fish are abundant. There is no surfing of any kind here, though. Camping is not permitted, and be sure to carry any trash out with you. McBryde Sugar Company is seriously considering closing the access road because of these two problems.

Back on the cane road paralleling the shore, continue driving in a northeasterly direction until you come to a barbed-wire fence. Park there and look for a gate formed by two twisted poles through the barbed wire with a faint trail on the rocky slope beyond. This is Grove Farm land and you need permission from them to pass through the gate. Follow the trail until you come to a bluff overlooking a gorgeous small beach. This is **Haula** (hot sun) **Beach**. There are no facilities here, but you have found paradise and should be alone. Ahead of you is the "head" of Haupu Range and if the cloud cover is right, you will see why it got the nickname "Hoary Head" Range. Haula Beach is safe most of the time – just observe the conditions before going swimming. Snorkeling is good when the ocean is calm, but there is no surfing.

The sand dunes of Mahaulepu are where the Hawaiian commoners in this region buried their dead. It was difficult to dig a gravesite in the hard, rocky earth with their wooden implements. A stroll on the dunes after a storm still turns up bones and artifacts. It is suggested that you not dig or look for them, but instead treat the area with respect.

Return west along Poipu Road to Lawai Road, which angles sharply to the left at the corner with the "Welcome to Poipu" sign. Another short jog to the left at the first "y" takes you over the bridge to **Koloa Landing**. Pull to the side of the road at the 5 mile marker and look down. All that remains of what was once Kauai's busiest port lies before you. In fact, until the decline of whaling starting in 1859, it was the third busiest port in the Hawaiian Islands, behind only Honolulu and Lahaina. There were often forty to fifty ships anchored offshore here. It was last used as a port in 1928, giving way to Nawiliwili. It is now a favorite spot for scuba diving and snorkeling because it is almost always calm.

HOONA BEACH TO PALAMA BEACH – MAP #4

Now back to Lawai Road to explore the rest of Poipu. Actually, the coast from here to Spouting Horn is called Kukuiula, but it is becoming regarded more and more as part of Poipu, so let's go along with that. Less than a mile after the turnoff, you come to **Kuhio Park** where there is ample room to pull over and stop. Behind you is a shallow, completely protected beach – **Hoona Beach**. There are seashells to find, tidepools to explore, and sand to build castles. It is probably the best beach on Kauai for children aged two to six. Farther down Lawai Road, past the point with a Thai-style home, is tiny **Keiki Beach**, the best on the island for infants younger than that. It offers a totally protected pond averaging a foot and a half deep, sandy bottom, brightly colored baby fish, aama crabs to chase, and toddlers can't wander more than a few feet away because of the walls on either side. Bring your own shade to both beaches, however.

Hoai Bay, where Kuhio Park is, was a prominent Hawaiian fishing village in pre-contact times and high chiefs of Kauai would often stay here. **Prince Jonah Kuhio Kalanianaole** was born in March 26, 1871 on the spot marked by the monument. He was a grandson of the last high chief of Kauai, Kaumualii. Prince Kuhio was adopted by Queen Kapiolani, wife of King Kalakaua, raised in Iolani Palace in Honolulu, and made a prince by royal decree. When the Organic Act of 1900 made Hawaii a Territory of the United States, Prince Kuhio was the first delegate to Congress in 1902. He continued as such until 1921. He died in 1922 at age fifty-one, and his body now rests in the Royal Mausoleum in Nuuanu Valley, Honolulu. He was the last heir of the Hawaiian monarchy, and is revered because of his heartfelt efforts on behalf of the Hawaiian people. His birthday is a State holiday and the occasion for a week of celebration on Kauai, concluding with a moving ceremony in this park. Notice the inscription on the bronze plaque: "Ke Alii Makaainana", which means "The Prince of the People."

There is much more of interest here. In the northwest corner is the small **Hoai Heiau**. Off to the right as you are facing the park from the road are old stone terraces and housesites. Beyond the fence are remnants of irrigation ditches, walls and other structures. The pond in front of you is actually an ancient fish pond. **Hoai Beach** is small and partially protected by an offshore reef. Sunbathing and swimming are the principle activities. Snorkeling is not particularly good and there is not much surf. There are no facilities here except a restroom in Kuhio Park.

Almost all visitors ask us why the three shacks with their surrounding piles of trash are allowed to desecrate this beautiful park. So far we have been unable to find satisfactory answers.

Just past the Beach House Restaurant is a great place for sunbathing, swimming and snorkeling and there is little or no surf onshore. Offshore are three world-famous board surfing spots. The beach has no Hawaiian name, but is traditionally called **Longhouse Beach** because of a structure previously on the site. The waters are protected by an offshore reef and are almost always calm.

Farther along Lawai Road is **Kukuiula Harbor** and **Kukuiula Beach**. The sandy beach is clean and always safe except during a severe Kona storm. Snorkeling is excellent to the right of the harbor entrance, but there is no surf. Showers, restrooms, picnic tables and barbecue facilities are near the boat launch. The word "kukuiula" means "red light of the kukui nut" because the burning of kukui nuts guided late fishermen safely home. This was the location of another Hawaiian fishing village, but the last evidence, a fishing shrine, was eradicated by Hurricane Iwa. It also destroyed all of the homes that were here, as well as the road you are driving on. The harbor was rebuilt after Iwa and is once again one of the best launching sites for small fishing and recreation boats.

SOUTH SHORE TOUR
HOONA BEACH TO PALAMA BEACH
MAP #4

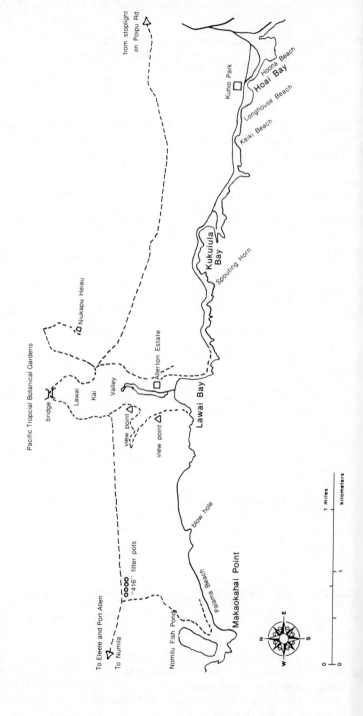

At the end of the well-paved part of the road is **Spouting Horn Park**. High swells force air out of an opening in a large lava tube, producing a moaning or wheezing sound, and spray comes out of another opening close by. It is this combination that distinguishes it from the many blow holes elsewhere in the islands and gives it the name "Spouting Horn." The height of the spray varies from two feet on a calm day to sixty feet when the swells are high. Heed the warning signs and don't go near either opening – footing is slippery. Shopping at the booths lining the walkway nearby is fun, and bargains can often be found here because of the low overhead. With a little bargaining, you may be able to talk the price down a bit as well.

Continue on the poorly paved road beyond Spouting Horn to a gate at the entrance to the Allerton Estate at Lawai Kai. If you want to see the Estate, park at the turnaround, walk up and over the bank on the mauka side and up the cane road. In ten or fifteen minutes you will come to places where you can peer down into the valley. It is breathtakingly beautiful, and scenes of "Fantasy Island" as well as a dozen motion pictures have been filmed here.

In ancient times Lawai Kai was filled with taro fields and an intricate irrigation system, remnants of which can still be seen. A small heiau on a hill near the west bluff was used for ceremonial circumcisions. An entire village site, waterfall and pool are just upstream from the lily pond. Lawai Kai was also a favorite fishing site of the Hawaiians, and they would shelter for the night in the caves near the shore. Many artifacts have been found in them.

Lawai Kai was first mentioned in written history when **Queen Emma** stayed there on her honeymoon as the bride of King Kamehameha IV in 1856. When her husband died in 1870, she returned there to live alone for several years in a cottage built for her on the east bluff. She planted the bougainvillaea which cascades down that bank today. Some years after she left, the property was sold to Alexander McBryde, and in 1899 he moved the cottage down by his house.

Robert Allerton, a millionaire from Chicago, bought Lawai Kai from the McBryde Estate in 1937, and with his adopted son, John Gregg Allerton, created a paradise in this valley. They built a new home to replace the McBryde residence in a style to complement Queen Emma's cottage, and restored the cottage itself. Much of the upper valley was in sugar cane under the McBryde Sugar Company until the Allertons purchased it. The railroad bed with its tunnels through the rock for the cane trains can still be seen on both banks. Just before his death in 1964, Robert Allerton was instrumental in creating the **Pacific Tropical Botanical Garden** in the upper part of the valley. He endowed it with one million dollars and it was chartered by Congress in that year. His ashes were scattered in Lawai Bay upon his death. John Gregg Allerton died in 1986 and the estate then became part of the Garden. A tour through the Garden and the Allerton Estate is truly an unforgettable experience. It can be arranged by calling the Pacific Tropical Botanical Garden, 808-332-7361. Call well ahead because the tours are often booked up for a week or more in advance. For more details, see "What To Do."

Lawai Kai Beach is a beautiful crescent of sand divided by Lawai Stream. The gentle surf is perfect for body surfing and body boarding, but not board surfing. Snorkeling is wonderful, especially along the eastern point. Because this is private property, permission to use the beach must be obtained from the Garden. You may also take one of the boat tours that come here but must remain below the debris and vegetation line. There are no facilities.

Now we will go exploring along the south shore to some out-of-the-way sites. These all require permission from the McBryde Sugar Company or others. Be sure you have your McBryde sticker with you. Return to the junction a mile south of Koloa where the large cane road intersects Poipu Road. Turn west on this and note your odometer reading. If the gate there is locked, try another time or enter the area from one of the small cane roads on Route 530 out of Koloa.

On the way is a heiau that was found only once by archaeologists in 1907, and has not been located by them since. It was rediscovered by one of the authors of this book, however. A hill is to your right about two miles from the start of this road. Take any cane road mauka and circle up behind the hill. The heiau cannot be seen from any road, but hike up on top of the hill and you will find the **Niukapu Heiau**, 50 by 100 feet, which commands a spectacular view.

At 2.3 miles from the start, the large cane road begins to descend and wind around Lawai Valley and crosses a bridge between upper Lawai Valley and Lawai Kai. At the top of the rise beyond the valley, 3.3 miles from the start, a small cane road leads to the left along the west rim. This goes south for approximately .2 mile where it widens slightly at a bend. Park here and enjoy the fabulous view of **Lawai Valley** and the Allerton Estate. Farther along after the cane road winds around a gorge, there is a second wide place with another view. Paths lead down from each to the valley floor, but both are on private property not covered by your McBryde permit, so you should not be tempted. Take the Pacific Tropical Botanical Garden tour instead (one of the authors of this book is a tour guide) or visit **Lawai Bay** on one of the boat tours, as we have suggested.

Now return to the large cane road and continue west until you see a line of brush marking a small stream about 4.3 miles from the entry at Poipu Road. Just beyond this on the left are four filter pots (used to keep small bits of matter out of the drip irrigation system) with the number 416 on them. Next to these, a small cane road leads towards the ocean. Drive down this, and in .4 miles you will see the **Nomilu Fish Pond**. A left turn beyond the gate there goes down the steep hill to a road paralleling the shore. At .2 miles from the gate the road widens, providing enough space for two cars to park. Look for a "cattle guard" opening in the barbed wire fence with a path beyond. About 100 yards down this path is half-mile long **Palama Beach**, where clear blue water breaks on crystal white sand. Sometimes the summer surf is rough here, but it is safe for snorkeling and swimming most of the time. At times an alongshore current sweeps seaward off the point, so swim well away from it. In the summer the surf is good enough for body surfing and body boarding, but the rides are short and the waves unpredictable. There is no board surfing. No facilities are here, but some shade is available.

The Palama family owns Makaokahai Point just to the west, but you are allowed to walk on the beach up to their property, which is posted, and from there you can see the fish pond up close. This is one of the most famous fish ponds in all of the Hawaiian Islands. The brackish water still abounds with fish. Stone terraces and burial caves are in the bluffs around it.

KOLOA TO KALAHEO - MAP #5

Return on the main road to Koloa and turn left on Route 530 to the west. The cane fields on either side were planted with pineapple until 1964. That industry died on Kauai because it is more labor-intensive than sugar cane. This is a good place to give you an idea of what is hidden from you on a casual drive on the main roads of Kauai. Iwipoo Road, to the left just before the old pineapple cannery, leads to two sites that are on private property, so you can't visit them. Off this road, hidden by trees, is a dilapidated building that once housed the Hop Sing Society, where Taoist ceremonies were once held. A fascinating overgrown cemetery is beside it. Farther along, hidden behind some houses, are two huge black monoliths with mysterious Hawaiian petroglyphs carved on them. Please don't trespass to look for either of these – we just thought you'd like to know that such things are out of sight all over Kauai almost everywhere you drive.

Just before the junction with Highway 50 is the defunct pineapple cannery on the left. Next on the right is a huge trinket store that residents of Kauai call "The Tourist Trap." We are not especially proud of this establishment, with its garish signs and crass commercialism.

Turn left on Highway 50 and be prepared to stop in exactly .2 mile, opposite a house with a wooden fence on the left. There is not much room on the right shoulder, so be careful getting out and crossing the highway. Go along the path on the right of the fence. This leads to a set of stairs going down. You have arrived at the ***Kobo Dai Ishi Shrine***. Kobo Dai Ishi was a great sage of the Shingon Buddhist Sect, and the original shrine in Japan was dedicated to him over a thousand years ago. This one was erected by Japanese immigrants in 1902. Along a path around the hillside to the right are eighty-eight small figures, each representing a different sin according to the Buddhist Sutra. Under each is a bit of earth taken from the equivalent site of the Kobo Dai Ishi Shrine on the island of Shikoku. Make your way down to the altar and you will see tokens, paper prayers and joss sticks still there. The building on the left is where the caretaker lived until he died in 1947. After his death the shrine fell into disuse and disrepair. Be careful – the wooden floor may collapse under your weight. The path around the hill has grown over, but the tradition is that if you walk the path of the eighty-eight, you will no longer be tempted by any of the sins. We rather like to be tempted, so didn't walk on it.

Continue on Highway 50 to ***Kalaheo*** (the proud day). This was formerly a labor camp for the sugar cane fields in the hills above, and was largely populated by Portuguese. Note their church, Iglesia Ni Cristo, on the right. Turn left at the traffic light and you pass a Portuguese sausage factory and Medeiros farm, where most of the eggs and chickens served on the island come from.

Continue .9 mile out of Kalaheo on Papalina Road, look to the right and you will see a small white sign indicating ***Kukuiolono Park***. The name means "light of Lono" because fires were built on the hill to guide Hawaiian seafarers. The entrance through the large gate cuts back at an angle to your right. This was the original entry to the Walter Duncan McBryde Estate on this hill, which is now a County park. The Japanese gardens date from the time the McBrydes lived here. Walter McBryde also

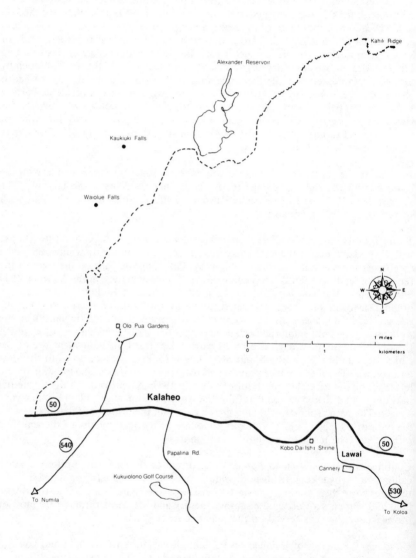

accumulated the legend stones there. The makai path leads to a pavilion from which there is a panoramic view. If you are there to watch the sunset, don't linger too long – the gate closes to cars at 6:30 p.m. But you can park your car outside and walk in.

The *Kukuiolono Golf Course* on the mauka part of the hill is used mostly by the local populace. Not many tourists have found this yet, and it is a delight. The atmosphere is laid back and friendly – it is the only course on Kauai where you can play barefoot without a shirt.

Continue west on Highway 50 .4 mile out of Kalaheo, where the entrance of the *Olo Pua* (named for a native tree) *Gardens* is on your right. Olo Pua was the home of the manager of the Kauai Pineapple Plantation from 1932 to 1962. Tours of the Garden were stopped just as we go to press, and the owner now plans to open the estate only for vacation rentals. This may change, so we left it in the book.

The next cane road to your right leads past the 100-foot *Waiolue Falls* and the smaller *Kaukiuki Falls*, both requiring difficult but short hikes, and *Alexander Reservoir*. From there an almost impassible jeep trail takes you to the top of *Kahili Ridge* for an unbelievable view. Remnants of the structure from which Hawaiian sentries stood guard are still on the ridge.

The macadamia nut trees on the mauka side of Highway 50 here represent one effort of Phil Scott, the progressive manager of McBryde Sugar Company, to diversify crops in the face of the gloomy outlook for the sugar industry. He is also experimenting with tea, coffee and patchouli.

KALAHEO TO SALT POND BEACH PARK – MAP #6

At the 14 mile marker is the *Hanapepe Lookout*. From here you look down into the lush Hanapepe Valley. If petroglyphs are your thing, turn left on the first cane road after the lookout. An irrigation ditch runs along your left. Continue until the road dead-ends at a barbed wire fence on the edge of Wahiawa Gulch. Turn right and stop at the first pile of black rocks that allows you access to *Wahiawa Stream*. On the banks of the stream on both sides along here are ancient petroglyphs. A heiau is just upstream on the east bank, and taro terraces are in the valley downstream.

Here is another secret, one that is easier to reach. Turn left on Route 540 from Highway 50 just before Eleele. Then right on the cane road just before coming to the mill, pass the mill on your left, turn right again and continue to the coast. Around Weli Point to the west is spectacular *Wahiawa* (place of milkfish) *Bay* and *Wahiawa Beach*. The swimming, fishing and snorkeling here are all fantastic. You can drive right down to the white sand beach and park there. There is no surf and the bay is well-protected and safe both summer and winter. There are no facilities here. The mill that you passed, referred to as New Mill or "Numila" by the Hawaiians, closed in 1974 and its machinery was moved to the Koloa Mill.

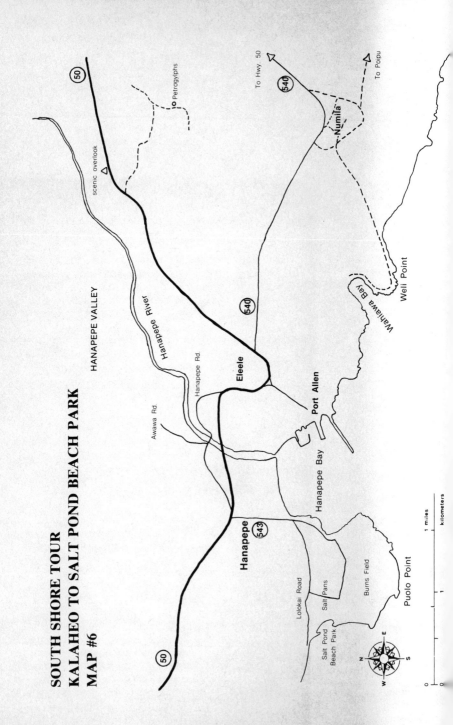

SOUTH SHORE TOUR
KALAHEO TO SALT POND BEACH PARK
MAP #6

50

HANAPEPE VALLEY

Petroglyphs

scenic overlook

To Hwy. 50

540

Numila

To Poipu

Hanapepe River

Weli Point

Hanapepe Rd.

540

Wahiawa Bay

Eleele

Awawa Rd

Port Allen

Hanapepe Bay

Hanapepe

543

50

Lolokai Road

Salt Pans

Burns Field

Puolo Point

Salt Pond
Beach Park

N
W E
S

0   1   1 miles
0   1   kilometers

Back on highway 50, continue past the turnoff for **Port Allen**, which was named for Samuel Cresson Allen, the Honolulu industrialist who was instrumental in its development during the 1930's and 1940's. He hoped to make it Kauai's principle port, but overlooked two geographic facts: Nawiliwili is more centrally located on Kauai and is considerably closer to Oahu. Port Allen is the major petroleum terminus for Kauai, however, handles other cargo as well and has a small boat harbor and navy pier. Across the harbor entrance is **Burns Field**, which from 1920 to 1930 was the only airport on Kauai except for several small landing strips.

Circle around Eleele, down the hill, and angle right into **Hanapepe** on Hanapepe Road. The name means "bay crushed by landslides", and it is. The main street of Hanapepe was used as the set for the television mini-series "The Thorn Birds." Cross over the 1911 bridge, park on the far side, and walk back on the bridge to see some of the old rustic buildings along the river. The road where you stopped is Awawa Road. It leads back into Hanapepe Valley, and along this is some of the best local color on Kauai. Four heiaus and numerous Hawaiian housesites are in the valley. Taro is grown here in thousand-year-old stone-lined taro ponds. You may see an aged Filipino caressing his rooster in anticipation of the cockfight next weekend. At a bend in the road is a nondescript two-story frame house. The top story is the old **Bart Dai Sin Temple**, cared for by Tai Hing Leong, with an exquisitely beautiful altar and statuary inside. When the Chinese farmed rice in this valley from about 1870 to 1910, this temple was the center of worship for them. There are no more Chinese here to worship now – only the old caretaker who wants to go to Honolulu to die. Sometime soon, he and the temple contents may be taken there so he can have his wish.

Find the feed store in Hanapepe, and beside it Shimonishi Orchids. Miyasuki Shimonishi has 1,600 varieties which he wholesales to various markets, but some are for retail sale. Miyasuki's daughter, Elsie, and her husband, Tom, will be happy to help you and provide tips on caring for orchids so you can carry a bit of the Garden Island home with you.

Hanapepe road then returns to Highway 50. Several interesting places on Highway 50 were missed while touring "downtown" Hanapepe, so you should turn left at the end of Hanapepe Road if you wish to return and visit them. Lappert's Aloha Ice Cream and Kauai Kookies are made in Hanapepe. And there is a small funky place on the main highway for delicious local food, The Leeward Diner.

The Soto Zen Temple on the makai side of the Highway is noted for its exquisite design and ornamental details both inside and out. The bronze bell was crafted in Japan.

History was also here in Hanapepe. The cane field and the bluff to the east of Hanapepe Valley was the scene of the bloodiest battle ever fought on Kauai as far as historians know. In 1824 a large group of chiefs led by Humehume, the son of Kaumualii, gathered their forces here against those of Liholiho from Oahu. In this battle, the Kauaians were defeated and the island remained under the domination of Kamehameha's lineage. Hanapepe was also the scene of a major strike by Filipino plantation workers in 1924 in which a score of them were killed.

Every February, a river raft race is held here in Hanapepe. Homemade rafts are paddled from the old bridge to the new one, sometimes in circles and often with disaster en route. It is all in good fun and the residents come out to applaud, sell their handmade wares and home-cooked food, and everyone has a wonderful time.

Just beyond town, turn left on Route 543 and then right again on Lolokai Road. The **salt ponds** on your left are still harvested. Every summer, descendants of those who have inherited the rights to these ancestral plots, the Hui Hana Paakai o Hanapepe, can be seen working them. Captain Cook described this activity exactly as it is done today, and he actually obtained his salt here. The salt workers mix the salt with ocherous red earth (which is more intense in color from here to Waimea) and regard the result as very tasty. It really is!

Continue on to **Salt Pond Beach Park**. It rarely rains here, all facilities are available, and camping is allowed with a County permit. The surf is safe and gentle all year round, but is usually enough to entertain a young body boarder. Shell hunting is best at the far west end. Snorkeling is good at either end, and there are many tidepools to explore. This is one of the two beaches on Kauai where there is a full-time lifeguard.

If you are not bored with archeological sites by now, a heiau is on Puolo Point, along with old housesites and a fishing shrine. Look along the shore to the west of the airfield.

Farther along Highway 50 at the 19 mile marker, a double row of trees lining the road is on your left. Down this is the Olokele Sugar Mill, and you can see how most of the sugar plantation headquarter buildings in the Hawaiian Islands were laid out a century ago. Nearby Kaumakani is a typical plantation camp.

KALUAPUHI BEACH TO WAIMEA – MAP #7

Small beaches can be reached by cane road all along here, but you need permission from Olokele Sugar Company or Gay & Robinson. The best of these is **Kaluapuhi** (the eel pit) **Beach**. At the intersection .7 mile beyond the 20 mile marker where the post office "U.S.P.O. Makaweli" is, turn right on the cane road and then immediately right again to parallel the highway. Continue to the underpass and go under it toward the ocean. Ignore the first turnoff to the left and the second to the right. Bear gradually left until the cane road runs along the shore. The secluded sandy beach is near Kaluapuhi Point. That is its chief feature – seclusion. Swimming is possible between the rock outcroppings, but no other activities. There is some shade but no facilities at this small beach.

If a really long beach is to your liking, stop after the 21 mile marker on the west side of the concrete bridge over the Aakukui (kukui roots) Stream. The bridge abutment has "Aakukui" stamped on it. Cross the road makai and look for the "cattleguard" opening through the barbed wire fence. Beyond this is a well-worn path to follow. A couple of hundred yards walk through Gay & Robinson pasture land (they graciously allow access without specific permission) will lead you to the beach. The water and sand are brownish from the Waimea River. Body surfing, body boarding and board surfing are all great in the summer months, but snorkeling is impossible.

Aakukui Beach has no facilities, but there is ample shade. This beach is sometimes called "Pakala's" in error. The small patch of sand to the south near Pakala Village (beyond a rocky point) is *Pakala Beach*. Aakukui Beach is also called *"Infinities"* by surfers because in the summer the left slides seem to go on forever.

The beach is well over a mile long and except when surfers are there, you will be alone. Walk west to see the old Robinson Estate where Eleanor Robinson still lives. But stay on the beach – don't trespass.

Back on Highway 50, huge banks of bougainvillaea mark the mauka boundary of the Robinson Estate, the entry to which is opposite mile marker 22. The next point of interest is *Fort Elizabeth*, or *The Russian Fort*, built for Russia by Dr. Georg Anton Shaeffer, a Hessian militant, in 1815. He was employed by the Russian Fur Company of Alaska and named the fort in honor of Tsar Alexander's consort. He also built two forts on the bluffs above Hanalei Bay, Fort Alexander and Fort Barclay, of which little remains today. His scheme was to persuade Kaumualii to turn over all of Kauai to Russia. Kaumualii acceded, Shaeffer hoisted the Russian flag, but Russia then declined the offer.

There is really not much to see – the fort was dismantled in 1864 – but you might pull in only because the restrooms are well-maintained. It is a regular tourist bus stop for this purpose.

For history buffs, a good account of this fort is in Joesting's *Kauai, The Separate Kingdom*, and brochures for walking tours are available on the site. The walls were piled together in the dry-stack method of the Hawaiians using rubble fill without mortar to a height of twelve feet. The five points of the fort where cannons were mounted faced the ocean and river mouth. Within the enclosure are remnants of the barracks, located surprisingly close to the magazine. The officers' quarters are at a more comfortable distance. Shaeffer also built a fort near the site of the Aloha Tower in Honolulu, which is how Fort Street there got its name.

On Highway 50 once again, note the protective dikes built along the *Waimea River* in 1950 because of the frequent flooding of the river. Many of the older buildings in town are on stilts for the same reason. At the entry into *Waimea* itself, *Lucy Wright Beach Park* is not of much interest to the visitor except that it marks the spot where Captain Cook first set foot. He walked up what is now Ala Wai Road to about where the first Japanese temple is now. A monument honoring him is in a small triangular park in the center of town. The word "Waimea" means "reddish water", and you can see why. The river constantly brings down silt from the red highlands above.

With a length of 19.5 miles including Poomanu Stream, this is the longest river on Kauai. There are numerous archeological findings in Waimea Valley, including a huge heiau at the junction of Waialae and Waimea Rivers.

Waimea is where the first missionaries to Kauai arrived in 1820. For a complete tour of town, stop at the Waimea Branch Library on the makai side of Highway 50 and ask for a walking tour map. Library hours are Monday and Wednesday, 12 noon to 8:00 p.m., Tuesday, Thursday and Friday 8:30 a.m. to 4:30 p.m., closed Saturday

SOUTH SHORE TOUR
KALUAPUHI BEACH TO WAIMEA
MAP #7

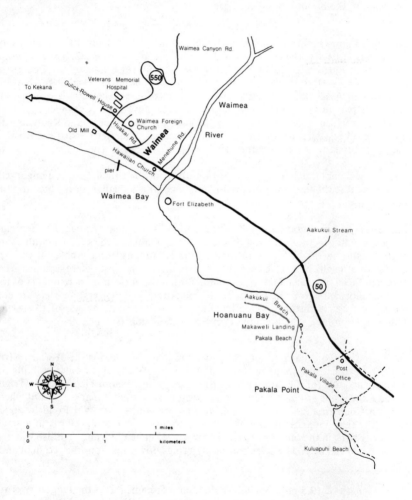

and Sunday. For a rapid tour, just go up Waimea Canyon Road to Huakai Road. One block to the right is the **Waimea Foreign Church**, built by the missionary George Rowell and his congregation in 1845 out of sandstone blocks because of the scarcity of finished lumber. One block to the left is a huge monkey pod tree sheltering the **Gulick-Rowell House**, which dates from 1829. Peter Gulick built the coral block foundation and walls and George Rowell finished it using imported lumber in 1846. It is the best unrestored example of early missionary architecture in the Hawaiian Islands.

Waimea Beach runs for over a mile and a half to the west from Waimea. Then beyond Kikiaola Small Boat Harbor there is another half-mile or so to Oomano Point. The dark sand here does not appeal to visitors, who have so many other beaches to choose from, so the beach will not be described here.

Keep your ears tuned as you walk around Waimea. A number of Niihauans live here, and it is the only place in Hawaii where you will hear Hawaiian used in everyday conversation. They have retained the Tahitian "r" for "l" and "t" for "k", and it is a delight to hear this older form of the language. Their church, **The Hawaiian Church**, is an inconspicuous wooden building on the highway opposite the police station. It was built in 1858 by Reverend Rowell, and services are conducted here in Hawaiian every Sunday. Down Pokole Road is a small park and fishing pier. Near there on the Highway is Yumi's – she makes fabulous fruit turnovers that are usually sold out by noon. Just out of town to the west is the frame of the Waimea Sugar Mill, built in 1885, which was ravaged by Hurricane Iwa. Farther west in the grove of coconut trees, the Kikiaola Land Company is converting original plantation housing into vacation cottages.

Waimea has one fascinating archeological site, the **"Menehune Ditch"** or **Kiki a Ola**, but there is not much to see. You may just want to read about it. The road next to the police station, named "Menehune Road" for the tourists, is marked by a Hawaii Visitors Bureau sign and leads inland to the ditch.

A half mile from the start is an item of interest before you get to the ditch. Turn left at the sign "Waimea Shingon Mission." At the mission are eighty-eight images depicting the sins of man, as at the Kobo Dai Ishi Shrine in Kalaheo. But look above the temple. There are several burial caves in the bluff and all still contain bones.

About 1.2 miles from the highway is a suspension bridge. Park here and walk about 150 feet. To your left is the Kiki a Ola, which means watercourse of Chief Ola. Its not what you can see – its what it signifies. This is the major – almost only – example of cut and dressed stone found in the Hawaiian Islands.

Only about sixty feet of the top of the ditch is still visible because of the thoughtless road construction. When Vancouver came to this spot in 1793, he described the height of the ditch wall as twenty-four feet above the level of the river with a base twenty feet thick. He didn't venture beyond this point but did record that it brought water from an intake on the Waimea River, so must have been some miles in length. He noted that the wall was wide enough on top for the Hawaiians to use as a pathway to the interior, and that the rocks used to build it were quarried seven miles away. The Hawaiians did not have the wheel, so the rocks had to be carried or rolled there on coconut logs – quite a feat! Small wonder the myth of the Menehune was invoked to explain it.

SOUTH SHORE TOUR
KEKAHA TO POLIHALE
MAP #8

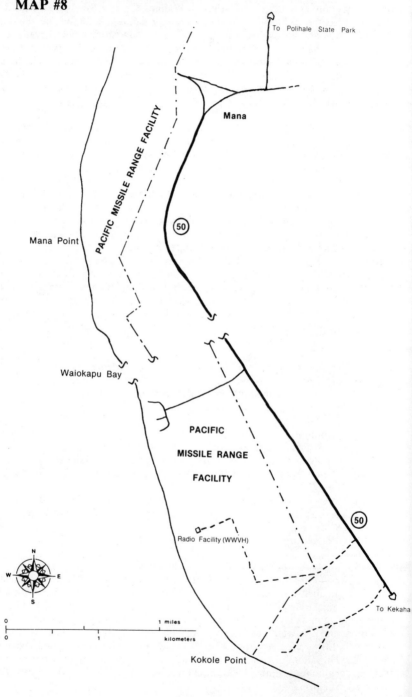

To Polihale State Park

Mana

PACIFIC MISSILE RANGE FACILITY

Mana Point

50

Waiokapu Bay

PACIFIC

MISSILE RANGE

FACILITY

Radio Facility (WWVH)

50

To Kekaha

N
W   E
S

0   1 miles
0   1
kilometers

Kokole Point

There is more to the history of this unprepossessing town. Starting about 1790 it was the center of the sandalwood trade that by 1824 had literally stripped the island of all sandalwood trees. During this period the Hawaiians were forced by their greedy chiefs to leave their taro patches and farms to gather sandalwood, which resulted in terrible famine and thousands of deaths from starvation. Waimea was also the main provisioning port of the early discoverers, and the betrayal of Kaumualii described in the "History" chapter took place here in 1821.

Waimea Canyon Road, sometimes called the Canyon Rim Road, was built in the 1950's and is the newest way to the Waimea Canyon and Kokee areas. It only *looks* older because it is poorly maintained. But it does have less traffic (tour busses are prohibited) than the older Kokee Road out of Kekaha (built in 1910), and some interesting views of the lower canyon, the south shore, and Niihau that are not visible on the older route. We advise going up on Kokee Road and returning on this one.

KEKAHA TO POLIHALE – MAP #8

For now we will continue along Highway 50. Look at the gas gauge – the last gas stations on this side of the island are in Waimea. Halfway between the 24 and 25 mile markers is Kikiaola Small Boat Harbor. It has a lot of use by local residents, but is not of interest to the visitor. Ignore the commercial sign at the start of Kekaha Road across from the boat harbor. It purports to direct you to Waimea Canyon, but its purpose is to take you past such things as an indifferent restaurant, an undistinguished souvenir shop, and the like along Kekaha Road.

As you approach **Kekaha**, there is a clear view of **Niihau** with **Lehua** to the right. What appears to be a separate island is Kawaihoa on the southern point of Niihau, which from Kekaha is just seventeen miles away.

As you round Oomano Point to enter Kekaha, the sand once again becomes lighter and the water clearer at **Kekaha Beach**. **Kekaha Beach Park** is thirty acres in size with a pavilion, restrooms and showers. The beach is beautiful and sunsets are spectacular from here. All of the wide sandy beach along the highway is inviting, but the best place to swim is just beyond Akialoa Road at mile marker 27, where the road diverges from the beach. There is room for parking here, the path to the beach is not over rocks, and the surf has a favorable break on the point. However, the beach is steep with a shorebreak causing a backwash, and there is almost always a current along shore to the east, so caution is advised. Body surfing and body boarding are only possible at the small point, and board surfing is very poor. The beach is hot with little or no shade, so bring your suntan oil and cold drinks.

The first turnoff to the left past Kekaha is a dirt road that leads to the National Guard Rifle Range and a drag strip. It also takes you to the same beach near Kokole Point, as does a second road a little farther on. In fact, this beach is nearly twelve miles long to Nohili Point. The portion from Kokole Point to Nohili Point, seven miles in length, is collectively called **Mana Beach**. The description given for Kekaha Beach also applies to this stretch, except it lacks any facilities. Ignore any guide books that tell you of access via the sanitary landfill road. This is all privately-owned land to the Pacific Missile Range Facility, and there is no beach access from the dump road.

Continuing on Highway 50, at mile marker 30 a road leads to the left with a sign "Radio Station WWVH." This station is maintained by the National Bureau of Standards and entry is prohibited. It is not an ordinary radio station, but transmits weather information and a time signal from its three atomic clocks. You can hear this transmission by dialing 335-4363. The time signal is used by navigators sailing the Pacific to check their chronometers.

Most of the flat land to your right was a swamp until Valdemar Knudsen began draining it in 1856 to raise cattle there. The ancient sea cliffs rise dramatically beyond the plain.

The *Pacific Missile Range Facility* consists of 1,885 acres along the Mana shore, with a complementary facility located on Makaha Ridge a few miles to the north. It is, in effect, a "high-tech" shooting gallery. Extensive sensors and sophisticated computers monitor dummy missiles fired from aircraft, surface ships and submarines. Some test-firing of missiles under development is conducted in an area just north of the airstrip. The Navy is understandably reluctant to allow access to the beach near where the test-firing is taking place or to the airstrip where there are frequent takeoffs and landings. In fact, their own personnel housing area is two miles south of these potentially dangerous operations.

But Bob Curtis, the Commanding Officer, has opened up a portion of Mana Beach near the personnel area to the public. Perhaps once a year the beach may be closed for such operations as a marine amphibious exercise, but otherwise it is always available for public use. You may call ahead (335-4229) to inquire about its availability if you wish, but you can almost always trust your luck and turn in at the main gate just past the 32 mile marker. You will be asked to show evidence of no-fault insurance, your driver's license, sign in, and then allowed entry. Go through the gate, turn left and continue 1.5 miles to "Recarea 3." This is, as we said, Mana Beach, but for some reason this place is called *"Major's Bay"* by board surfers, with *"Major's Point"* to the left. This is a spot for professional surfers only. Swimming is also hazardous here almost all the time because of the strong southward currents, high surf crashing on the shore, and backwash, so no ocean activities are advisable. Sunbathing is the only activity here, and no facilities are available. A little later on when we describe Polihale, we will tell you about the one safe spot on this stretch of beach.

Past the Pacific Missile Range Facility gate, Highway 50 curves inland. Nearby Mana was once a thriving sugar plantation camp, but now is little more than a ghost town. Part of "The Thorn Birds" was filmed here.

A Hawaii Visitors Bureau sign indicates the cane road to take left and follow for five miles to *Polihale State Park*. It almost never rains here, so the three-mile long *Polihale Beach* is a good place to come if it is raining elsewhere. But swimming is even more dangerous than at Mana Beach. We have mentioned the leftward current and the steep shore causing a shorebreak and backwash, but north of Kokole Point the velocity of the current along the beach sometimes reaches three or four knots. When it sweeps out from any small point, it takes swimmers right with it.

One place *is* safe and delightful. At 3.4 miles, the cane road curves right at a sand dune by a large tree. Take the fork to the left and park on the right almost immediately. Don't try to drive on the sand even with a four-wheel drive. It is so soft that only oversize tires will make it. Walk north along the beach until you see a hollow in the coral about the size of a swimming pool. This is *Queen's Pond*, which is clear, calm and safe except in the highest winter surf.

The name *Barking Sands* is sometimes applied loosely to the whole area from Polihale to Kekaha, probably because of the name of the naval facility along much of this shore. However, it is appropriate only for the half-mile long sand dune fifty to sixty feet high north of Nohili Point and the immediately adjacent mile-long beach. *Barking Sands Beach* is the most dangerous of all on this side of the island, so will not be described. The name comes from an interesting phenomenon. When the sand on the dune has the right humidity and salt content, you can shuffle your feet and make the sound of a dog barking – sometimes like a Pekingese, sometimes like a German shepherd.

Polihale State Park is 140 acres in size and has all facilities. Camping requires a State permit. At the north end the dirt road comes to an end at a day use area. About 100 feet beyond this, in the scrub growth on the talus slope, are remnants of *Polihale Heiau*. From here the spirits of the dead entered ''Po'' (the nether world of the Hawaiians), a cavern beneath the ocean offshore. About a hundred yards north of the heiau at the foot of the bluff is *Polihale Spring*. The only way to locate it now is to dig a hole at low tide and fresh water will seep in. It was once important to the Hawaiians as the only source of fresh water for miles around. If you are an archeology buff, a dwelling site where artifacts have been found is in a niche above the heiau. Other housesites and terraces are in Haeleele Valley just south of Polihale Bluff. Another heiau is at the base of the Haeleele Bluff, the *Kapaula Heiau*.

The best-kept secret of Polihale is that tiny Niihau shells can be found on the beach. Most visitors walk right over them because they are too small to see unless you sit down and look for them.

This is the end of the south shore tour, but an even more delightful experience awaits you!

171

WAIMEA CANYON AND KOKEE

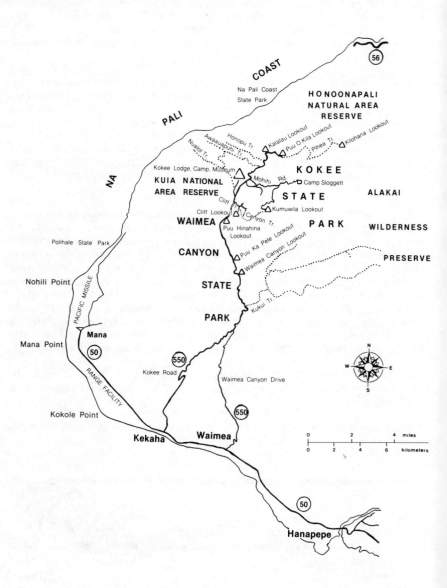

WAIMEA CANYON AND KOKEE TOUR

The trip up to Waimea Canyon and the Kokee area is worth at least a day by itself. If you would like to camp and hike here, a week would not be enough. But most visitors include it as part of a one-day area tour of the south shore, and should set aside at least two or three hours for it. This area is totally untropical and one of the most beautiful on Kauai. Vistas of the multi-hued Waimea Canyon, spectacular panoramas of Na Pali Coast, the exotic ohia lehua, tree ferns, fragrant maile and mokihana, forests of kukui, sugi pine, and koa trees, and swooping tropic birds will be just a few of your rewards.

A few tips first. Bring a bird book and binoculars. Even if you are not a birdwatcher, those you see will intrigue you. The streams in this area are intermittently contaminated by hikers and animals, so the drinking water is not reliably safe. Bring your own beverages or stop at the Kokee Lodge where the water is filtered and hyper-chlorinated. The name Kokee means to bend or wind and the road *is* winding, so those who are susceptible to car sickness are forewarned. The temperature is about ten degrees cooler at the 4,000 foot altitude, even chillier if it is overcast, so bring along a sweater. When the trade winds are blowing, the views often mist in – Kalalau by midmorning and Waimea Canyon by late morning – so go early if you can. When a storm is in the vicinity of Kauai, the whole area may be socked in all day. Call Weather Information (245-6001) to be sure. The Air National Guard Aircraft Control and Warning Station at Kokee (335-6556) will also answer your questions about the weather as a courtesy. If you plan to go off the main road you should have a four-wheel drive vehicle.

To get to the Waimea Canyon/Kokee area, going up take **Kokee Road**, the older access route from Kekaha. This route is about seven miles long and then joins the newer **Waimea Canyon Road** out of Waimea. **Waimea Canyon State Park**, with 1,800 acres, starts just beyond the junction and runs along the edge of the canyon to Puu Hinahina Lookout. Then comes **Kokee State Park**, with 4,345 acres and forty-five miles of trails incorporating Kalalau and Puu o Kila lookouts. Outside of these two parks are various forest reserves under the jurisdiction of the District Forester.

Set your odometer at the start of Kokee Road. From about five miles on you will see the many koa trees toppled by Hurricane Iwa. They look like gray ghosts now. Majestic redwoods begin shortly beyond. From time to time, you also see glimpses of the canyon and the southern coast.

At 7.6 miles you come to the junction with the newer access road. But here is a surprise – the first mile marker after that is 7, when your odometer reads 7.9! This is because the older access road is that much longer, and the mile markers start at the beginning of the *new* route.

The **Iliau Nature Loop** trailhead is at 9.6 miles by your odometer and about halfway between the 8 and 9 mile road markers. The trail is nearly level, only .3 mile long, and takes less than half an hour. There are many species of endemic plants that have been labeled. You will also have an awesome view of the canyon and **Waialae Falls** on the other side. Unfortunately, the area is not well-maintained and many plant labels are missing. The iliau plant along the trail is related to the rare silversword of Haleakala, Maui. From this loop, the **Kukui Trail** is the "short" route to the canyon floor, about two hours down and three up. From there you have a choice of three other trails. None of these will be described on this tour.

The **Waimea Canyon Lookout** is at 11.2 miles by your odometer, or a little past the 10 mile road marker. Here you will have your first good view of Waimea Canyon – one mile wide, ten miles long, and 3,000 feet deep. Some have compared it to the Grand Canyon, but those of us who live on Kauai think of it as just a grand canyon. From here you can see the three main tributary canyons: Poohau, Koaie and Waialae.

At 13.7 miles by odometer, or nearly to the 13 mile road marker, a picnic area is on your left. The side road that goes by this leads to Hale Koa, a Seventh Day Adventist Camp. Opposite is **Puu Ka Pele** itself, and just beyond is the **Puu Ka Pele Lookout**. The name means "Hill of Pele", and this hill is geologically the oldest spot on Kauai. It was here that Hawaiians came to select the best koa trees from the nearby forest to make their canoes. The trees were felled, hauled here and rough-carved, then dragged to the coast for finishing. Traces of the route to Kekaha can still be detected. Stone adzes and other implements used in canoe making can be found near Puu Ka Pele. A heiau about forty feet square and several housesites are on the makai side of the hill.

Next, at 14.6 miles by the odometer, is the **Puu Hinahina Lookout**. It was named for the hill to the east where hinahina plants are abundant.

At 15.1 miles is Halemanu Road, which leads to the start of three trails. The **Cliff Trail** is .1 mile from the end of the road to the **Cliff Overlook**, which we suggest if you have time. The **Canyon Trail** leads to the **Kumuwela Lookout** by way of 800-foot **Waipoo Falls** with pools below it to splash in, but would take at least three hours. The **Black Pipe Trail** starts so far in that we recommend returning another day to hike it. The NASA Tracking Station facilities are on both sides of the road for nearly a mile along here. The ridge on the left is Kaunuohua Ridge where many burial caves have been found.

At about 15.8 miles, down to the right, are privately-owned cabins on land leased from the State. At 16 miles by the odometer, to the right, is Faye Road (pronounced Fy-yuh) which loops back to join the main road after giving access to trails in the **Halemanu Forest**. At 16.4 miles is the ranger station and the turnoff to **Kokee Lodge** and the **Kokee Natural History Museum**. The museum is free (donations accepted) and well worth a visit. The Lodge serves lunch from 11:30 a.m. to 3:30 p.m. daily and has a dozen rental cabins. A green glade is beyond both with a picnic area and space for tent camping and trailers at the far end. The Nature Trail .1 mile long starts between the Museum and the Lodge. Much of the flora of this area can be seen along this trail and its byways, but none is labelled.

Back on Route 55 (550 except in the State Parks), Kumuwela Road to the YWCA's **Camp Sloggett** is opposite the picnic area, and Mohihi Road is just past that opposite the camping area. Methley plums that ripen at the end of May are most abundant along these roads. The roads join together and several trails lead off from them. **Awaawapuhi** and **Honopu** trails to lookout points over Na Pali start from the road on your left along here; the other trail to Na Pali and Nualolo starts near the ranger station.

Next on the left is the 150th Aircraft Control and Warning Squadron of the Hawaii Air National Guard. This is where you may have called to inquire about the weather in Kokee. Wild ginger is abundant beside the road beyond here.

The road divides at mile marker 18. The left fork goes to the **Kalalau Lookout,** and the right takes you one mile farther on to the **Puu O Kila** ("Kila's hill"; Kila was a heroic chief) **Lookout,** with a more dramatic view of Kalalau Valley from a height of 4,120 feet above sea level. For us, this is the most beautiful view on the island. The **Pihea Trail** starts beyond this and leads to a lookout over the **Alakai Swamp** about one mile in. The first part of this trail is on the abandoned Na Pali Coast Road Project which was to lead to Hanalei. We are all thankful that the project was abandoned.

This is the end of our tours of the island of Kauai. We think you will agree that you have seen more natural beauty with more variety than is to be found on any other island of its size in the world.

WHAT TO DO

Kauai offers an almost unlimited number of recreational activities to enjoy. Our suggestions are listed below alphabetically.

BEACHES

Most visitors come here for our beaches. Nature has had more time with Kauai, so we have more sandy shoreline than any of the other Hawaiian Islands.

BEACH INDEX

Virtually all of the beaches listed above were described, with directions, in the chapter "What to See." The rest are described in this chapter under "Snorkeling" or "Surfing."

But more needs to be said about those beaches that are sometimes dangerous. Over one million visitors a year are coming to Kauai now, and most spend at least some time at the beach. Many of our visitors have had experience only in swimming pools or at relatively gentle and protected beaches where there are lifeguards. Tragically, swimmers drown here every year when a little caution could have prevented their deaths. To give you a rough idea of the problem, more than 1,000,000 persons went to the beaches of Southern California *every day* of 1986, with only four deaths from drowning that year. Considerably less than that number visited the beaches of Kauai during *the entire year* of 1986, and eleven drowned! That works out to something like a 1,000 times greater risk here than that in Southern California, which is an area that is fairly representative of most mainland beaches.

OCEAN SAFETY

Let's talk about the dangers. In order to do so, we have to clear up some terms. First of all, there is no such thing as an "undertow." A **backwash** occurs when waves break on a steep shore and the water sweeps back out between waves. The term "undertow" was probably coined by someone who got caught in a backwash just as an incoming wave was breaking over him. Nor is there such a thing as a "riptide." A **rip current**, yes. The word "rip" comes from the word riparian, which means that it resembles a river. Currents along shore do not normally have this characteristic, but those going out to sea often do. So all currents that course seaward like a river are properly called rip currents, no matter what their cause.

Most of the surface currents around Kauai are caused by the prevailing wind acting over hundreds of miles of fetch on the ocean surface. These currents commonly sweep along the east and west shores of Kauai at one to three knots. They are dangerous only if they carry a swimmer into heavy surf, onto sharp coral or other hazard, or if the shoreline deflects the current out to sea – when it may carry a careless swimmer with it. The most dangerous type of current is one with a seaward set, a true rip current. This is the one for which the standard advice is given to swim parallel to shore until it is possible to swim back in.

On Kauai, rip currents are most often caused by a high surf breaking over an offshore reef. This raises the water level inside the reef. The excess water must go back out to sea and always finds an opening through the reef to do so. If the opening is narrow, the seaward current through that opening can easily reach a velocity of three or four knots, and sometimes more.

A good example of this is the opening to the left at Kee Beach. Under calm conditions, the lagoon inside the reef is like a lake, with no current through the opening at all. But we have been there when the surf was breaking ten to twelve feet high over the reef, causing a current out through the opening of five or six knots. If a swimmer is caught in a rip current like this, there is no way to combat it. Even if he stayed calm, let himself be carried out to sea, and then swam parallel to shore, he would then face the task of getting back over the sharp reef with the huge surf pounding on it. His only chance would be to tread water, signal for help, and hope for rescue.

Look for currents carefully before you enter the water. If you are not certain, ask one or two locals who appear to be knowledgeable. A good motto is "if in doubt, stay out." Then test your conclusions by standing for a few moments in knee-deep water. While swimming, look at landmarks ashore frequently and come in at once if it is difficult to remain in place.

Another danger often unforeseen by visitors is the effect of strong winds on *inflatable objects*. The usual precaution advised is that the person using them should do so only where he can get to shore on his own if he were to lose it, or if it were to suddenly deflate. With the trade winds on Kauai sometimes reaching twenty to twenty-five knots during the summer, one additional precaution must be added: Don't use them if the wind is strong and blowing along the shore or out to sea.

One serious hazard that is not expected by most visitors is a *rogue wave*. It is not uncommon for two or more waves to fuse at sea and come ashore with a height at least twice that of the other waves. This does not cause much difficulty for swimmers or surfers, but is extremely hazardous for those walking on rocks and exploring tidepools, especially when it is high tide. People are lost every year this way. Always be careful when you walk close to the surf, keep a sharp lookout, and never turn your back to the oncoming waves.

Never swim alone. If you are not a strong swimmer, it is best to swim only at the two beaches on Kauai where there are full-time lifeguards – Salt Pond Beach Park and Poipu Beach Park. Part-time "contract" guards are sometimes at other beaches. Look to be sure they are there. An empty lifeguard stand won't do you much good.

Many of our visitors want to attain a glistening bronze tan while they are here. There are two immediate problems besides the long-range one of skin cancer. The first is sunburn. Most may not appreciate that in this latitude the sun is stronger than they may be accustomed to. The worst time is from 11:00 a.m. to 3:00 p.m., when the rays are more direct. Until you have had a few days to judge the effect of the sun on your skin, remain in the sun for a limited time only and wear a hat and shirt, or blouse. While in the water you do not feel the infra-red or hot rays of the sun, but the water allows the ultra-violet rays which burn to pass right through. Somewhat the same thing happens on a cloudy day. You know about sunscreens and blocks, so use the ones that work best for you. You will perspire more here, and probably swim more often, so use the water-resistant or "waterproof" kind and reapply it frequently. But here is the second problem. The most common skin disorder affecting visitors, even leading sunburn, is something called Papulovesicular Light Eruption or PVLE. This consists of a lot of bumps and blisters on the skin from long hours in the sun *with* a sunscreen. The screens allow the longer ultraviolet rays right through, which causes this, while screening out the shorter wavelengths that cause sunburn. So a word to the wise.

The sea life on Kauai presents a whole new array of hazards for most visitors. Here are the important ones:

Sea Anemones – These are attached to rocks, and some have stinging cells on their tentacles. It is safest not to touch any unless you are wearing gloves.

A word here that is applicable to all **stinging marine animals.** They have millions of microscopic capsules called nematocysts, each of which has a tiny dart that injects a toxin when stimulated. When you are stung, it is important to remember that many more nematocysts may be on your skin that are not yet stimulated. If you rub the area, you may be stung more – even on the hand you rub with. The best thing to do is destroy the unstimulated nematocysts with white vinegar. Ammonia and unseasoned meat tenderizer also work well. Do not use a tenderizer, however, if you are allergic to papain. If there is no visible part of the stinging marine animal such as tentacles on your skin, and if none of the above remedies are available, scrub the area with wet sand and water. This may help some, but unfortunately most of the toxin will already have been injected into the skin and cannot be removed.

Barracudas – These do not deserve their reputation, at least on Kauai. Here they are seldom more than three feet in length and are mostly curious, so they just circle you. They are easily frightened away.

Clams – The large tridacna clams that grab divers in "B" movies are no threat at all. Ours are small and couldn't hold a finger. The larger ones elsewhere in the tropics close too slowly to be dangerous.

Cone Shells – Most have a small dart at the tip with which they inject venom, and the darts can penetrate gloves. Be careful when handling them. If you are injured by one, see a physician immediately.

Coral – Many kinds of coral are irritating, and we even have some of the worst of all – fire coral – in Hawaiian waters. Stinging corals have nematocysts as described for anemones, and the treatment is the same. A coral abrasion is something else. Proteinaceous toxic material is left in the wound, and this continues to irritate and retard healing for days afterward. This invariably means infection. Scrub the abrasion thoroughly as soon as you can with soap and water, using a soft brush. Then keep an antibiotic ointment and bandage on the abrasion (with frequent changes) until it is healed.

Jellyfish – Some of these are similar to sea anemones, but on rare occasions the worst one is blown in from the ocean – the Portuguese Man-of-War. It has an inflatable blue "sail" and tentacles that may be ten to fifteen feet long. The toxin can cause a severe reaction, even anaphylactic shock. The best and simplest thing to do is avoid them. Leave any beach where you see them lying on the sand or floating on the surface of the water. If you are stung, follow the advice given for anemones and see a physician without delay.

Eels – Moray eels are not usually aggressive, but if you poke your hands in holes in the reef and one is there, it will defend itself and inflict a nasty laceration. Their jaws are extremely strong and they hang on like a bulldog. If you are snorkeling underwater, you may not be able to come up for air.

Sometimes films are shown here on television with divers feeding the eels – even from their mouths! These eels are *not* "trained and friendly" as the films imply. They just know where to grab the tastiest food. On occasion they don't like what is offered and take off a nose or finger instead. Don't ever try this yourself. It is utterly irresponsible to show films such as this to the unsuspecting public.

Sea Snakes – These are rare in Hawaiian waters and they are not aggressive. Just avoid them – their bite is extremely venomous. They are easily distinguished from eels because they breathe air and therefore spend most of their time on the surface.

Sea Urchins – You see these spiny creatures all over the ocean bottom, especially in shallow water. A few have a toxin on their spines. Home remedies such as vinegar or urine do not work. The latter is even a little awkward on a public beach! Try to remove the spines with tweezers – if you can't, see a physician.

Octopus – These have a sharp beak underneath, so either handle them with care or not at all. They are shy and either flee in a black cloud of "ink" or hide. The huge, aggressive ones are only in "B" movies.

Sting Ray – These are not common on Kauai, but in some areas where the water is shallow they may lie partially covered by sand. Always shuffle your feet as you walk in these places. The barb in their tails injects a powerful venom.

Surgeon Fish – There are many species in Hawaiian waters that have a small scalpel on each side of their tails. Handle these with care.

Scorpion Fish – Also called stone fish, they are masters at disguise and lie motionless on the coral or rocks. Their thirteen dorsal spines are hollow with a venom sack at the base on either side. If you should step on one of these, see a physician immediately.

Sharks – We have seventeen species in Hawaiian waters, but only four species are potentially dangerous to man, and they are not numerous. One or two encounters – mostly sightings – occur every year on Kauai. In all the Hawaiian Islands, there have been only seventeen documented attacks in the last 100 years. Your chances of being struck by lightning are greater.

Avoid murky water, be constantly alert when you are snorkeling, and if spearfishing, pull your catch behind you on a long stringer. Do not go in the water with open cuts.

If you should see a shark while in the water, just swim slowly away. Strong, slow, regular movements tend to disinterest them, but any irregularity or fluttering that might resemble an injured fish might attract them. If you are present when someone is attacked by a shark, get them ashore as quickly as possible. Sharks tend to make one slashing attack, then cruise leisurely nearby waiting for the victim to bleed to death before returning to feed, so there is not that much danger to the rescuer. Apply direct pressure to the laceration to stop the bleeding, and call 911 for help. Most of those attacked by sharks who are helped this way survive.

Good reference books to read about Hawaii's fascinating marine life are Ann Fielding's *Hawaiian Reef Fishes*, *Hawaiian Marine Shells*, by E. Alison Kay, and *Seashells of Hawaii* by Stephen Quirk and Charles Wolfe.

BICYCLING

The two-lane belt road around Kauai has bicycle paths in a few locations, but they disappear without warning. This road is narrow, barely accommodating two cars abreast, with variable shoulders and heavy traffic. For these reasons, bicycling on the belt road (Highways 50 and 56) and similar roads is strongly discouraged. However, there are many enjoyable places on Kauai to bicycle and drivers are courteous.

Bicycle rental agencies:

Aquatics Kauai, Kapaa – 822-9213
Peddle & Paddle, Hanalei – 826-9069
South Shore Activities, Poipu – 742-6873
Sheraton Coconut Beach – 822-3455

Bicycle tours are conducted by North Shore Bike Cruise and Snorkel, Inc., Kapaa – 822-1582.

Rental rates are about $10 a day or $50 a week. Bike races are held from time to time during which the traffic is controlled, so these are safe for entrants. If you bring your own bike, several repair shops are on the island.

A good reference book is *Bicycling in Hawaii* by R. Immler.

BIRDWATCHING

Land birds are abundant in Alakai Swamp, reached by the Alakai Swamp Trail. However, most visitors do not care to make the long hike into Alakai. With binoculars, a number of land birds can be seen from the Puu Ka Pele, Puu Kila and Kalalau Lookouts in the Kokee area.

The best place to see marine birds is at the Kilauea National Wildlife Refuge. There are also many marine birds along Na Pali Coast and in the Mahaulepu area on the southern coast.

Water birds can be seen at the Hanalei National Wildlife Refuge and the Huleia National Wildlife Refuge. They are also numerous at the Alekoko Fish Pond, Wailua Reservoir, and Waita Reservoir.

Because Kauai is the only major island in Hawaii that does not have the mongoose, we have more birds here than the other islands. The mongoose is notorious for its depredations on eggs and young nestlings. We would have more birds if dogs and cats were not let loose by residents. Feral goats and pigs also interfere with the natural habitats of land birds.

Three excellent references are the *Audobon Book* listed in the back of this guide, Peterson's *Field Guide to the Western Birds*, which comes with a cassette of bird calls, and *Hawaiian Birdlife*, by Andrew Berger.

BOATING

Boating is a popular activity on Kauai and takes many forms – a Zodiac tour along Na Pali Coast, a snorkel cruise, a catamaran sail, deep sea fishing, sunset sailing, whale watching, and others.

Before we list the firms offering these, we would like to put in a few premonitory paragraphs. The number of boats and operators engaged in this activity has been burgeoning in the last few years, and accidents have increased alarmingly. The United States Coast Guard Marine Safety Office in Honolulu has admitted that its resources are inadequate to regulate boating activities on Kauai, so those enjoying them have to assume some responsibility themselves. The rule is *caveat emptor*.

The most common cause of accidents on Kauai is the decision of a Zodiac captain to set out for Na Pali in unfavorable weather. Some may enter caves on that coast without due precautions for rogue waves, cut too close to the point leaving Hanalei Bay and capsize in the surf, or use excess speed on the return leg of the Na Pali run in the winter. As the boats come crashing down over the high seas, passengers are often injured. Three weeks ago, as we write this, two visitors sustained crushed vertebrae this way. Then we have fishing and dive boats breaking down or springing leaks at sea without emergency equipment on board.

Because of this trend, we decided to list only United States Coast Guard-inspected boats with licensed operators, but we found that the Privacy Act prevents our getting most of the information we needed.

Here is what you have to know for your own safety. Any vessel that carries more than six passengers commercially must be inspected regularly by the Coast Guard, but those carrying six or fewer are not legally required to have any inspection whatsoever. Any reputable operator of a boat that carries six or fewer passengers has a voluntary inspection by the Coast Guard Auxiliary. Therefore, *any* boat you go on should have been inspected by one or the other and have a current inspection decal displayed on the vessel. Look for it and don't go on a boat that does not have one. This is not the sticker on the bow with the current year – that is the registration tag. The inspection decal is larger, has a Coast Guard or Auxiliary seal on it, and should be located somewhere amidships. Both inspections are thorough and cover seaworthiness, the number of Coast Guard-approved flotation devices (life jackets), fire extinguishers and other emergency equipment.

Watch out for tricky talk – only *devices* are "Coast Guard approved." You *buy* them that way. Vessels are *certificated* and operators are *licensed* – neither are "approved."

The second thing to look for is evidence of operator competence. The law requires that operators of vessels carrying *any number* of passengers commercially must be tested and licensed by the U.S. Coast Guard. Further, the original copy of the operator's license must be posted and clearly visible whenever that operator is in charge of a vessel carrying passengers. In cases where this is not practical, the original license must be immediately available and presented upon inquiry by any passenger. Always ask to see the license of the operator before you get on board. It may be awkward, but you owe it to yourself and others. We show up half an hour early, chat with the operator first, then ask.

If you suspect a violation, call or write Captain C.W. Grey, Officer in Charge, Marine Inspection, U.S. Coast Guard Marine Safety Office, 433 Ala Moana, Honolulu, HI 96813-4909, telephone 808-541-2063. The life you save may be your own.

Although we couldn't obtain the complete information we wanted, we did spend a considerable time looking into boating activities and learned a few things. First, all of the boats going to the Fern Grotto on the Wailua River are certificated and operated by licensed captains. Second, no fishing vessel or dive boat on Kauai takes more than six passengers, and none of those we looked at were voluntarily inspected by the U.S. Coast Guard Auxiliary. Only about half of these operators were licensed.

As a result of our looking around and asking questions, we assembled a partial list of firms with both certificated boats *and* licensed operators, but it should be emphasized that this list is not complete:

Blue Odyssey Adventures - Operates the "Blue Odyssey", certificated for twenty passengers. Snorkeling, fishing. Out of Hanalei, 826-7568.

Blue Water Sailing - A 42' ketch-rigged sailing yacht, the "Lady LeAnne II" is certificated for ten passengers. Snorkeling, sunset sails, whale watching, sport fishing, exclusives on request. Sails out of Port Allen October through May, and out of Hanalei Bay June through September. Office in Kapaa, 822-0525, or 335-6440.

Captain Andy's Sailing Adventures - A trimaran, "The Cetacean II", certificated for twenty passengers. Snorkeling, sailing, sunset cruises, sightseeing. Out of Kukuiula Harbor, office in Kapaa, 822-7833.

Fantasy Island Adventures - Two inflatable craft certificated for seventeen and twenty passengers. Snorkeling, sightseeing. Out of Kukuiula Harbor, 742-6636.

Hawaiian World and Seascape - The "Jubilee", certificated for forty-two passengers, and a Zodiac certificated for eighteen. Scuba diving, fishing, sightseeing Out of Hanalei, 826-9045.

Lady Ann Cruises - The "Lady Ann", certificated for forty-four passengers. Sightseeing, snorkeling, fishing. Out of Nawiliwili Harbor, 245-8538.

Na Pali Adventures - One Zodiac, "Hawaiian World", certificated for eighteen passengers. Na Pali tours and whale watching. Out of Hanalei, 826-6804.

Na Pali Kai Tours - Two Zodiacs certificated for thirty passengers each. Na Pali Coast tours primarily, but sometimes operates out of Port Allen in rough weather. Office in Kapaa, 822-3553.

Na Pali Zodiac - This was the first company on Kauai to offer Na Pali tours on Zodiac craft, and is by far the most experienced. Clancy Greff, "Captain Zodiac", has six Zodiacs which are certificated for seventeen passengers each, and is adding more boats. Out of Makua Beach, 826-9371.

Ocean Ventures - Two Zodiacs, each certificated for sixteen passengers. Snorkeling and other tours. Out of Hanalei, 826-6151.

Playtime Charters - The "Dena D", certificated for twenty-eight passengers. Snorkeling, whale watching. Out of Port Allen, 335-5074.

Sea Kauai - Two Zodiacs, each certificated for seventeen passengers. Na Pali tours. Out of Hanalei, 828-1488.

Approximately 90% of the boating done by visitors to Kauai is a **Na Pali cruise**, so we will offer some tips on this:

1. It is best to go in the summer months when the ocean is calmer, caves can be entered, and snorkeling is possible at deserted beaches. October to March trips started only a few years ago because of the demand, but at times during these months the trips are truly hazardous.

2. Try to go on the twenty-three foot Zodiacs - they ride better than the smaller ones.

3. Sit on the starboard (right) side so you won't get a "crick" in your neck. Most of the sightseeing is on the outward bound leg.

4. Look for whales in season, flying fish, turtles and porpoises. You may be the first to spot them while the operator is otherwise occupied.

5. The morning tours are usually calmer than the afternoon ones, but the all-day tour with lunch on a lonely beach may be worth the bouncy ride back.

6. If you have well-fitting fins, mask and snorkel, bring them. The ones supplied leave something to be desired.

7. Bring your camera. Plastic bags are provided to protect it and other personal articles.

In August of 1987, the Na Pali Queen, a 130-foot boat capable of carrying 150 passengers, arrived on Kauai to go into service on the Na Pali run out of Port Allen. This is a six-hour luxury ride, air-conditioned, with buffet lunch and open bar on the return trip. The cost is $100 per person. We cannot comment because we have not yet taken the trip. Telephone 335-5078 for information.

Whale watching is the next most common boating activity. Every winter starting in November, humpback whales from arctic waters begin to arrive off the southern shore of Kauai to mate and give birth. Most go on to Maui and the Big Island, but about sixty stay and cavort in our waters. In May and June they begin returning to their arctic feeding grounds. Virtually everything that floats offers whale watching during the season.

Federal Law protects this endangered species from any action that disturbs them. For information on their protection, contact the National Marine Fisheries Service, P.O. Box 3830, Honolulu, HI 96812, 808-946-2181.

CONCERTS

The Kauai Concert Association schedules six or seven concerts a year featuring well-known artists. Watch the paper or television information channel.

FISHING

Besides shore fishing, which is very popular with local residents on Kauai, other types of fishing are available. Rainbow trout fishing is allowed in eight Kokee streams and the Puu Loa Reservoir the first sixteen days of August and thereafter on weekends through the end of September. Certain reservoirs are open for small-mouth bass fishing year-round. For information on freshwater fishing, write the Division of Aquatic Resources, P.O. Box 1671, Lihue, Kauai, HI 96766, or call 808-245-4444. Bass Guides of Kauai, 808-822-1405, is a private organization that conducts fishing excursions to out-of-the-way reservoirs.

Another type is deep sea fishing, and about a dozen firms operate such boats. Look on our list above or in the yellow pages under "Boats for Charter" and "Fishing Parties." On Kauai, a fishing license is required for freshwater fishing, but not for saltwater fishing.

Three good reference books are C.M. Morita's *Freshwater Fishing in Hawaii*, *Modern Hawaiian Gamefishing*, by J. Rizzuto, and *Shore Fishing in Hawaii*, by Edward Hosaka.

Equipment and supplies can be purchased or rented at several places on Kauai.

FOLK/SQUARE DANCING

Folk dancing at the Kalaheo Neighborhood Center on Mondays at 7:30 p.m.; square dancing at the Lihue Neighborhood Center on Fridays at 7:30 p.m.

GARDEN TOURS

Moir Gardens, Poipu – Six acres of cacti and succulents. 10:00 a.m. daily. Free. Telephone 742-6411.

Olo Pua Gardens, Kalaheo – Recently closed for tours, but may resume so information is provided. Twelve and one-half acres. Tours were formerly Monday, Wednesday and Friday, 9:30 a.m., 11:30 a.m., and 1:30 p.m. Admission $6.00. Reservations. Telephone 332-8182.

Pacific Tropical Botanical Garden, Lawai – 286 acres. Two and one-half hour van and walking tour of the Garden and the Allerton Estate. Tours Monday through Friday, 9:00 a.m. and 1:00 p.m. Currently, admission is $10.00 per person (membership is $25.00, which also allows you to visit the 1,000 acre Limahuli Garden, in Haena.) Reservations *are* required. Telephone (808) 332-7361, but it is best to write two or three weeks ahead to P.O. Box 340, Lawai, Kauai, HI 96765. A good reference book to read about the Garden is *Queen Emma and Lawai*, by David Forbes.

Smith's Tropical Paradise, adjacent to the Wailua Marina – 30 acres with a Japanese garden, Filipino and Polynesian villages. Open 8:30 a.m. to 4:30 p.m. daily. The present entrance fee is $3.00 for a walking tour and $5.00 for a narrated tram ride. No reservations required. Call 822-4654 for information.

If you would like to learn more about Hawaii's unique plant and floral life, excellent books to read are *Ethnobotany of Hawaii*, by Beatrice H. Krauss, *Hawaiian Flowers & Flower Trees*, by Loraine Kuck and Richard Tongg, and *Trailside Plants of Hawaii's National Parks*, by Charles H. Lamoreaux.

GLIDERS/SAILPLANES

Call Sailplanes Kauai, 335-5446.

GOLF

Kauai has four golf courses, and all are open to the public:

Kukuiolono Golf Course, Kalaheo – Nine holes. Wide fairways and few traps. Beautiful view. Relaxed atmosphere. Green fee is $5, carts (optional) $5. Telephone 332-9151.

Kiahuna Golf Club, Poipu – Eighteen holes, par seventy. Designed by Robert Trent Jones, Jr. Windy, narrow fairways. Green fee is $50 including cart. Telephone 742-9595.

Wailua Golf Course, Wailua – Eighteen holes. Municipal, but an excellent course. Lots of sand and water hazards. Green fee is $10 weekdays, $11 weekends. Carts (optional) $11.50. Telephone 245-2163.

Princeville Makai, Princeville – Twenty-seven holes consisting of three nine-hole courses that can be played in any eighteen-hole combination. All designed by Robert Trent Jones, Jr. Tight fairways, lots of hazards. Green fee is $44 for non-residents, $27 for those staying in Princeville, carts (mandatory) $26. Telephone 826-3580. A new nine-hole course is being added as we go to press.

The *Westin Kauai Resort*, Nawiliwili – opened in September, 1987. One Jack Nicklaus-designed eighteen-hole course is expected to be ready by February, 1988. A second eighteen-hole course of professional calibre with ample gallery space will open later in 1988. Green fee will be in the $50-$60 range and carts will probably be required, rental rate unknown. Telephone 245-5050.

If you have difficulty obtaining tee times, or want any other specialized service, contact: *Golf Services Unlimited* in Wailua, telephone 822-0522.

HEALTH CLUBS

There are four health clubs on the island:

Hanalei Athletic Club, Princeville – Telephone 826-7333.
Kauai Athletic Club, Lihue – Telephone 245-7877.
Poipu Beach Fitness Center, Waiohai Resort, Poipu – Telephone 742-9391.
The Westin Kauai Resort, Nawiliwili – Telephone 245-5050.

All of the above may be used for a daily fee.

HELICOPTER TOURS

As we write this, sixteen firms offer helicopter tours of Kauai. There were only three as recently as 1979. A similar increase is seen on the other islands. The whirlybird may soon be designated the official State bird of Hawaii! Last year, 150,000 visitors enjoyed helicopter flights on Kauai.

Although a helicopter tour of this island might well be one of the most spectacular experiences of your life, a dark side does exist. There have been twelve commercial helicopter crashes in Hawaii during the last sixteen months, with six deaths and twenty-three injuries. This contrasts with just four crashes in the entire previous decade. On Kauai, two accidents in 1986 alone injured eight people.

Some companies are cutting down on their pilot training and maintenance (two of the largest firms on Kauai have recently been cited for this by the FAA), some take chances on the weather and flight patterns, and others have a high pilot turnover rate.

In 1986, the FAA declared the helicopter operations out of Lihue Airport to be "unsafe." But Peter Bechner, manager of the FAA's Flight Standards District Office in Honolulu, added "We are not a criminal enforcement department." The State cannot directly control such operations because of the overriding Federal Airspace Law, but *could* control them through its authority to lease heliports with appropriate contracts. It just has not been done. Furthermore, it takes years to learn how to fly above the unusual terrain of Kauai, and nearly as long to learn enough about the island to make the narration interesting.

For all these reasons, we decided to recommend just one helicopter firm. **Jack Harter** operates a one-man, one-helicopter operation. He was the first on Kauai, having started in 1962, has a perfect safety record, and his helicopter maintenance is meticulous. His wife, Beverly, handles the business end. He makes only three flights per day, and insists that they be an hour and a half in length in order to cover all points of interest. He is careful in flight and will cancel and re-schedule if the weather is marginal or worse. He is also the most knowledgeable helicopter pilot on the flora, fauna and history of Kauai. Because he is not interested in increasing the size of his operation, he has never advertised.

You can call when you get here (245-3774), but he is usually well booked-up, so it is best to call from your home two or three weeks ahead of time or write P.O. Box 306, Lihue, Kauai, HI 96766. If you decide to go with another helicopter firm, two reliable ones are Will Squyres and South Sea.

Once in any office, be sure to look for the FAA Certificate of Approval on the wall. By law, all certified carriers must display this. We are sometimes asked about an "air-taxi" certificate, apparently because another guidebook mentions this, but there is no such thing.

If you have any safety questions, call the FAA office in Honolulu, 808-836-0615.

What may be a fabulous tour (we have not taken it yet) has just started as we go to press. Bruce Robinson has formed **Niihau Helicopter, Inc.** and makes helicopter flights from Burns Field in Hanapepe to the "Forbidden Isle" of Niihau twice daily. The flights tour Niihau but stay away from the one town so as not to disturb the inhabitants. The helicopters land but passengers cannot leave the landing site. This is the first and only firm to use the much safer twin-engine Augusta 109. Each flight is two hours in length and includes either a Na Pali Coast or Waimea Canyon tour. The cost is $235. Telephone 338-1234 for information.

For about half the cost you can take a fixed-wing airplane tour of the island. This is safer than the single-engine helicopter flights with two "ifs": If they use a twin-engine airplane and if they do not try stunts like flying into the canyons and zooming the ridges.

The two companies on Kauai offering these flights are:

Garden Island Aviation – Flies a twin-engine Cessna, telephone 245-1844.

Blue Sky Aviation – Flies a single-engine Cessna out of both Lihue Airport and Princeville Airport, telephone 828-1344. A crash last year killing all aboard that may have violated both "if's" above discourages us from recommending this firm until the results of the investigation are known.

Some companies based at Honolulu International Airport have fixed-wing flights to all islands, with short stopovers on some. See your travel agent for details regarding these.

HIKING AND CAMPING

This section is for the serious hiker, so it includes camping. The first thing to do is obtain information. Write the Hawaii Geographic Society, P.O. Box 1698, Honolulu, HI 96806, and ask for their information packet. The present price is $6.00. A good book on the subject is by Robert Smith, *Hiking Kauai*, but his times required for hiking the trails are not always accurate and since it was written in 1977, it describes some trails that are now closed. It is available at local bookstores and also may be ordered from the Hawaii Geographic Society for $7.00. A better book, Craig Chisolm's *Hawaiian Hiking Trails*, describes fewer Kauai trails, but these are sufficient for the visitor.

The Hawaiian Trail and Mountain Club, P.O. Box 2238, Honolulu, HI 96804, or telephone 808-734-5515, is mostly concerned with group hikes on Oahu but they have an excellent information kit applicable to all islands. The present price is $1.00. The Sierra Club has a chapter on Kauai – for information write The Sierra Club, Kauai Group, P.O. Box 3412, Lihue, Kauai, HI 96766.

In addition, several organizations conduct hiking trips on all islands:

Wilderness Hawaii – P.O. Box 61692, Honolulu, HI 96822.
Pacific Quest, Inc. – P.O. Box 2, Haleiwa, HI 96712.
Sea Trek Hawaii – P.O. Box 1585, Kaneohe, HI 96744.
Paradise Isles Adventures, Inc. – 501 Lilikoi Lane, Haiku, HI 96708.

Good maps are essential. The University of Hawaii Press Reference Map of Kauai is the basic one for roads and general orientation. This is available from the Hawaii Geographic Society and bookstores on Kauai. The eleven U.S.G.S. Quadrangle Topographic Maps are more detailed but not designed for hikers. They can be purchased at several locations on Kauai or from Maps and Miscellaneous, 404 Piikoi Street, Suite 213, Honolulu, HI 96814, or Pacific Map Center, 94-529 Ukee Street, #7, Waipahu, HI 96797. Maps that show the hiking trails can be obtained from the State Division of Forestry, P.O. Box 1671, Lihue, Kauai, HI 96766, and the Division of State Parks, same address.

For camping along the Na Pali Coast, at Polihale, or in the glade near the Kokee Museum, a State permit, which is free, must be obtained from the Division of State Parks. For camping elsewhere in Kokee, permits are issued by the Division of Forestry and are also free. Permits for camping in the County beach parks are issued by the Department of Parks and Recreation for a small fee. Addresses for all are given in the chapter "Obtaining Helpful Information."

Some precautions. For longer hikes, bring at least one canteen of water per person and carry tablets to treat the water in the streams. Take along a small backpack, even for a day hike, containing food, matches, whistle, unbreakable mirror, knife, first-aid kit and flashlight. A compass is of limited value because of the terrain. A long-sleeved shirt, a windbreaker, and long trousers are all good ideas. Appropriate footwear is essential, along with good socks. Be sure to check the weather prediction before you start out and allow ample time to reach your destination. Always hike with at least two companions, one of whom is familiar with the trail, unless it is a well-used one where other hikers are frequently encountered. Inform family and friends of your departure time, your estimated arrival time, and your itinerary.

Try never to be on the trail when darkness approaches. In this latitude, darkness comes quickly and you should not move once your visibility is impaired. Remember that all volcanic rock on Kauai is crumbly and may give way underfoot.

Underbrush can mask a hole in the trail or a precipitous dropoff. Stay on established trails at all times. Keep yourself oriented by frequent reference to your map. Watch for flash floods around streams during rainy season. If one occurs, seek high ground immediately and wait for the crest to subside.

A lightweight backpacking stove is a good idea. The wood on the ground is often wet and campfires are not allowed unless you can extinguish it with water when you are through. Never taste or eat any strange fruit or seed. Many of these resemble fruits you know but are poisonous. And always carry out everything you carry in.

The one store on Kauai for hiking and backpacking equipment and supplies is Hanalei Camping and Backpacking, Inc., in the Ching Young Village in Hanalei, telephone 826-6664. Most equipment that you need can be rented or purchased there.

Here are our favorite trails.

WAIMEA CANYON AREA:

The Kukui Trail – Rather strenuous, but it is the shortest route into Waimea Canyon. About five miles round trip. It starts off the Iliau Loop Trail and through a 2,000 foot drop takes you to the canyon floor. Although the first part of the trail is well-maintained, it is overgrown on the second. Follow the cairns and quarter-mile markers carefully. The views of Waimea Canyon and Waialae Falls are spectacular. At a widened area, a ninety-degree turn to the left down a barren hillside leads to Wiliwili Camp next to the river, where there is a large swimming hole.

The Koaie Canyon Trail – About six miles round-trip, and easier than the Kukui Trail. It starts at the end of the Kukui Trail at Wiliwili Camp. The name of the canyon comes from the koaie tree, which resembles the koa tree. Its hard wood was used by the Hawaiians to make spears. You pass by ancient Hawaiian rock walls, terraced areas and the remains of old housesites. There are pools along Koaie stream in which you can splash to cool off. Watch for flash floods. At the trail's end is a secluded shelter and a larger pool nearby.

TO OVERLOOK THE ALAKAI SWAMP:

The Pihea Lookout Trail – About six miles round trip and somewhat strenuous. The start is at Puu o Kila Lookout. Views of Kalalau along the first half-mile and at 1.1 miles, the Pihea Lookout offers a dramatic view of Alakai Swamp. Along the way are fragrant mokihana trees, maile vines and beautiful ohia lehua trees. The trail ends at Mohihi Road.

The Kawaikoi Stream Trail – About 2.5 miles round-trip and not very strenuous. The trailhead is 2.5 miles past the State Park headquarters. Take Mohihi Road (driveable in a passenger car when it is dry) to the sign "Sugi Grove." The trail starts amid Japanese sugi pines (cedar) and redwoods, goes along the south side of Kawaikoi Stream, loops, and returns on the north side. Sugi Grove is a great place to picnic.

OVERLOOKING NA PALI COAST:

The Awaawapuhi Trail – About six miles round-trip and strenuous. Much of it has not been cleared since Hurricane Iwa, so caution is advised. The trailhead is 1.5 miles past the State Park headquarters at telephone pole number 1-4/2P/152 on the left side of the road. This trail offers the most dramatic views of Na Pali Coast of any. A loop return is possible on the Nualolo Trail which intersects it at the three mile point. About .3 mile beyond the intersection is a lookout 3,000 feet above Na Pali Coast. You should be cautioned that footing is unstable here – the first drop is over 2,000 feet!

HANALEI VALLEY:

The Hanalei River Trail – Starts at the end of the Hanalei Valley Road in Hanalei Valley. Stay on the trail and don't stray into the Wildlife Refuge. You will be hiking through taro fields, and mango, guava, orange, and pomelo trees along the way. There are two stream crossings and a bamboo forest before you arrive at a beautiful glade by a stream perfect for picnicking.

SHORE HIKE:

Start at Moloaa and end at Kilauea five miles later by way of Kaakaanui Beach and Waipake Beach. Beautiful beaches and coastal views. It is best to wear tabis (reef walkers) – there is some wading and rock hopping.

A shorter hike, just over a mile, starts at Kauapea Beach and goes along a beautiful shoreline past waterfalls to Kalihiwai.

STREAM HIKE:

Start where Waioli Stream crosses Highway 56, and go as far as you like. You pass by ancient Hawaiian rock walls, dikes and irrigation ditches. The flowers and bird life are fabulous. You will be in the stream a lot, so tabis are the best footwear for this hike.

SCENIC HIKE:

The Kuilau Ridge Trail – This is the most scenic trail on the island and about four miles round-trip. Starts about a mile beyond the University of Hawaii Agricultural Experimental Station on Route 580. It passes a picnic site at one and a 1-1/4 miles, then climbs a ridge through hala, ti, and wild orchids, and past innumerable small waterfalls to a viewpoint near where Opaekaa Stream starts.

AND THE MOST DRAMATIC OF ALL:

The Kalalau Trail – This is the original Hawaiian trail, with very little improvement, and it begins at Kee Beach where Highway 56 ends. About one-half mile from the start is a spectacular view of Kee Beach one way and of the rugged Na Pali Coast the other. At one mile is a small spring, but don't be tempted to drink. Hanakapiai Valley is approximately two miles in. During the summer **Hanakapiai Beach** is beautiful, but during the winter there may be little or no sand. At all times the surf is extremely treacherous with a strong east-to-west current, so never swim there.

The real reward is hiking two miles inland to the **Hanakapiai Falls** and pool. Note the weather before you start because of the danger of flash flooding. The first quarter mile goes along the stream and is easy. The first crossing is at three-quarters of a mile. If it is difficult to cross there, it is best to turn back. The three crossings up ahead are even more difficult. The valley is narrow and the trail follows the stream, so you can't get lost. In the lower area you will see old taro terraces and rock walls. A little farther in are the ruins of an old coffee mill. The last half mile is the most strenuous, but the most entrancing. The lush green growth, pools and small water-falls will lure you on, and when you finally get to the Hanakapiai Falls which cascade in three tiers down 300 feet into a natural pool, you will receive your reward. Bathe in the pool below the falls only briefly because of the danger of falling rocks. One person has been killed here by one. If you want to lounge a while, find another pool away from the falls.

The trail is more strenuous to Hanakoa, and that four miles is serious hiking with switchbacks for the first mile. Seasoned hikers camp overnight at Hanakapiai and take this stretch in the cool of the morning. Watch for falling rocks. The first view of Hanakoa Valley is 4-3/4 miles from the start at Kee. There is no beach here, only a small rocky cove. The rain and mosquitoes discourage camping at Hanakoa. One friend of ours who tried it zipped her sleeping bag all the way up and used her snorkel to breathe. She didn't tell us how the mosquitoes tasted.

The next five miles is also strenuous through endless switchbacks and the trail is hazardous. At times it is two feet wide with a 1,000 foot drop. By now it is after-noon, warmer, and you are tired. But the views are breathtaking. After the six mile marker, the area becomes increasingly more arid. Then the drop into Kalalau Valley and a soak in the stream. **Kalalau Beach** is wide and beautiful in the summer, but almost disappears in the winter. Don't swim at any time. The best place to cool off is in the waterfall at the west end.

The next day you may feel like hiking to Big Pool, with its water slide, and exploring the valley. Beyond Kalalau, and accessible only by sea, are the valleys of Honopu, Awaawapuhi and Nualolo, among others. A fine beach is at **Nualolo Kai**.

There is one professional hiking guide on Kauai:

Local Boy Tours – P.O. Box 3324, Lihue, Kauai, HI 96766, telephone 822-7919.

To complete the camping picture, trailer camping is allowed only at Polihale and Kokee. To rent trailer campers, contact the following:

Beach Boy Campers – P.O. Box 3208, Lihue, Kauai, HI 96766, telephone 245-9211.

Holo Holo Campers, Inc. – P.O. Box 1604, Lihue, Kauai, HI 96766, telephone 245-4592.

HORSEBACK RIDING

We have two stables on Kauai:

CJM Country Stables, Poipu – Telephone 245-6666.

Po'oku Stables, Hanalei – Telephone 826-6777.

For those staying at the Kahili Mountain Cabins, horses are available there.

HUNTING

Feral pigs, goats, black-tailed deer, pheasants, quail and partridge are the main game on Kauai. For information, write or call the Hawaii Department of Land and Natural Resources, Division of Forestry and Wildlife, P.O. Box 1671, Lihue, Kauai, HI 96766, telephone 245-4433.

JET/WATER SKIING/PARASAILING

Kauai Jet Ski Rentals – This is the only rental outlet, telephone 822-9240. Those who do this should be aware that Kauai is a quiet place and visitors come for the peace and natural beauty. Jet skiing is offensive to residents and visitors alike, so please be considerate.

Adventures Unlimited of Kauai, Lihue – Telephone 245-8766, offers water skiing and parasailing.

Terheggen International Ski Club, Kapaa – Telephone 822-3574, water skiing.

Water Ski Kauai, Kapaa – Telephone 822-3388.

KAYAKS

Island Adventures, Nawiliwili – The major firm offering guided tours of Na Pali coast, the Huleia River, to Kipu Kai, and to other areas, telephone 245-9662.

Beach Activities Center, Sheraton Princeville Hotel – Offers a trip up the Wailua River, telephone 826-6851.

Kayak Kauai – offers inflatable kayaks for rent as well as tours, telephone 826-9844.

Peddle & Paddle, Hanalei – Canoes are available for rent, telephone 826-9069.

MOPEDS

Mopeds are available at:

Adventures Unlimited, Lihue – Telephone 245-8766
Honda Two Wheels, Kapaa – Telephone 822-7283
Peddle & Paddle, Hanalei – Telephone 826-9069
Rent-a-Jeep, Lihue – Telephone 245-9622
South Shore Activities, Poipu – Telephone 742-6873

Visitors are cautioned against using the main belt road (Highways 50 and 56) because of the narrow road, heavy traffic, and unreliability of the shoulders in event of emergency. Serious accidents occur frequently. Try to find byways with low hills.

MOUNTAIN TOURS

Four-wheel drive tours of out-of-the-way places in the Kokee area are conducted by Kauai Mountain Tours, telephone 245-7224.

MOVIES

Kauai has three movie theatres:

Plantation Cinemas 1 and 2 – A twin theatre in the Coconut Plantation Marketplace, Wailua, 822-9391.
Kilauea Theatre and Social Hall, Kilauea, 828-1722.
Kukui Grove Cinemas 1 & 2 – A twin theatre adjacent to the Kukui Grove Shopping Center, 245-5055.

Most of the movies are the horror, shoot-em-up and car-chase type, but some good ones are shown, too. Watch the paper or call for current program information.

VCR's and video movies are available for rent at many outlets and offer a better selection.

Sometimes excellent free movies are shown at neighborhood centers and branch libraries. Watch the paper for schedules.

MUSEUMS

Grove Farm Homestead, Lihue – Described more completely in "What to See." Tours are two and one-half hours, conducted by docents on Mondays, Wednesdays and Thursdays at 10:00 a.m. and 1:15 p.m. Small admission charge. Reservations are required and accepted up to three months ahead of time by writing Grove Farm Homestead, P.O. Box 1631, Lihue, Kauai, HI 96766, or telephone 808-245-3202. An informative book about Grove Farm Homestead, written by Bob Krauss and William Alexander, is *Grove Farm Plantation*.

The Hawaiian Trading and Cultural Center, Hanalei – Hawaiiana. Open daily 10:00 a.m. to 5:00 p.m. Free. Telephone 826-7222.

The Hanalei Museum, Hanalei – Hawaiian artifacts and old photographs. Open daily 10:00 a.m. to 5:00 p.m. Free. Telephone 826-6783.

The Kauai Museum, Lihue – This is the principal museum on Kauai and was described in "What to See." It has ethnic heritage as well as geological exhibits, with a featured display. Located at 4428 Rice Street, Lihue, Kauai, HI, 96766. Open Monday through Friday, 9:30 a.m. to 4:30 p.m., Saturday 9 a.m. to 1 p.m. Small admission charge, children free. Telephone 245-6931.

Kilohana Plantation, Puhi – A restored 1930's plantation estate with agricultural exhibits, and a 19th century plantation camp. Open daily from 9:00 a.m. to 4:30 p.m. Free. Telephone 245-7818.

Kokee Natural History Museum, Kokee State Park – Open daily from 10:00 a.m. to 4:00 p.m. Geographic maps of Kauai and exhibits of Kauai's endemic bird and plant life. Free, but donations are accepted. Telephone 335-9975.

The Waioli Mission House – Described more extensively in "What to See." Dates back to 1830. Open Tuesdays, Thursdays and Saturdays from 9:00 a.m. to 3:00 p.m. A half-hour guided tour is provided by a volunteer docent. Free, but donations are welcome. No reservations necessary. Telephone 245-3202. *Waioli Mission House* by Barnes Riznick is an excellent book to read if you are interested in learning more about the House.

RUNNING/JOGGING

Although there are marvelous places to walk almost everywhere on Kauai, we are talking about exercise here. Race-walking, which looks like most of the work is done by the hips and elbows, would fit in. There is some disagreement about the definitions of running versus jogging. It all depends on how fast you go – as one of us stated in another book we wrote, running is when you take less than ten minutes to do a mile; jogging is the term if you need a few more minutes than that!

Good routes are to be found in all areas. Hotels, condos and athletic clubs can advise you about the best ones near where you are staying. Be sure to keep well-hydrated and take precautions against the sun. Carry identification with you and run on the road shoulders facing traffic whenever possible. No solitary runners that we are aware of have been molested on Kauai, but this sometimes occurs on Oahu in isolated places.

Once again you are cautioned about our belt road, Highways 50 and 56. These are narrow, with heavy traffic, and the shoulders frequently disappear. We advise that you run or jog elsewhere. If you are caught on *any* road with a car coming, step off the pavement for your own safety. The roads were designed and built for four-wheel vehicles, not runners, and you will never win a confrontation.

A good reference is *Hawaii, a Running Guide*, by Murchie and Ryan.

SHOPPING

Kukui Grove Shopping Center is the largest shopping center on Kauai. It, together with nearby Lihue, is where the local residents do their shopping. If you want an everyday item, try *Gems, Sears, Longs, JCPenney* and *Woolworth* in this area. But there are also shops here that appeal to visitors. *See You In China* has jewelry, vacation wear and other things. *Linda's Creation* has coral jewelry. *Stones Gallery* is probably the best art gallery on the island. *Rainbow Books* and *Walden Books* are the two major bookstores on Kauai.

In the Hanalei area, the *Ching Young Village Shopping Center* has two places of interest: *Hanalei Camping and Backpacking*, and *On The Road to Hanalei*, which has Pacific Island Kapa (tapa) cloth.

Ola's, near the Hanalei Dolphin Restaurant, is a fine small art gallery featuring local artists and craftsmen.

The Princeville Gallery, featuring local artists, in the Princeville Center. Also at the Princeville Center is *Kauai Kite and Hobby*, with a large selection of colorful kites and windsocks, and *Toucan's* for resort wear.

In Kilauea, *Kong Lung Store* should not be missed. We call it our "Gumps of the Pacific." Designer muumuus and other items of clothing are available here. It is perhaps the finest gift store on the island, and immediately adjacent is a creative florist and a fine jeweler. *The Lighthouse Gallery* next to Kong Lung Store is also worth a visit.

The Sheraton Princeville has some interesting shops, including a *Gems Creations* and a branch of *Kahn Gallery*.

The Coconut Plantation Marketplace has over seventy stores, most of which are tourist-oriented. A few are a touch above the rest: *Kahn Gallery*, *Reyn Spooner*, with traditional Hawaiian clothes, and branches of *Liberty House*, *Andrades* and *McInerny's*. Others that deserve a browse are *Kauai Gold*, *The Poster Shop*, *Sandalworks*, *Plantation Stitchery*, *Port of Kauai*, and *Hale Keiki*, which has toys and togs for the younger set.

In the Kapaa and Waipouli area, there are many shops that cater to the tourist trade. One that stands above the rest for quality is *Jim Saylor's Jewelers*.

Just north of Lihue is the *Kapaia Stitchery*, with Hawaiian prints, quilt patterns and needlepoint kits. Near Hanamaulu is *The Lady Jane Company, Inc.*, with woodcraft, designer clothing and gifts. Local artists also display their wares on the lawn outside.

Kilohana, in Puhi, is a restored plantation home with several fine shops. The ones we like the most are: *Stones*, *Island Memories*, *Kilohana Galleries*, *Sea Reflections*, and *Half Moon Trading Company*.

Koloa has its share of shops as well. Those that interest us are: *J. Bianucci Jewelers*, *Hawaiian Kite Company*, and *Tonga Handicrafts*. Outside Koloa along Poipu Road is a small collection of stores collectively known as *Poipu Plaza*. Here, *The Station Two* specializes in needlepoint designs and gifts. Near there in the Kiahuna Shopping Village is a variety of interesting shops. Among these are *The Ship Store Gallery* with nautical and fine art, *Elephant Walk* for handicrafts, *Pomare*, a resort apparel store, and *Traders of Kauai* for gifts. In the Waiohai Resort is *The Gallery* with an exquisite selection of artwork.

On the west side in Hanapepe is *The Station* with needlepoint designs and gifts.

The best place to buy Niihau shell leis and other handicrafts of the Pacific is the *Kauai Museum* in Lihue. Here you are certain of their quality and authenticity. Many shops on the island sell imperfectly matched and strung Niihau shell leis at excessive prices, or offer woodcraft that is 95% made in the Philippines with only the finishing touches added in Hawaii so they can qualify for the label "Made in Hawaii."

SNORKELING/SCUBA DIVING

Kauai is on the fringe of the coral belt, so the coral is not as profuse as it is on some tropical islands. But the water is clear and the sea life abundant. Because the water is calmer along the southern shores, most of the best snorkeling and scuba diving spots are there.

Most hotels rent snorkeling equipment and some give lessons. Any of the six dive shops on Kauai will take care of both your snorkeling and scuba needs:

Aquatics Kauai - 822-9213
Dive Kauai - 822-0452
Fathom Five Divers - 742-6991
Kauai Divers - 742-1580
Ocean Odyssey Dive Shop - 822-9680
Sea Sage Diving Center - 822-3841

The three firms that have been here the longest are **Fathom Five, Kauai Divers** and **Sea Sage**. We have had personal experience with these three and can recommend them. Most of the dive shops offer snorkeling tours and introductory scuba lessons in swimming pools at various locations around the island. All offer shore dives, certification courses and boat dives. This discussion will not include boat dives, but those who wish to go on one should ask about the following spots along the south shore: Sheraton Caverns, General Store, Brennecke's Ledge, Oasis Reef, Turtle Bluffs and Fishbowl. If the weather is right, Mana Crack, Oceanarium and Truckstop on the north shore are worth inquiring about, as are Aquarium and Dragon's Head on the east shore.

Let's begin at the beginning with tips for snorkelers:

1. Buy or rent masks with tempered glass and clean them before each use with hot water and detergent to remove deposited face oil.
2. Ensure a good mask fit with the assistance of an experienced salesman or beach activities person. The best test is to place the mask on your face without the strap and inhale. If it stays, the fit is okay.
3. Buy or rent fins that float. For walking on rocks and coral, the shoe type fin is best. Snorkelers do not need the powerhouse fins sold to scuba divers. As a matter of fact most scuba divers do not need them, either.
4. Get gloves if you plan to touch any coral or pick up certain sea animals. There will also be times when you need to grasp rocks in strong wave action or current and you will be glad you have them.
5. Practice first in a pool standing at the shallow end, then swim around at the deeper end. The first time in the ocean you may want to snorkel on a body board or air mattress to give you confidence.
6. Never snorkel alone.
7. Always observe ocean conditions before you enter the water, and check your location frequently.
8. Never dive the north shore sites during winter months.
9. Be aware of your body condition and return to shore *before* you become fatigued.

Good reference books about snorkeling and scuba diving in Hawaiian waters are *Skin Diver's Guide to Hawaii*, by G. Freund and *Skin and Scuba Diving Guide for the Hawaiian Islands*, by D. Wallin. We should also mention W.A. Gosline's *Handbook of Hawaiian Fishes*, *Underwater Guide to Hawaiian Reef Fishes*, by John Randall, which is waterproof and can be used underwater (plastic cards are also available to use this way, but they are not as complete), and *Hawaiian Reef Animals*, by Edmund Hobson and E.H. Chave.

And now for our favorite snorkeling and shore diving spots clockwise around the island, from the north. Exact directions are in the chapter "What to See":

Kee Lagoon – The entry is easy and the depth varies from three to twelve feet inside the lagoon. On an exceptional day in the summer when it is flat calm, you might venture out the channel opening to depths of forty feet where there are ledges, ravines and caves.

Kailio – Farther to the east, past Kailio Point, the lagoon behind the reef is similar but often rougher.

Makua Beach (Tunnels) – To the right between the inner and outer reefs, you will be in six to eight feet of water with a sand bottom and dead coral heads. Fish are tame and like to be fed. Scuba divers prefer to go to the left where there are caves and ledges along the outer reef and depths to seventy feet, but must be careful of the surf near the surface and the current at any depth.

Puu Poa Point and **Kenomene** – Usually dangerous, but on a flat summer day you might take a look.

Anini Beach and **Kalihikai Beach** – Many areas here have dead coral and are not too interesting, but if conditions permit going out an opening in the reef, both the coral and the sea life are abundant.

Kauapea (Secret) Beach – This beach can be particularly hazardous during the winter. On an ideal summer day, however, a leisurely swim along the shore to the right toward Kilauea Point takes you to a sharp dropoff with dramatic vistas. Under ideal circumstances, the more adventurous might want to venture off Kilauea Point to the small island of Mokuaeae.

Kakiu Point and along shore near Pohaku Malumalu – Good if the conditions are calm.

Waiakalua – All along here is great, depths six to twelve feet, sandy bottom, but be careful of currents going out the reef openings.

Papaa Bay – Exquisite on the north side. Coral and sandy bottom, depths to twenty feet.

Kuaehu Point – Similar, but not as protected.

Anahola Bay – Near Kahala Point to the right is an interesting spot, but usually rough.

Lae o Kailiu and ***Lae Lipoa*** – The best reefs are on either side of the points themselves. Good only when conditions are calm.

Lydgate State Park – Inside the protected area is an ideal spot for children to learn or for the novice snorkeler to gain experience. The fish are tame and they love to be fed. The depth does not exceed six feet.

Ahukini Landing – Usually undiveable because of trade winds, but a good place when Kona winds close out the south shore sites. May be murky after heavy rains. The safest entry is over the rocks just to the left of the jetty. If conditions are calm, you can swim around the jetty or enter directly to seaward from the parking lot by the sign, over the rock ledge. There is more to see on the seaward side. Depths average thirty to forty feet.

Mahaulepu – Easy entry, lots of caves and fish.

Poipu Beach Park – The depths are only ten to fifteen feet, but the visibility is good, there is a lot to see, and conditions are generally calm. A short hike across Nukumoi Point takes you to the cove in front of the Waiohai Resort where you will find abundant sea life on the western side of Nukumoi Point. The small cove in front of the Poipu Beach Hotel has fish that will make you feel guilty if you don't bring something! Luncheon meat works best.

Koloa Landing – Almost always diveable. This is sheltered from all but the strongest Kona winds. Easy entry down old boat ramp. The water is a bit murky on entry because of Waikomo Stream, but a short swim will carry you to clear water either left or right. Depths are up to thirty feet and the point just to your left, Laiokahala, offers dramatic views if surf conditions permit.

Kukuiula Harbor – Always calm, easy entry. Best reef is off harbor entrance, depth twenty feet.

Longhouse Beach – The small sand beach adjacent to the Beach House Restaurant is protected by an offshore reef, so it is almost always calm. It affords an easy entry and has much that is interesting to see, including a lot of the old Beach House Restaurant that was destroyed by Hurricane Iwa. Depths are up to eight or ten feet. The most interesting areas are toward the point on the right. Those who are experienced and are accompanied by a companion may venture out beyond the reef, where it is fantastic.

Wahiawa Bay – A sandy entry and rocks on either side of the bay with abundant sea life. It is protected out to the points – the left is best – and always safe except in strong Kona conditions.

Makaokahai Point – A rewarding spot on a calm day.

Salt Pond Beach Park – Snorkel anywhere along the beach inside the reef, where depths rarely exceed six feet. The water is generally clear and surf conditions favorable. This is also an excellent area for a beginning scuba diver to practice.

Paweo Point – Small sand beaches all along here. During the summer the surf can be high. The water is clear and there is abundant sea life, but not much coral.

Koki Point – There is coral and good visibility all the way from Kaumakani to Kaluapuhi, but the best spot is south of Koki Point.

Lawai Kai and ***Kipu Kai*** – These are the two most spectacular spots on Kauai, but are off privately owned valleys and are therefore inaccessible by land. However, some snorkel and scuba tours do go there; be sure to ask about them.

Kauai has one recompression chamber at the Veterans Memorial Hospital in Waimea, but the team has to be flown over from Honolulu. Consequently, most cases requiring recompression are flown directly to Kewalo Basin on Oahu.

SURFING

Visiting board surfers usually find out about the best spots from local surfers and then check out conditions at those spots on the day they want to go with KUAI Surfline, telephone 335-3611.

Some suggested spots, clockwise around the island from the north, are:

Kawaiaka (Cannon's) – At 9.2 mile marker in Haena. Park across from the green chain link fence, walk along the fence to the beach, enter at cut in the reef. Offshore lefts in winter. Shallow with strong currents.

Makua (Tunnels) – Off Haena Point. Surf is frequently ten feet in the winter. It is also windy with shallow coral reef.

Waikomo – Near the point, west side of Hanalei Bay. Lefts in winter.

Middles – The middle of Hanalei Bay. Huge walls with long lefts in the winter.

Pinetrees – Off the ironwood trees between Waioli Stream and the Hanalei Pavilion, Hanalei Bay. Humungous rights and lefts in the winter over sandy bottom.

Puu Poa – Off the point, east side of Hanalei Bay. Right walls in winter. Three takeoffs: Impossibles, Flat Rock and The Bowl.

Kalihiwai Bay – West side of bay. Right slides in the winter.

Anahola Bay – Beach break in winter.

Alakukui Point (Horner's) – Just beyond the small point north of Coco Palms Resort. Good left shoulders in high winter swells, but often choppy.

Wailua Bay (Coco Palms Resort) – Beach breaks summer and winter. Sandy bottom.

Ninini Point – Nawiliwili Harbor near the lighthouse. The surf is usually small, but sometimes there are good left slides in summer.

Brennecke's – Great for body boarding. Body surfing too, at high tide, if you watch out for rocks on the bottom.

Waiohai – In front of the Waiohai Resort. This is best at high tide and in the summer, as are all the south shore surfing places. Inside tubes over a shallow reef. Usually crowded in the afternoons.

First Break – Farther out and slightly to the north. This is good in a south swell, and the rights have a good peak.

Longhouse (also called "P.K.'s" for Prince Kuhio) – Off the Beach House Restaurant. There are long, hollow lefts in the summer with a consistent south swell.

211

Center's – A little farther out and to the north of P.K.'s. This is shallow over part of the run, but there are usually smooth rights in the summer.

Acid Drop (or The Drop) – A little farther to the north. There are steep sudden peaks due to the sharp dropoff of the bottom, and a rocky beach awaits you. Short lefts and longer rights in the summer only.

Salt Pond – The trade winds are offshore here, but both right and left tubes happen in the summer with a strong south swell.

Aakukui (Pakala's or Infinities) – Best in summer, but usually reliable year-round just off Pakala Village. Long lefts after long paddle out. Shark sightings in the brown water.

Waimea Rivermouth – Avoid. Shark sightings more frequent than any other spot on Kauai.

Oomano Point, Kekaha – Usually good rights all summer long. Shallow reef.

Kokole Point (Rifle Range) – Beach break in summer.

Mana Beach (Major's) – This is only good during the winter when the swells from the northeast wrap around the island. There are then long tubes to the right. Good peaks with both rights and lefts off the point (Major's Point). Strong currents at both. For top surfers only.

Polihale – There are strong currents here also and the surf is favorable only at times during the winter. Again, only for pro's.

Two good reference books about surfing in the Hawaiian Islands are *Surfer in Hawaii: A Guide to Surfing in the Hawaiian Islands*, by R. Grigg and R. Church, and *Surfing Hawaii*, by Bank Wright. *Hawaii Surfing Map*, has descriptions of ninety-seven surfing spots.

Wave skis are the latest thing here. Call Wailua Surf, 822-3035, or Hawaiian Islands Wave Ski Company, 332-9364.

TENNIS

There are public courts in Lihue, Kalaheo, Kapaa, Hanapepe, Koloa and Waimea, but they are not well-maintained. Two more recently-constructed ones in Wailua Homesteads and Wailua Houselots are still in good condition. Most condos and hotels either have excellent tennis courts or an arrangement with a nearby resort that does. Some have lights. Instruction, equipment and clothing are available at many places on the island.

THEATER

The surprisingly talented Kauai Community Players present several productions each year, plus a summer musical. Watch the papers or television information channel.

WINDSURFING/BOARD SAILING

Action Windsurfing, Koloa – 742-6118
Aquarius Beach Center, Coconut Plantation Marketplace – 822-7172
Brennecke Ocean Sports, Poipu – 742-6570
Garden Island Windsurfing, Princeville – 826-9005
Hanalei Sailboards, Hanalei – 826-9732
Island Adventure, Lihue – 245-9662
Kalapaki Beach Center and Ocean Sports, Nawiliwili – 245-5955
Peddle & Paddle, Hanalei – 826-9069
Sailboards Kauai, Lihue – 245-4635
Sea Star Kauai, Lihue – 245-3732
Waiohai Beach Service, Waiohai Resort, Poipu – 742-7051

Several hotels also rent equipment and give lessons. Ask at the beach activities center where you are staying.

The two best places for beginners are Anini Beach Park and Kalapaki Beach. Anini has steadier winds and is favored. If you drop by the park on any good day, you will find at least one of the above organizations there with a truck full of stuff to rent. Lessons are available also. It is surprising that after a short time of instruction using a mockup board on the beach and an hour or so of practice in the water, anyone can have fun at this.

This concludes our list of recommended activities. If you discover any more on your own, let us know about them.

We would like to end our book with a quotation about Hawaii by Mark Twain. He visited here more than a century ago and fell in love with the islands. Since then, time has not been kind to them. Kauai is now perhaps the only island about which he could rhapsodize today as he did then:

"No alien land in all the world has any deep strong charm for me but that one, no other land could so longingly and so beseechingly haunt me, sleeping and waking, through half a lifetime, as that one has done. Other things leave me, but it abides; other things change, but it remains the same. For me its balmy airs are always blowing, its summer seas flashing in the sun; the pulsing of its surfbeat is in my ear; I can see its garlanded crags, its leaping cascades, its plumy palms drowsing by the shore, its remote summits floating like islands above the cloud wrack; I can feel the spirit of its woodland solitudes, I can hear the splash of its brooks; in my nostrils still lives the breath of flowers..."

RECOMMENDED READING

Alexander, Arthur C. *Koloa Plantation 1835-1935*. Honolulu: Kauai Historical Society (updated to 1985).

Armstrong, R. Warwick. *Atlas of Hawaii*. Honolulu: University of Hawaii Press. 1983.

Barrere, Dorothy B. *Hula: Historical Perspectives*. Honolulu: Bishop Museum. 1980.

Bennett, Wendell C. *Archeology of Kauai*. Honolulu: Bishop Museum. 1931.

Berger, Andrew. *Hawaiian Birdlife*. Honolulu: University of Hawaii. 1981 (2nd Edition).

Bishop, Isabella Bird. *Six Months in the Sandwich Islands*. Honolulu: University of Hawaii Press. 1964.

Carlquist, Sherwin J. *Hawaii: A Natural History*. Garden City, NY: National History Press. 1970.

Carr, Elizabeth B. *Da Kine Talk: From Pidgin to Standard English in Hawaii*. Honolulu: University of Hawaii Press. 1972.

Chisholm, Craig. *Hawaiian Hiking Trails*. Lake Oswego, Oregon: The Fernglen Press. 1986.

Cox, J. Halley. *Hawaiian Petroglyphs*. Honolulu: Bishop Museum. 1970.

Cox, J. Halley & Davenport, W.H. *Hawaiian Sculpture*. Honolulu: University of Hawaii Press. 1974.

Damon, Ethel M. *Koamalu, A Story of Pioneers on Kauai*. Privately printed. 1931.

Daws, Gavan. *Shoal of Time*. Honolulu: University of Hawaii Press. 1974.

Day, A. Grove. *A Hawaiian Reader*. New York: Appleton. 1959.

Day, A. Grove. *The Spell of Hawaii*. New York: Meredith. 1968.

Day, A. Grove. *Hawaii And Its People*. New York: Meredith. Rev. 1968.

Elbert, Samuel & Pukui, Mary. *Hawaiian Grammer*. Honolulu: University of Hawaii Press. 1979.

Fielding, Ann. *Hawaiian Reefs and Tidepools*. Honolulu: Oriental Publishing Co. 1979 (2nd Edition).

Forbes, David. *Queen Emma and Lawai*. Honolulu: Kauai Historical Society. 1984.

Fornander, Abraham. *Account of the Polynesian Race: Its Origin and Migrations*. Rutland, Vermont: Tuttle. 1981.

Freund, G. *Skin Divers Guide to Hawaii.* Honolulu: Pacific Sports. 1969.

Gosline, W.A. *Handbook of Hawaiian Fishes.* Honolulu: University of Hawaii Press. 1960.

Grigg, R.W. & Church, R. *Surfer in Hawaii: A Guide to Surfing in the Hawaiian Islands.* Dana Point: John Severson Publications. 1963.

Hawaii Audobon Society. *Hawaii's Birds.* Author. 1984.

Hinds, Norman E. *The Geology of Kauai and Niihau.* Honolulu: Bishop Museum. 1930.

Hobson, Edmund S. & Chave, E.H. *Hawaiian Reef Animals.* Honolulu: University of Hawaii Press. 1972.

Hosaka, Edward Y. *Shore Fishing in Hawaii.* Honolulu: Petroglyph. 1973.

Ii, John Papa. *Fragments of Hawaiian History.* Honolulu: Bishop Museum Press. 1959.

Imler, R. *Bicycling in Hawaii.* Berkeley: Wilderness Press, 1978.

Joesting, Edward. *Kauai: The Separate Kingdom.* Honolulu: University of Hawaii Press. 1984.

Judd, Gerritt P. *Hawaii: An Informal History.* New York: Macmillan. 1961.

Kamakau, Samuel M. *Ka Po'e Kahiko: The People of Old.* Honolulu: Bishop Museum Press. 1964.

Kanahele, George. *Hawaiian Music.* Honolulu: University of Hawaii Press. 1979.

Kay, E. Alison. *Hawaiian Marine Shells.* Honolulu: Bishop Museum. 1979.

Kirch, Patrick V. *Feathered Gods and Fishooks.* Honolulu: University of Hawaii Press. 1985.

Krauss, Beatrice H. *Ethnobotany of Hawaii.* Honolulu: University of Hawaii, Department of Botany. 1974.

Krauss, Bob and Gleasner, Bill. *Kauai.* Honolulu: Island Heritage. 1978.

Krauss, Bob and Alexander, William P. *Grove Farm Plantation.* Palo Alto: Pacific Books. 1965.

Kuck, Loraine E. & Tongg, Richard. *Hawaiian Flowers & Flower Trees.* Rutland, Vt.: C.E. Tuttle. 1958.

Kuykendall, Ralph S. and Day, Arthur G. *Hawaii: A History.* Englewood Cliffs, N.J.: Prentice-Hall. 1978 (Revised).

Lamoreaux, Charles H. *Trailside Plants of Hawaii's National Parks.* HVNP: Hawaii National Historical Association. 1978.

Lewis, David. *We The Navigators.* Honolulu: University of Hawaii Press. 1972.

Lind, Andrew. *Hawaii's People.* Honolulu: University of Hawaii Press. 1980.

Malo, David. *Hawaiian Antiquities.* Honolulu: Bishop Museum. 1971.

McDermott, J., Tseng, W., Maretzki, T., Eds. *People and Cultures of Hawaii.* Honolulu: University of Hawaii Press. 1980.

McDonald, Marie A. *Ka Lei: The Leis of Hawaii.* New York: Topgallant. 1978.

MacDonald, Gordon A. & Abbott, Agatin T. *Volcanoes in the Sea.* Honolulu: University of Hawaii Press. 1983.

Morgan, Joseph. *Hawaii, A Geography.* Boulder, Co.: Westview. 1983.

Moriarty, Linda P. *Niihau Shell Leis.* Honolulu: University of Hawaii Press. 1986.

Morita, C.M. *Freshwater Fishing in Hawaii.* Honolulu: State of Hawaii Division of Fish & Game, Department of Land & Natural Resources. 1974.

Mulholland, J.F. *Hawaii's Religions.* Rutland, VT: Tuttle. 1970.

Murchie, N. & Ryan, P. *Hawaii, A Running Guide.* Honolulu: Oriental Publishing Company. 1981.

Peebles, Douglas and Ronck, Ronn. *Kauai, A Many Splendored Island.* Honolulu: Mutual Publishing Co. 1985.

Pukui, Mary K. & Elbert, Samuel H. *Hawaiian Dictionary.* Honolulu: University of Hawaii Press. 1971.

Pukui, Mary K., et al. *Place Names of Hawaii.* Honolulu: University of Hawaii Press. 1974.

Pukui, Mary K. *The Echo of Our Song: Chants and Poems of the Hawaiians.* Honolulu: University Press of Hawaii. 1973.

Quirk, Stephen & Wolfe, Charles. *Seashells of Hawaii.* Honolulu: WW Distributors. 1974.

Randall, John E. *Underwater Guide to Hawaiian Reef Fishes.* Kaneohe, HI: Treasures of Nature. 1981.

Riznick, Barnes. *Waioli Mission House.* Lihue: The Grove Farm Homestead. 1987.

Rizzuto, Jim. *Modern Hawaiian Gamefishing.* Honolulu: University of Hawaii Press. 1977.

Rizzuto, Shirley. *Hawaiian Camping*. Berkeley: Wilderness Press. 1979.

Schleck, Robert J. *The Wilcox Quilts*. Lihue: The Grove Farm Homestead. 1986.

Seiden, Allan. *Kauai, The Garden Isle*. Honolulu: Island Heritage. 1986.

Smith, Robert. *Hiking Kauai*. Berkeley: Wilderness Press. 1983.

U.S. Weather Bureau. *Climate of Hawaii*. Washington, D.C.: U.S. Government Printing Office. 1967.

Wallin, D. *Skin and Scuba Diving Guide for the Hawaiian Islands*. Honolulu: Worldwide Distributors. 1978.

Wenkam, Robert. *Hawaii's Garden Island: Kauai*. New York: Rand McNally. 1980.

Wichman, Frederick B. *Kauai Tales*. Honolulu: Bamboo Ridge. 1985.

Wilcox, Carol. *The Kauai Album*. Lihue: Kauai Historical Society. 1981.

Wright, Bank. *Surfing Hawaii*. Los Angeles: Tivoli Printing Co. 1972.

INDEX

219

221

READER RESPONSE – ORDERING INFORMATION

Dear Reader:

We hope you have had a pleasant visit to Kauai. Since our book expresses our own opinions on places to stay, restaurants, and things to see and do, we would sincerely appreciate hearing of your experiences. Any updates or changes would also be welcomed. Please mail comments or suggestions to the publisher.

FREE!
To keep our readers current on the most recent island changes, Paradise Publications has introduced *THE KAUAI UPDATE*. A complimentary copy of this quarterly subscription newsletter is available by writing the publisher (Newsletter Dept.) and enclosing a self-addressed, stamped, #10 size envelope.

Traveling to MAUI? A "must purchase" for the visitor bound for Hawaii's Valley Isle is *MAUI, A PARADISE GUIDE* by Greg and Christie Stilson. This is the original comprehensive Maui island guide. It provides information on 50 of Maui's best beaches, 200 restaurants and more than 150 hotels and condominiums. Recreational and tour activities are featured as well as historical sights. Island transportation, traveling with children or the physically impaired, weddings and honeymoons and childrens activities are just a few of the topics covered in General Information. Accurate descriptions and personal recommendations are provided for each subject. This easy to use guide is multi-indexed with maps and illustrations.

Also available is *THE MAUI UPDATE*, a quarterly subscription newsletter.

KAUAI, A PARADISE GUIDE by Don & Bea Donohugh
$9.95 U.S. currency plus $2 shipping
MAUI, A PARADISE GUIDE by Greg & Christie Stilson
$9.95 U.S. currency plus $2 shipping

THE MAUI UPDATE — Quarterly subscription newsletter – $5/year
THE KAUAI UPDATE — Quarterly subscription newsletter – $5/year

★ To order, or receive additional information on other Hawaiian publications which may be hard-to-find in mainland bookstores, write:

PARADISE PUBLICATIONS
8110 S.W. Wareham
Suite 100
Portland, OR 97223